MW01487485

# Professional Stock Trading

# Professional Stock Trading

## System Design and Automation

FIRST EDITION
With 140 Chart Examples

MARK R. CONWAY
AARON N. BEHLE

Copyright @ 2003 Mark R Conway, Aaron N Behle. All rights reserved.

Published by:

Acme Trader LLC
237 Moody Street, Suite 565
Waltham, MA 02453

No part of this publication may be reproduced, stored in a retrieval system or transmitted in any form or by any means, electronic, mechanical, photocopying, recording, scanning or otherwise, except as permitted under Sections 107 or 108 of the 1976 United States Copyright Act, without either the prior written permission of the Publisher. Requests to the Publisher for permission should be sent to support@acmetrader.com or to the address above.

This publication is designed to provide accurate and authoritative information in regard to the subject matter covered. It is sold with the understanding that neither the author nor the publisher is engaged in rendering legal, accounting, futures or securities trading, or other professional service. If legal advice or other expert assistance is required, the services of a competent professional person should be sought.

> *– From a Declaration of Principles jointly adopted by a Committee of the American Bar Association and a Committee of Publishers*

TradeStation, EasyLanguage, GlobalServer, HistoryBank.com, StrategyBuilder, and PaintBar are trademarks and tradenames of TradeStation Group, Inc. FirstAlert is a trademark of Neovest, Inc. NYSE and OpenBook are trademarks and tradenames of the New York Stock Exchange. The Bullish Consensus is a trademark of Market Vane Corporation. All other product names and logos are trademarks of their respective owners. Any such designation of trademark has been printed in initial caps, and the publisher has taken every precaution in preparation of this book. The publisher assumes no responsibility for errors or omissions, or for damages resulting from the use of the information contained herein.

The publisher acknowledges *Technical Analysis of* STOCKS & COMMODITIES for its permission to reprint portions of articles written by the authors in August 1998 and May 2002.

ISBN 0-9718536-4-9

Library of Congress Cataloging-in-Publication Data

Conway, Mark R., 1961-
    Professional stock trading : system design and automation / Mark R.
Conway, Aaron N. Behle.-- 1st ed.
        p. cm.
Includes bibliographical references and index.
    ISBN 0-9718536-4-9 (hardcover : alk. paper)
  1. Stocks--Charts, diagrams, etc. 2. Stocks--Data processing. 3.
Commodity exchanges--Data processing. 4. Investment analysis--Data
processing. I. Behle, Aaron N., 1971- II. Title.
    HG4638 .C66 2002
    332.63'2--dc21

                                                        2002006516

Printed in the United States of America.

This book is printed on acid-free paper.

*To the Conway Family and the Force.* AB

*This book is dedicated to my family, friends, and partner.* AB

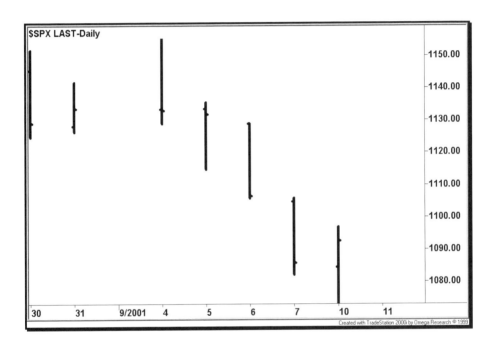

*We shape our buildings,*
*and afterwards*
*Our buildings shape us.*

Winston Churchill

# Preface

*The most incomprehensible thing*
*About the world is that*
*It is at all comprehensible.*
Albert Einstein

The beginning of a trading career is filled with excitement — independence, freedom, and the potential to make money. After building up a starting stake and reading as many books about the market as possible, the new trader is ready to wade into an ocean of stocks with a raft of ideas. As the trader soon discovers, however, a good idea does not always translate into a good trade. A long string of losing trades will have the trader jumping from one idea to another without realizing that having a "system" is just a single cornerstone of trading success.

The most popular trading books focus on technical analysis and pattern identification, suggesting an underlying order to the stock market. Unless the trader has a framework for trading these patterns, the process of trading can be both subjective and overwhelming. When certain patterns stop working, the trader will abandon them just before they resume working again, resulting in a never-ending quest for profits.

This is the first book to give a trader a complete, automated framework for trading stocks: a model that encompasses money management, position sizing, order entry, and a set of trading systems. Nothing is left to chance during the execution process, while the trader is freed to create. The model imposes discipline on the mechanics of trading, not on the creative aspects of system design.

The reader should have several years of trading experience and a background in technical analysis. Proficiency in either trading systems development with a language such as EasyLanguage® or software development using a computer programming language such as Visual Basic will complete the experience.

Chapter 1 is a presentation of the trading model and its components. First, we present a summary of the trading systems. Then, we establish the system standards for position sizing, trade entry and exit, and filtering. Finally, we complete the model with a brief analysis of some common technical analysis indicators and their impact on system performance.

In each of Chapters 2 through 7, we design and develop a trading system based on a single concept. We define the system rules, code it in accordance with the trading model, and then present some examples of actual trades with charts and rationale.

In Chapter 8, we create two market models using two different approaches. First, we apply all of the trading systems to various market and sector indices to create a bottoms-up model. Then, we adapt the pattern trading system to a set of sentiment indicators to create a top-down model, comparing the results of each model.

Chapter 9 takes the professional trader through a real-time trade analysis from the closing bell of one day to the opening bell of the next. The daily cycle of position management and chart review is described in detail.

Chapter 10 presents a different perspective on day trading. After a brief Level II tutorial, we show how any trading system can be adapted to intraday time frames. Here, we introduce several day trading techniques that integrate traditional technical analysis with direct access tools.

Chapter 11 is the complete implementation of a trading model, including source code for money management, position management, and a complete set of trading systems. The code can be compiled into TradeStation, and the executable code can then be run as a professional trading platform.

In writing this book, we acknowledge the achievements of some of the lesser-known yet influential technicians who approached the market from an applied scientific perspective: Dunnigan, Gartley, Schabacker, and Taylor. We can only imagine their reaction to the images of charts and indicators being drawn in real-time as a soothing voice tells the trader when to buy and when to sell.

The next generation of trading software is already being written to merge the world of trading with the world of software – the integration of price streams with scripting languages, the transparency of database access to many sources of market data, and the dynamic composition of new types of market instruments synthesized from the fine granularity of multiple data feeds. The evolution of trading from art to science is just beginning.

*Mark Conway*
*Aaron Behle*

San Diego, California
April 2002

# Contents

# Table of Figures

# 1 Introduction

*Millions of human hands at work,*
*billions of minds…a vast network,*
*screaming with life: an organism.*
*A natural organism.*

Max Cohen, *Pi* the Motion Picture

Π In the movie *Pi*, Max Cohen is a brilliant number theorist trying to detect hidden order in the chaos of the stock market, an infinitely long string of numbers scrolling through the universe. During his relentless pursuit of the answer, he is stricken with migraine headaches, confronting powerful antagonists along the way. His singular obsession exemplifies the never-ending search for the ultimate solution – a master key to the market.

An avid student of the market may be compelled to translating license plates into stock symbols or composing phrases from symbols, e.g., EYE LUV U[1]. The market can easily become an obsession as one jumps from one trading system to another without gaining a single insight and losing capital during the process. Immersion in technical analysis is a cornerstone of success, but managing risk and temperament are equally important.

In this book, we do not follow the path taken by Max Cohen. Instead, we present a diversity of trading systems as an integrated, scientific approach to professional stock trading. The elements of portfolio management, position management, and trading system have been synthesized into a practical blueprint. Some would claim that trading is as much art as science, and we agree. Our main point is that inspiration is built into the trading model and reflected in the design of the trading system. Such an accomplishment frees the trader to focus on just executing trades.

Trading is insight through observation. A professional trader exploits two or three unique insights to consistently pull money out of the stock market. Over time, the trader builds up a portfolio of trading systems and techniques, just as a

---

[1] VISX (EYE:NYSE), Southwest Airlines (LUV:NYSE), and US Airways Group (U:NYSE).

doctor or lawyer accumulates experience through casework. Attaining success is the application of wisdom and the ability to match technique with various market conditions.

Most traders have a bias as to the direction of the market and position themselves accordingly; however, market-neutral strategies are becoming popular for professionals who are tired of trading on the gerbil wheel of Level II quotes and one-minute charts. By going into every trading day with both long and short opportunities, the trader lets the market pick the direction.

The last point to emphasize is that *price leads news*. Instead of reacting to the news or analyst recommendations, strive to develop trading systems that detect unusual price movement. Deploy a diversity of trading systems, and watch for combinations of signals in the same direction. When signals conflict, avoid the trade.

## 1.1 Acme Trading Systems

In the following chapters, we present a group of trading systems named the *Acme Trading Systems*[2]. The Acme systems were derived empirically – they are based on historical studies of daily and intraday price patterns that occur with regularity in the stock market. We use the inductive process preferred by some of the traders profiled in the *Market Wizards* books [27, 28], who discovered price anomalies in diverse instruments such as mutual fund sectors, futures, and options. In contrast, many of the current systems are based on deductive, top-down combinations of technical analysis indicators.

The Acme Trading Systems do not rely on traditional technical analysis, mainly because technical indicators derived from price lag the real price action. Moreover, because many traders use these indicators as a foundation for their systems, their overuse renders them ineffective; instead, the indicators are more useful as trade filters, not as trade signals.

The main strength of the Acme systems is that they are mechanical, and nothing is left to chance. They take long and short positions with specific entry and exit points. Each of these systems has been programmed in a trading programming language[3], EasyLanguage®. Consequently, a trader can run stock scans each night and then generate real-time order alerts for the following day.

---

[2] The word *acme* represents the highest point, the pinnacle of success. In contrast, the Acme Company supplied the ill-fated Wile E. Coyote with explosives and other Rube Goldberg contraptions designed to capture Road Runner. We chose the name Acme because a trader will occasionally feel the pain of Coyote on the path to success.

[3] Refer to Chapter 11 for the full source code. For further information, get the EasyLanguage reference guide from TradeStation Group.

For those of you watching business television during the day, we have one recommendation: Turn it off. Trading is hard enough without having to listen to a money manager pumping his latest highflier down 30%. Remember that his dual motive is to keep his job and to take your money for self-preservation. The so-called business reporters are usually the last to know about breaking news; experienced traders know that media hype is a *fade*, i.e., doing the opposite of the emotional choice. The bottom line is that nobody knows where the market is headed, even though many pretend to know so. Let price be the guide.

The trading systems have been designed with one goal in mind: consistent profitability based on a unique market insight. They are all based on high probability price patterns that do not appear frequently in a single stock, but can be found often in a universe of over ten thousand stocks. The systems are shown in Table 1.1.

**Table 1.1.** Acme Trading Systems

| *System* | *Identifier* | *Timeframe* | *Complexity* |
|---|---|---|---|
| Float | Acme F | Daily, Weekly | High |
| Multiple patterns | Acme M | Intraday, Daily | Medium |
| Narrow range | Acme N | Intraday, Daily | Low |
| Pair trading | Acme P | Intraday | High |
| Rectangle | Acme R | Intraday, Daily | Low |
| Volatility | Acme V | Daily Only | Medium |

The trading systems span the spectrum of complexity. If just starting out, then focus on the Acme N and R systems. Both systems are based on simple bar formations. The calculations are minimal, so sophisticated trading software is not required, although automation will make the systems easier to trade.

The Acme M and V systems are designed for the intermediate trader. Each requires knowledge of technical analysis to identify certain bar patterns. As the trader becomes more proficient at identifying the various market patterns, the M System becomes more powerful in the trader's hands. The Acme V System is a riskier strategy but is based on a single concept. Use this strategy with smaller positions at first to experience the volatility.

The Acme F and Acme P Systems are the most technical systems for the advanced trader. The F System requires extensive calculations and works best with trading software such as TradeStation® or MetaStock®. The P System requires a real-time trading platform with multiple chart windows.

Finally, in the spirit of open source, we encourage the trader to make each system his or her own. Experiment with the source code, the input parameters, and the trading filters to create or derive new systems. Trading system development is a laboratory, and each trader has to "own" the system to trade it effectively. Watch the systems work in real-time to confirm that trading entries and exits are realistic in terms of slippage and liquidity.

## 1.2 System Summary

The *Acme F System* is based on the technical work of W.D. Gann and a book by Steve Woods called *The Precision Profit Float Indicator* [38]. The system uses the float of a stock to analyze supply and demand patterns created by custom float indicators. The F System then pinpoints breakout and turning points by combining float turnover points with geometric patterns such as triple bottoms and retracement patterns such as pullbacks.

The *Acme M System* identifies combinations of bar patterns. For example, a bar that forms a Tail and a Test is a combination of two distinct bar patterns (these patterns are discussed in Chapter 3). The M System scans for bars that have two, three, or even more patterns. The success rate of this system is directly proportional to the number of identified patterns. Associated with each bar pattern is a set of qualifiers. For example, a bar may be a narrow range bar, or a bar may overlap its 50-day moving average. Since technicians attach significance to these conditions, they are denoted on the chart.

The *Acme N System* is based on a simple concept: identify *narrow range* bars on strongly trending stocks, entering a trade in the direction of the trend on a breakout of the narrow range bar. The appeal of this system is that the risk on the trade is limited to the range of the narrow range bar, but the reward is high because the trending stock is in transition from low to high volatility.

The *Acme P System* is a *pair trading* strategy that has been gaining popularity because it is a *hedged* trade, i.e., the trader enters both a long trade and short trade simultaneously. The allure of pair trading is that it is a strategy with little risk; however, no stock is immune to the risk of a trading halt or an earnings warning. As with every other system, specific entry points, exit points, profit targets, and stop losses are defined.

The *Acme R System* is based on a simple pattern: the *rectangle* [2, 11]. The theory behind the rectangle is that it represents a period of consolidation where traders have already taken positions over several days, but the stock has not moved decidedly in either direction. Once the stock breaks the rectangle range, the move is usually explosive; further, the narrow range of the rectangle allows the trader to reverse direction if the initial move is a head fake.

The *Acme V System* goes against all the trading truisms such as "the trend is your friend", "don't try to pick bottoms", "never catch a falling knife", etc. In general, these observations are correct, but at times the trader wants to catch the knife and hold it for a few days before releasing it. This system is called the V system because the chart formation traces the letter V. The system exploits this pattern with a statistical method known as *linear regression*.

The M and N systems are swing-trading systems. Performance improves linearly with higher values for momentum indicators such as the ADX. The performance of the other systems does *not* improve with such filters. Although each system can be improved with proper optimization, none of the systems has been optimized to avoid overstating results.

## 1.3 Chart Indicators

Each Acme system has corresponding chart indicators that alert the trader to specific market conditions; these indicators are known as *lines and letters*. Each indicator is presented in the relevant chapter along with its related system. A summary of each indicator is shown in Table 1.2. Note that the *Range Patterns* indicator is actually a series of PaintBars™ designed to identify various types of narrow range bars.

**Table 1.2.** Acme Indicators

| System | Indicator | Description |
|---|---|---|
| Acme F System | Float Box | Channel lines |
| | Float Channel | Channel lines |
| | Float Percentage | Histogram |
| Acme M System | Market Patterns | Text on Bar |
| | High Zone | PaintBar |
| | Low Zone | PaintBar |
| Acme N System | Range Patterns | PaintBar |
| | Range Ratio | Separate Plot |
| Acme P System | Spread | Separate Plot |
| Acme R System | Rectangle | Lines on Chart |
| Acme V System | Regression Curve | Line on Chart |
| Acme Market System | Market Model | Text on Bar |

## 1.4 A Trading Model

Given a set of trading systems, we construct a framework for trading them within the context of an overall portfolio. This Trading Model has three main components:

- ❏ Portfolio
- ❏ Systems
- ❏ Trade Manager

The *Portfolio* is a dynamic set of trading positions, as shown in Figure 1.1. It specifies the uniform money management criteria, passing them to each of the Systems. The *Systems* enter trades, creating positions based on the equity and position-sizing model. As the Systems run, the *Trade Manager* monitors profit targets, stop losses, and holding periods, closing any positions that meet the exit criteria; closed positions are sent to a trade log file for spreadsheet analysis.

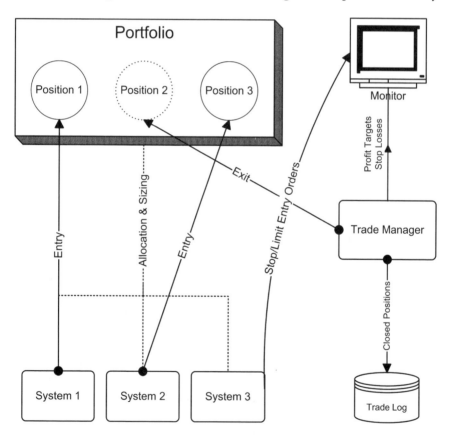

**Figure 1.1.** Trading Model

Although not shown in the diagram, each system is designed with a specific set of trading filters. The trader has the option of turning the filters on or off to compare filtered performance with unfiltered performance for benchmarking.

## 1.4.1 Portfolio

Costs are associated with both the Portfolio and the Trade Manager. Portfolio costs are items such as your own salary, data and exchange fees, and other fixed expenses such as software subscriptions and news services. The trading costs encompass commissions, slippage, and margin interest.

### Capital

Many traders underestimate the initial trading capital and return required to be a full-time trader. If trading is your profession, then running it as a business is the only way to determine whether or not it will be a profitable endeavor. If the trader has no other source of income, then cost-of-living expenses will have to be withdrawn from the trading account on a regular basis. A full-time trader starting out should set aside at least six months of living expenses and add these expenses to the fixed costs.

The trader calculates fixed costs on a monthly basis. Achieving consistent profitability is difficult enough, so every cost must be quantified. For the full-time trader, the added expenses translate into requiring a higher return on capital. A trader with a $100,000 account who must pay several thousand dollars in monthly expenses has significant hurdles to overcome, as shown below.

To estimate monthly trading income, start with known quantities: equity, portfolio costs, trading costs, and tax rate. Then, based on each trading system, estimate the number of trades per month and the amount of capital that will be allocated to each trade. Determine how many positions will be maintained simultaneously, and estimate how often the average position will be turned over. For example, if the average holding period is three days, and the portfolio has four positions at any one time, then the estimated number of trades per month is $22 \times (4 \div 3) \approx 29$, assuming twenty-two trading days per month.

Table 1.3 shows the expected monthly income for a trading account with $100,000. The fixed costs are $1000 per month, and the commissions and slippage per round trip total $200. The number of trades per month is estimated at 20, and 50% of equity is allocated to each trade, implying a two-day holding period. The dollar amount per trade can either be calculated from actual trading records or extracted from a historical performance report. For example, the average Acme trade (win & loss) based on a hypothetical $50,000 allocation per trade is about $425 per trade. Using the table as a guide, a trader in the 30% tax bracket could theoretically earn a monthly return of approximately 4.95%.

The other way to derive the average trade amount is to start with the percentage return per trade or a geometric mean[4] [35, 36]. In Table 1.3, to compute the Average $ Per Trade, multiply the Equity by the % Allocation per position, then multiply by the % Return Per Trade, and finally subtract the Trade Cost (commissions and slippage). The Net Income is the Monthly Gross minus Taxes minus the Portfolio Cost.

**Table 1.3.** Expected Monthly Income

| Equity | 100000 | # Trades | 20 | | |
|--------|--------|----------|-----|---|---|
| Portfolio Cost | 1000 | % Allocation | 50% | | |
| Trade Cost | 200 | Tax Rate | 0.3 | | |

| % Return Per Trade | Average $ Per Trade | Monthly Gross | Taxes | Net Income | Monthly % Return |
|--------------------|---------------------|---------------|-------|------------|------------------|
| 0.50% | 50 | 1000 | 300 | -300 | -0.30% |
| 0.75% | 175 | 3500 | 1050 | 1450 | 1.45% |
| 1.00% | 300 | 6000 | 1800 | 3200 | 3.20% |
| 1.25% | 425 | 8500 | 2550 | 4950 | 4.95% |
| 1.50% | 550 | 11000 | 3300 | 6700 | 6.70% |
| 1.75% | 675 | 13500 | 4050 | 8450 | 8.45% |
| 2.00% | 800 | 16000 | 4800 | 10200 | 10.20% |

## Fixed Costs

To receive real-time quotes, a trader must complete exchange agreements[5] and pay monthly fees for the data feed. Standard trading tools are typically bundled by a direct access broker so that the trader pays one monthly fee for a certain level of service. In many cases, the monthly fee will be waived or rebated based on the number of trades; the credit is usually applied the first week of the following month to your account.

---

[4] The geometric mean is a mathematical term for describing the growth per trade.
[5] The exchanges distinguish between *professional* and *non-professional* traders. Generally, if you are associated with the securities industry or you are subscribing on behalf of a business, then you must register with the exchanges as a professional subscriber and pay more.

If your trade volume is very high, then negotiate with the broker for a lower commission rate. Commissions should be no greater than one cent per share, or $10 per 1000 shares. Other fixed costs are:

- ❑ Technical analysis software,
- ❑ Real-time news sources such Bloomberg or Dow Jones, and
- ❑ Subscriptions to advisory services and other publications.

Depending upon the requirements of the trading systems, monthly costs will vary from as little as several hundred dollars to several thousand dollars. Paying more for advanced trading tools such as stock screeners (e.g., FirstAlert) and services (e.g., a Bloomberg terminal) may be worth the additional cost. Software costs can be expensive and have a significant impact on the bottom line for smaller accounts (review Table 1.3).

### *Margin*

Think of margin as a length of rope, and recall the well-known idiom about hanging. The typical investor with a brokerage account gets 2:1 margin, and the pattern day trader gets 4:1 intraday margin. The question is whether or not a trader with a great system should use margin. First, frame the question in terms of risk as a percentage of equity, i.e., how much one is willing to lose on a single trade. Suppose the trader has a $100,000 account and is willing to lose no more than 2% of equity on any single position. The maximum loss per trade is $2,000.

Now, suppose the trader wants to leverage the position on 2:1 margin. The position size is doubled but the percent risk is still 2%. If the trader has designed a stop loss based on this risk value, then positions will be stopped out more often because the maximum loss per trade has not been adjusted to reflect the doubled size of the position. To maintain the efficacy of the system, the trader would have to increase the percent risk to 4%, thereby increasing the maximum loss per trade to $4,000. This change affects the integrity of the portfolio, as its past and future performance may not be able to bear 4% risk on every trade.

Returning to the great system, suppose the maximum loss of our system has been 1.5% of equity for a series of several hundred trades, and the percent risk is initially set to 2%. Given that the maximum loss has been only 1.5% of equity (but with no assurance as to future performance), the trader may decide to use margin in our theoretical account of $100,000. The formula is:

$$Margin = Equity \times (Risk \% \div Maximum \ Loss \%) \qquad (1.1)$$

In our example, the trader's margin would be $100,000 \times (2 \div 1.5) = $133,333. The expected highest loss would be $133,333 \times 1.5\% = $2,000, or 2% of equity.

Before using margin, however, be skeptical of the highest percentage loss number and think of scenarios where that number could be exceeded [30]. Further, do not use margin on a system with limited historical data or a short back testing period (e.g., a relatively new issue or instrument). Finally, examine the maximum consecutive losers to determine whether or not the system has an exceptional losing string.

## Position Sizing

Position size for all of the Acme Trading Systems is calculated from the models described in Tharp's book *Trade Your Way to Financial Freedom* [34]. The sizing models are as follows:

- ❑  Equal Value Units Model
- ❑  Percent Risk Model
- ❑  Percent Volatility Model

The Equal Value Units Model is simple. Allocate a fixed percentage of equity to each position in the portfolio. For example, if account equity of $100,000 is to be spread equally among 4 positions, then $25,000 is allocated to each position, regardless of price. If Stock A is trading at a price of 10, then Stock A's position size is 25000 ÷ 10 = 2500 shares. If Stock B is trading at a price of 25, then the position size of Stock B is 25000 ÷ 25 = 1000 shares. The problem with this model is that it does not consider volatility in the equation, so Stock A may have a much greater impact on the portfolio than Stock B, or vice versa.

The Percent Risk Model is based on the maximum number of units (e.g., points for stocks) one is willing to lose on any single trade. The formula is:

$$Position\ Size = Equity \times Risk\ \% \div RiskUnits \tag{1.2}$$

For example, if Equity is $100,000 and the Risk Percentage is 2%, then the trader may decide that a two-point stop loss is appropriate. The position size in this case is 100,000 × .02 ÷ 2 = 1000 shares. As a practical consideration, the trader must select an appropriate stop loss per stock and not apply the same value universally to a portfolio of stocks. The weakness of this model is that it is unit-based and not percentage-based. Instead, the stop loss value should be derived from a standard percentage loss such as 4%. Still, even the use of a fixed percentage is not optimal.

The Percent Volatility Model is the default model for the Acme systems. It is the only model to standardize across volatility. The difference between this model and the Percent Risk Model is the calculation of the Average True Range (ATR) denominator. This model adjusts to the inherent volatility of each stock because it uses the ATR, in contrast to the Percent Risk Model where the trader selects risk. The formula is:

$$Position\ Size = Equity \times Risk\ \% \div ATR \tag{1.3}$$

For example, suppose a trading account has \$100,000, and the trader wishes to lose no more than 2% on any one trade. If the stock's ATR is two points, then the number of shares is 100,000 × .02 = 2000 ÷ 2 = 1000 shares. If the ATR is four points, then the number of shares is 2000 ÷ 4, or 500 shares. As volatility increases, the number of shares decreases.

**Example 1.1.** Function *AcmeGetShares*

```
{*********************************************************************
AcmeGetShares: Calculate the number of shares based on risk model

RiskModel = 1, Equal Value Units Model
RiskModel = 2, Percent Risk Model
RiskModel = 3, Percent Volatility Model
*********************************************************************}

Inputs:
    Equity(Numeric),
    RiskModel(Numeric),
    RiskPercent(Numeric),
    RiskUnits(Numeric);

Variables:
    MinimumShares(200),
    RiskShares(0),
    ERP(0.0),
    Length(20);

ERP = Equity * RiskPercent / 100;

If RiskModel = 1 and Close > 0 Then
    RiskShares = MaxList(MinimumShares,
    100 * IntPortion(Equity / (100 * Close)));

If RiskModel = 2 and RiskUnits > 0 Then
    RiskShares = MaxList(MinimumShares,
    100 * IntPortion(ERP / (100 * RiskUnits)));

If RiskModel = 3 and Volatility(Length) > 0 Then
    RiskShares = MaxList(MinimumShares,
    100 * IntPortion(ERP / (100 * Volatility(Length))));

AcmeGetShares = RiskShares;
```

Each of the position sizing models is encoded in a common function that can be called by all of the trading systems in the portfolio. The *AcmeGetShares* function[6] shown in Example 1.1 is written in EasyLanguage; it calculates the position size

---

[6] The *Volatility* function in the code is based on the Average True Range over a certain period of time.

based on the equity and the selected position-sizing model. The number of shares is calculated and returned to the trading system calling the function.

By standardizing the number of shares traded across all equities, risk is spread evenly across the entire portfolio. Thus, the *AcmeGetShares* function is called by every trading system in the portfolio. An EasyLanguage example of calling the function is shown below in Example 1.2:

**Example 1.2.** Calling the *AcmeGetShares* Function

```
Inputs:
    Equity(100000),
    RiskModel(3),           {Percent Volatility Model}
    RiskPercent(2.0),
    RiskATR(1.0);           {Applies only to Percent Risk Model}

    {Calculate shares based on risk model}
    N = AcmeGetShares(Equity, RiskModel, RiskPercent, RiskATR);
    Buy N Shares;
```

### 1.4.2 Trade Manager

The Trade Manager is like an octopus; it is the brain of a trading operation with its arms in every trade. The trader must decide whether or not to use stop or limit orders, to use profit targets or not, how to implement stop losses, and how long to hold a position.

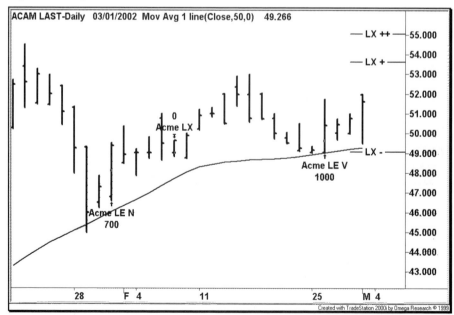

**Figure 1.2.** Visual Cues

The Trade Manager helps the trader with visual cues, showing the action points of the trade. Knowing the profit targets and stop losses a priori gives a trader confidence and reinforces discipline when exiting a trade. Figure 1.2 shows an example of these visual cues.

Improper settings can turn a winning trading system into a losing one; the strength of a trading system depends not only on its design but also on a balance between the maximum profit potential of a position and the holding period. For example, if the distribution of trades shows that the average return of a winning trade is 2% in two trading days and 2.5% in three trading days, then the trader should be taking profits after two days [32].

The trader should go through the exercise of experimenting with and without profit targets, testing different holding periods, and adjusting entry and exit parameters. For example, the trader may decide not to enter long positions one tick above the previous day's high but instead wait for a little more confirmation based on a percentage of the average true range, e.g., 25% of the ATR.

### Naming Convention

Each of the Acme Trading Systems has a designated letter (*SystemID*) that is part of the naming convention for trading signals. Each signal name contains a two-letter identifier containing the order type: Long (L) or Short (S) combined with either Entry (E) or Exit (X). Entries have a SystemID, and exit signals have an identifier appended to the order type specifying either a profit target or a stop loss. An example of an entry is **Acme SE M**, an Acme M short signal. An example of an exit is **LX++**, a multi-day profit target for a long entry. Refer to Table 1.4 for the list of qualifiers used in a signal name.

**Table 1.4.** Signal Qualifiers

| Symbol | Description |
|--------|-------------|
| LE | Long Entry |
| LX | Long Exit |
| SE | Short Entry |
| SX | Short Exit |
| + | Daily Profit Target |
| ++ | Multi-Day Profit Target |
| - | Stop Loss |

## Trade Entry

Except for the Acme P system, all of the Acme Trading Systems enter trades on stop orders. Typical swing trading systems will enter long trades on a break of the previous day's high plus one tick and enter short trades on a break of the previous day's low minus one tick. Because a previous day's high or low tends to be tested, each Acme system adds or subtracts a percentage of the ATR for long and short entries, respectively. This percentage gives the trader further confirmation on entries and prevents a trade from being prematurely stopped out on exits.

For trade entries, the percentage of the ATR is known as the *EntryFactor*, a parameter common to all of the systems. The default EntryFactor is 0.25. For example, if the ATR of a stock is 1.6 and the EntryFactor is 0.25, then a long trade will be entered if the previous day's high is exceeded by $1.6 \times 0.25 = 0.4$, and a short will be entered only if the previous day's low is exceeded by 0.4. The Acme systems use the ATR as a standard for trade entry, trade exit, position sizing, and for other range calculations (see Table 1.5).

**Table 1.5.** Acme System Entry Stops

| System | Buy Stop | Short Stop |
|--------|----------|------------|
| Acme F | High + (EntryFactor * ATR) | Low – (EntryFactor * ATR) |
| Acme M | High + (EntryFactor * ATR) | Low – (EntryFactor * ATR) |
| Acme N | High + (EntryFactor * ATR) | Low – (EntryFactor * ATR) |
| Acme P | n.a. | n.a. |
| Acme R | RectangleHigh + (EntryFactor * ATR) | RectangleLow – (EntryFactor * ATR) |
| Acme V | Close + (EntryFactor * ATR) | n.a. |

The chart in Figure 1.3 shows an example of a long N entry stop. A horizontal line is placed above the high of the bar *plus* the percentage of the ATR. On the following day, if the price reaches that line, then a buy order is triggered. What if the stock gaps open above the buy stop the following day? The answer depends on the size of the gap and the level of the stop relative to the price pattern the past few bars.

Let's examine the definition of a gap more closely. A gap reflects some news in the market, the sector, or the stock itself. There may be no news at all, which makes the gap even more significant. The key to understanding gaps is that the gap price is the price—what happens *after* the gap is the trader's action point. The trader may want to define an entry condition on an intraday chart, i.e., set a stop above or below the first five-minute bar. Experiment with different chart intervals to find the best intraday interval for gap continuations.

The code for the Acme Trading Systems does not filter gaps for its entries, to the detriment of each system's performance. Although EasyLanguage can reference the open of tomorrow's bar, the end-of-day scanner cannot generate alerts for the next day because of the unknown open. The code can be changed to restrict gap entries by using stop limit orders; otherwise, just ignore gaps that exceed a certain percentage of the ATR.

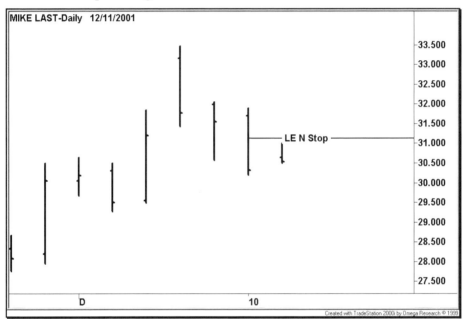

**Figure 1.3.** Trade Entry

## Trade Exit

The Acme Trade Manager defines three criteria for exiting trades:

- ❑ Stop Loss
- ❑ Single-Bar Profit Target
- ❑ Multi-Bar Profit Target

Together, the *ExitFactor*, a percentage of the ATR, and the total number of *StopBars* determine a trade's stop loss point. The ExitFactor is similar to the EntryFactor because it is used as an offset in the stop order. The number of StopBars indicates how many bars to consider when calculating the stop loss. The Trade Manager calculates the lowest low of the last StopBars bars for long exits and the highest high of the last StopBars bars for short exits. Thus, the EasyLanguage code for long exit stops is:

$$SellStop = Lowest\ (Low,\ StopBars) - (ExitFactor \times ATR) \qquad (1.4)$$

Similarly, the code for short exit stops is:

$$CoverStop = Highest\ (High,\ StopBars) + (ExitFactor \times ATR) \qquad (1.5)$$

The Profit Targets are percentages of the ATR determined by *ProfitFactor*. The Trade Manager defines two types of profit targets, a *single-bar target* and a *multi-bar target*. The single-bar target looks for a wide-range move on any given bar, and the multi-bar target looks for a wide-range move multiplied over a range of bars. The EasyLanguage code for the single-bar profit target for a long position follows:

$$SellTarget1 = High + (ProfitFactor \times ATR) \qquad (1.6)$$

The single-bar profit target for a short position is:

$$CoverTarget1 = Low - (ProfitFactor \times ATR) \qquad (1.7)$$

The default ProfitFactor is 0.9; the Trade Manager expects almost a full ATR move in the trade's direction. When a sell target is reached using a limit order, then half of the position is exited.

The multi-bar profit target is a double ProfitFactor move over half of the holding period (the variable *ProfitBars*). For example, if the holding period is five days, then the sell target is $2 \times 0.9 = 180\%$ of the ATR in three days. The code for the multi-bar profit target for a long position follows:

$$SellTarget2 = High[ProfitBars] + (2 \times ProfitFactor \times ATR) \qquad (1.8)$$

The multi-bar profit target for a short position is:

$$CoverTarget2 = Low[ProfitBars] - (2 \times ProfitFactor \times ATR) \qquad (1.9)$$

The complete code for the Acme Trade Manager is shown in Example 1.3:

**Example 1.3.** Signal *Acme Trade Manager*

```
{****************************************************************
Acme Trade Manager: Set stops and profit targets
****************************************************************}

Inputs:
    SystemID(""),
    {Position Management Parameters}
    ExitFactor(0.25),
    StopBars(1),
    ProfitTarget(True),
    ProfitFactor(0.9),
    HoldBars(5),
    DrawTargets(True),
```

```
{Trade Logging}
LogTrades(False),
LogFile("Orders.txt");

Variables:
    ATR(0.0),
    ATRLength(20),
    ATRFactor(0.0),
    ProfitBars(0),
    SellStop(0.0),
    SellTarget1(0.0),
    SellTarget2(0.0),
    CoverStop(0.0),
    CoverTarget1(0.0),
    CoverTarget2(0.0);

ATR = Volatility(ATRLength);
ATRFactor = ProfitFactor * ATR;
ProfitBars = IntPortion(HoldBars/2) + 1;

SellStop = Lowest(Low, StopBars) - (ExitFactor * ATR);
ExitLong("Acme LX-") Next Bar at SellStop Stop;
If ProfitTarget Then Begin
    SellTarget1 = High + ATRFactor;
    ExitLong("Acme LX+") CurrentContracts/2 Shares Next Bar at
    SellTarget1 Limit;
    SellTarget2 = High[ProfitBars] + (2 * ATRFactor);
    ExitLong("Acme LX++") CurrentContracts/2 Shares Next Bar at
    SellTarget2 Limit;
End;
If BarsSinceEntry >= HoldBars - 1 Then
    ExitLong("Acme LX") Next Bar on Open;

CoverStop = Highest(High, StopBars) + (ExitFactor * ATR);
ExitShort("Acme SX-") Next Bar at CoverStop Stop;
If ProfitTarget Then Begin
    CoverTarget1 = Low - ATRFactor;
    ExitShort("Acme SX+") CurrentContracts/2 Shares Next Bar at
    CoverTarget1 Limit;
    CoverTarget2 = Low[ProfitBars] - (2 * ATRFactor);
    ExitShort("Acme SX++") CurrentContracts/2 Shares Next Bar at
    CoverTarget2 Limit;
End;
If BarsSinceEntry >= HoldBars - 1 Then
    ExitShort("Acme SX") Next Bar on Open;

{Draw Exit Targets on the Chart}
If DrawTargets Then
    If MarketPosition = 1 Then
        Condition1 = AcmeExitTargets(SystemID, SellStop,
        SellTarget1, SellTarget2)
    Else If MarketPosition = -1 Then
        Condition1 = AcmeExitTargets(SystemID, CoverStop,
```

```
      CoverTarget1, CoverTarget2);

{Log Trades for Spreadsheet Export}
Condition1 = AcmeLogTrades(LogTrades, LogFile, SystemID);
```

Figure 1.4 shows an example of the profit target and stop loss levels using the function *AcmeExitTargets*. This function draws horizontal price levels on the chart to display the stop loss and profit targets. The stop loss is denoted by LX -, and the multi-bar profit target is denoted by LX ++. The multi-bar profit target is similar to Darvas's box theory [7], where stock prices move upwards in a series of stacked boxes with defined ranges.

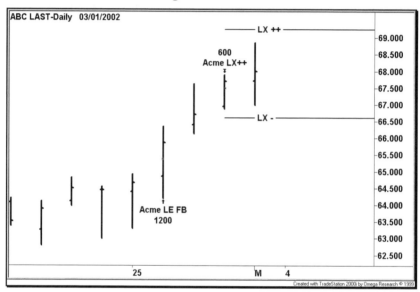

**Figure 1.4.** Trade Exit

The trader may wish to change the Trade Manager to implement different stop loss and profit target strategies, e.g., exit a long trade on the close if the close is below the open. By changing the Trade Manager, each of the Acme strategies can be tested with various trade exit techniques. One suggestion for changing the Trade Manager is to use different profit factors for the single-bar target and the multi-bar target. For example, the trader may want a 1.2-ATR move in one day and a 2.0-ATR move in two days.

### Holding Period

In the Trade Manager, the trader has the option of turning off profit targets to depend only on the holding period. When selecting a holding period, the trader wants to maximize the deployment of capital before the law of diminishing returns takes hold, i.e., how fast can the trades be turned over without sacrificing profit factor. The trader may wish to optimize the *HoldBars* parameter over a portfolio of stocks to determine the optimum holding period.

Many swing-trading techniques have holding periods of three to five days. Taylor defined a cycle of three days with each day representing a Buying Day, a Selling Day, and a Short Sell day [33]. The cycles vary according to sector; technology stocks have short cycles of two to three days, while cyclical stocks have cycles lasting up to thirty days. An example of a 30-day cycle is the retail sector, where same-store sales data are released the first week of every month.

### 1.4.3 The Trading System

So far, we have built an infrastructure for the core of the Trading Model. Now, we want to focus on the trading system itself. As an analogy, think of the Trading Model as the car and the Trading System(s) as the engine. If the engine is broken, then the car is not going to move. Unless the systems have an edge, the Portfolio is going to stay in Park.

Trading system design is difficult because a trader has to overcome reliance on canned technical analysis–some software packages make it too easy to plug in a moving average crossover system or a channel breakout system. By tweaking parameters, a trader tries to get results that he or she wants, a dangerous form of human optimization. The main issue is that any system can appear profitable in a narrowly defined time frame or on a narrowly defined portfolio. The key to any trading system is to look for consistent profitability across a wide range of stocks and markets over long periods of time. The job of *back testing* is essential to good system design [30].

The first question a trader must ask about a known trading system is "If the system is so good, then why is it published?" The answer is that the system may be a decent trading system, but certainly no one in his or her right mind would give away a great trading system. Obviously, a great system has to be traded, not sold. This question even applies to the trading systems in this book. Each of the Acme systems has a historical edge and a decent profit factor, but the best trading systems are in the hands of the people making money with them. We have enhanced the Acme systems as a departure point for systems with better profit factors. If a trader designs a system with a profit factor of 2.0, then he or she will be motivated to make the system even better through a process of iteration.

So how does one design a trading system? Without hesitation, we claim that the best systems result from a combination of market observation and total immersion in technical analysis. The wisdom acquired through reading, studying, analyzing, and observing leads to an explosion of creativity–simple concepts are combined to create a great trading system or technique. A trader soon discovers that the best systems are self-germinating.

The professional trader experiences breakthrough moments when all of the disparate technical elements that have been floating around in one's mind for years synthesize to produce inspired, original techniques. Some traders get there faster than others, but one day the trader realizes that money can be pulled out of the market consistently. Once the trader gets to that point, all of the external noise is eliminated. He or she stops going to chat rooms, turns off the television, and cancels all subscriptions. Ultimately, the pursuit is just pure trading.

## Design

The design of a successful trading system is based on a discovery that yields a statistical edge. We find an edge through number crunching, not from designing around technical indicators. The objective is to find recurring patterns in daily, weekly, or even intraday data. The process is iterative and painstaking, a cognitive panning for gold.

The best systems alternate winning streaks with relatively flat periods of drawdown. Look for consistency across parameter sets and across time frames, and exploit as much historical data as possible. Experiment with combinations of profit targets and stop losses [30]. For example, if the profit target is 1.5 times the ATR and the stop loss is 1.0 times the ATR, determine the winning percentage and then chart the trade distribution like a probability curve as shown in Figure 1.5. Plot the number of trades on the Y-axis and the percentage return on the X-axis. Repeat this exercise for risk/reward ratios of 1:1, 1:2, and 1:3. The trade distribution plot should resemble a normal curve that is shifted to the right with a peak in profitable trades to the right of zero.

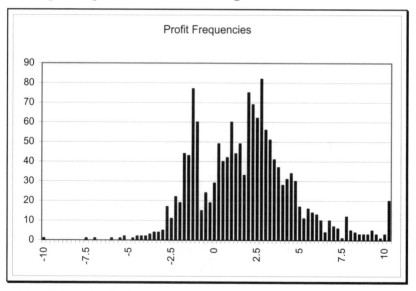

**Figure 1.5.** Trade Distribution

As discussed, Average True Range (ATR) is the standard for all Acme trading systems. Entry and exit points are percentages of the ATR. Consequently, profit targets and stop losses must be adjusted to the appropriate time frame. For example, if the ATR of a stock is two points, then the profit target for a three-day holding period may be twice the ATR. The multiplier of the ATR for a profit target is a constant that is adjusted to the holding period.

Similarly, the multiplier of the ATR for a stop loss is also a constant. For the day trader using a five-minute chart and a holding period of several hours, the profit multiplier may be 0.5 times the ATR and the stop multiplier may be 0.3 times the ATR. Day trading and systems trading are not mutually exclusive, as one might be led to believe.

Over time, the professional realizes that trading is a game of statistics and probability [12]. Traditionally, most trading books have focused on entry and exit points, e.g., a one-point stop loss or a 2% stop loss. When designing a trading system, start with the goal of finding a strategy that is profitable 50% of the time, but the ratio of the average win to the average loss is 2:1.

The winning percentage changes as the risk/reward parameters are adjusted. In general, the lower the risk, the lower the winning percentage will be. Tightening a stop reduces the number of winners but reduces risk as well. In contrast, loosening a stop increases the number of winners but increases risk. Trading is an equation – all parameters must be balanced to find the optimal stop loss settings and profit targets. The trader must adjust the parameters to fit his or her risk profile. A higher winning percentage may feel more comfortable, but the trader may be sacrificing profit for comfort.

### Rules

After a system has been designed, the entry and exit rules must be defined. Each Acme trading system conforms to a standard format with rules for both long and short positions, as shown in Table 1.6:

**Table 1.6.** System Rules

| Rule | Description |
|---|---|
| Long Entry | Define buy setup conditions and buy order |
| Long Exit | Define sell conditions and sell order |
| Short Entry | Define short sale setup conditions and sell short order |
| Short Exit | Define cover conditions and cover order |

### 1.4.4 Trade Filters

The trader now has the decision of applying trade filters to the system. Depending upon the design of the system, certain filters are more relevant than others. For example, one of the swing trading systems, Acme N, is the only one using the ADX. Since N is a pullback system, the performance is directly proportional to the minimum price, historical volatility, and ADX. The higher these values are set, the better the results will be [4]. In contrast, the Acme R system is based on the rectangle, a consolidation pattern where a higher ADX does not improve overall performance.

Table 1.7 shows the filters for each trading system. The Acme P system is the only system that does not use trade filters, but a volatility filter could be applied to it. Each system was tested on all of the trade filters – the ones that improved testing results were kept, while the others were discarded; however, there may be other filters that could further improve performance.

**Table 1.7.** Acme Trade Filters

| System | ATR | MA | MP | HV | NR | ADX | DMI |
|--------|-----|-----|-----|-----|-----|-----|-----|
| F | | ✔ | ✔ | | | | ✔ |
| M | ✔ | | ✔ | | | | |
| N | | ✔ | ✔ | ✔ | ✔ | ✔ | |
| P | | | | | | | |
| R | ✔ | | | | | | |
| V | | ✔ | | | ✔ | | |

| | |
|------|------------------------------|
| ATR | Average True Range |
| MA | Moving Average |
| MP | Minimum Price |
| HV | Historical Volatility |
| NR | Narrow Range |
| ADX | Average Directional Index |
| DMI | Directional Movement Index |

The most interesting comparison of trade filters was the difference between the Moving Average filter and the Directional Movement Index filter. Some swing traders use the DMI to determine whether a stock is in an up trend or a downtrend. Overall, the performance of the moving average filter (above or below the average) was better than the DMI filter (positive or negative DMI ratio). The

Acme N system uses the moving average filter as an alternative to the DMI. A combination of the MA and DMI filters would further improve performance but reduce the number of signals.

The trade filters are grouped into two categories: price filters and technical filters. The ATR, MP, and NR filters are price filters derived from a stock's trading price and range for the current bar. The MA, HV, ADX, and DMI filters are technical filters based on historical price calculations. The trader is free to modify the code to add other filters.

Note that the *FiltersOn* parameter is an input parameter to each of the Acme systems. By turning this parameter on or off, the trader can compare the performance of the raw system versus the filtered one.

### Average True Range (ATR)

The range of a bar is the difference between its high value and low value. The *True Range* factors in any gap between the current bar and the previous bar. If the current bar's high is lower than the previous bar's close, then the ATR calculation uses the previous bar's close as the *True High* because of the gap down. If the current bar's low is higher than the previous bar's close, then a gap up has occurred, and the previous bar's low is the *True Low*. Thus, the True Range is the difference between the True High and the True Low. Finally, the *Average True Range* is the average of the True Range over a range of bars, e.g., twenty as shown in Figure 1.6.

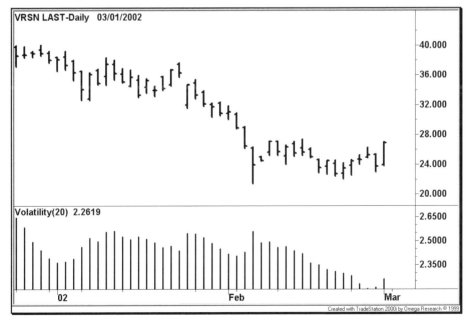

**Figure 1.6.** Average True Range

Average True Range is a measure of volatility. One might assume that a higher ATR implies a more volatile stock, but while ATR is a good initial volatility screen, a better screen is to divide the ATR into the stock price. So, if Stock A has an ATR of two and a price of 50, and Stock B has an ATR of two and a price of 40, then Stock A has a *Volatility Percentage* (VP) of $2 \div 50 = 4\%$, and Stock B has a VP of $2 \div 40 = 5\%$. Consequently, Stock B is more volatile.

Fortunately, even after stock prices converted from fractional to decimal in 2001, many stocks continue to have large daily ranges. In 1995, the ATRs of the popular companies to trade (Sun Microsystems, 3Com, and Applied Materials) ranged in the vicinity of three to four points. In 1999, many Nasdaq stocks had double-digit ATRs, some of which are shown here:

- Redback Networks (**RBAK:Nasdaq**): 16
- Yahoo (**YHOO:Nasdaq**): 11
- eBay (**EBAY:Nasdaq**): 11
- Copper Mountain (**CMTN:Nasdaq**): 9
- CMGI, Inc. (**CMGI:Nasdaq**): 8

Only three years later, we still find it difficult to believe that stocks were having daily ten-point swings. Since the heady days of 1999, the ATR of the typical momentum stock has declined to two or three points again as of this writing in early 2002.

### Moving Average (MA)

Much of technical analysis is self-fulfilling. The professional trader's job is to watch what other traders are watching. Because the 50-day moving average ($MA_{50}$) is so closely monitored, signals that occur here should be more profitable percentage-wise[7]. The general principle is that a stock in an up trend tends to pull back to the $MA_{50}$ as a support level (Figure 1.7). In contrast, a stock in a downtrend will pull up to the $MA_{50}$ as a resistance level (Figure 1.8).

The Acme F, N, and V systems use the 50-day moving average as a trade filter. The rules are simple. If trade filtering is on, then a long entry is allowed if the stock is trading above its $MA_{50}$. Similarly, a short entry is allowed only if the stock is below its $MA_{50}$. Because of its importance, the moving average is a pattern qualifier for the Acme M System. It alerts the trader to a stock near its average by placing the letter "A" above and below the bar.

Technicians use the 50-day MA to take positions on either side of the line. If a stock in a long uptrend breaks down below the average, then a trader goes short. If a stock in a long downtrend breaks above the average, then the trader goes long. As with any strategy in the market, however, nothing is ever that

---

[7] We test this assertion in Chapter 6 and reveal the answer.

simple. The $MA_{50}$ gets penetrated often in either direction, and the prevailing long-term trend usually wins out.

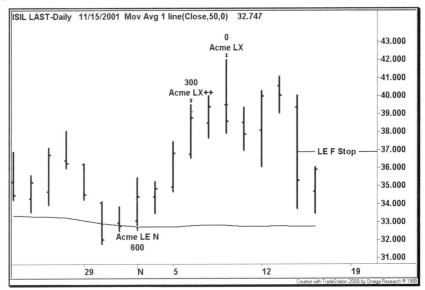

**Figure 1.7.** Long Entry at 50-day Moving Average

The best way to determine whether or not the trend has changed is to use an ATR factor for confirmation. To confirm an uptrend, do not go long until the price exceeds one ATR above the average. Likewise, for a downtrend, do not go short until the price falls one ATR below the average.

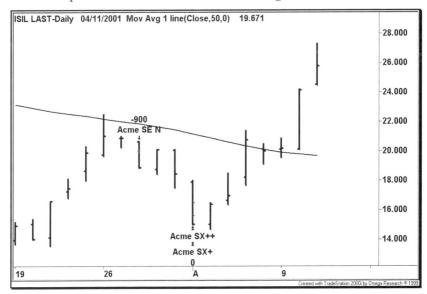

**Figure 1.8.** Short Entry at 50-day Moving Average

## Minimum Price (MP)

The conventional wisdom is that the professionals ignore stocks that trade for less than \$20 per share. The problem is that a minimum price screen filters out many volatile stocks, while less volatile high-priced stocks pass the minimum price screen. For example, if Stock A is trading at \$60 and has an ATR of 1.5, and Stock B is trading at \$10 with an ATR of 1.2, a screen based on a minimum ATR of 1.5 eliminates the more volatile Stock B. To compare the volatility of the two stocks, we divide the ATR by the stock price to calculate the Volatility Percentage. For Stock A, the VP is 1.5 ÷ 60 = 2.5%. In contrast, the VP for Stock B is 1.2 ÷ 10 = 12.0%. A volatility measure is a better trade filter than Minimum Price, although using both is an even better trade filter.

For low-priced stocks, screen for both volatility and liquidity. At the time of the chart in Figure 1.9, Ariba had a 20-day Volatility[8] of over 1.5 and traded under \$10 per share. Further, the stock traded an average of several million shares per day. As a result, the stock passed the filtering process and had two trades during this period with gains of approximately 20%. For the trader starting out with a smaller stake, these volatile, low-priced stocks are a logical choice.

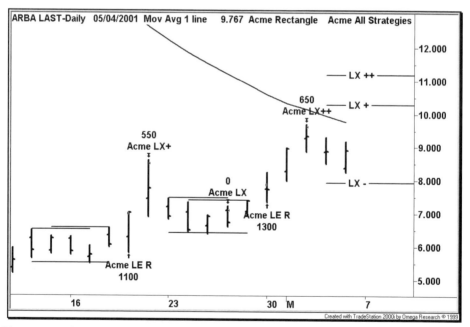

**Figure 1.9.** Ariba Low-Priced Stock Example

---

[8] The TradeStation *Volatility* function calculates the Average True Range, so the two terms in this context are equivalent.

A trader wants the three V's: volatility, volume, and a small vig[9] [21]. Volatility creates the opportunity to go long or go short, volume provides the liquidity to get in and out of the position, and the small vig limits the amount of money that lands in the pocket of the market maker or specialist.

### Historical Volatility (HV)

Each stock has *Historical Volatility* (HV). It is an annualized percentage that measures the standard deviation of a stock's price changes over a period of time, e.g., the percentage change of today's close compared to yesterday's close for the last thirty days. The historical volatility calculation assumes that stock prices fall in a lognormal distribution and is derived according to the Black-Scholes options model [5].

**Example 1.4.** Function *AcmeVolatility*

```
{********************************************************************
AcmeVolatility: Calculate the annualized historic volatility
********************************************************************}

Inputs:
    Length(Numeric);

Variables:
    DaysInYear(365),
    DaysInMonth(30),
    DaysInWeek(7),
    TimeFactor(0.0);

AcmeVolatility = 0;

If Close > 0 and Close[1] > 0 Then Begin
    If DataCompression >= 2 and DataCompression < 5 Then Begin
        If DataCompression = 2 Then {Daily}
            TimeFactor = DaysInYear
        Else If DataCompression = 3 Then {Weekly}
            TimeFactor = DaysInYear / DaysInWeek
        Else If DataCompression = 4 Then {Monthly}
            TimeFactor = DaysInYear / DaysInMonth;

        AcmeVolatility = StdDev(Log(Close / Close[1]), Length) *
        SquareRoot(TimeFactor);
    End;
End;
```

---

[9] Vig is an abbreviation for *vigorish*, the bookmaker's percentage of the total amount put up by the bettors. The standard service charge is 4.55%.

The EasyLanguage code for calculating HV is shown in Example 1.4. The HV can be calculated for daily, weekly, or monthly charts. Depending on the chart's time frame, the function calculates a multiplier to determine the annualized HV. The HV calculation uses a sample bar range based on the input parameter *Length* to extrapolate the annualized volatility from the closing price changes for the sample period. The steps for calculating the HV are as follows:

- Calculate the *TimeFactor* based on the chart periodicity.
- Compute the standard deviation of the sample based on the natural logarithm of the closing price percentages using the last Length bars.
- Multiply the standard deviation by the TimeFactor to determine the annualized HV.

For a daily chart, the TimeFactor is simply the number of days in the year. For a weekly chart, it is the number of days in the year divided by the number of days in a week. Historical volatilities are measured over various periods of time, but the 30-day HV ($HV_{30}$) is common in many options models. The $HV_{30}$ gives the trader an estimate of a stock's travel range. For example, a stock trading at $20 with an $HV_{30}$ of 20% will have traded 20 × 0.2 = 4 points above and below the current price approximately 68%[10] of the time during this period, based on a normal distribution [29]. The $HV_{30}$ of the stock in Figure 1.10 is 1.36, or 136%, which is extremely high.

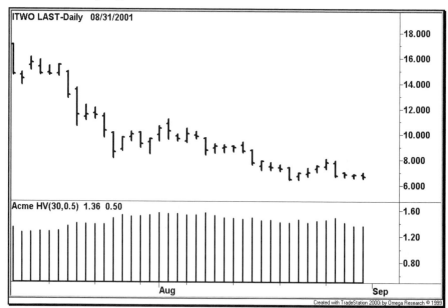

**Figure 1.10.** Historical Volatility

---

[10] Based on the normal probability curve, 1 standard deviation = 68%.

In general, we require a minimum HV reading of 0.5 to filter out non-volatile stocks; however, higher readings are desirable. The trader should experiment with various HV values to scope his or her universe of stocks. The IVolatility Web site at http://www.ivolatility.com has the 30-day HV readings as well as *Implied Volatility* (IV) readings.

### Narrow Range (NR)

Crabel pioneered the use of Narrow Range (NR) bars by assigning them to categories such as NR4 and NR7 [6]. For example, an NR4 bar is the bar with the narrowest range of the last four bars. Other variations of narrow range bars have since been developed, combining them with inside days to produce other patterns such as the ID/NR4 day [3].

A narrow range bar can also be defined by framing its range in the context of the ATR. By definition, a narrow range bar's range must be less than the ATR, but the NR bar is generally defined by a smaller percentage of the ATR. For example, if a stock's ATR is two, and the NR percentage is 60%, then a bar with a range of 2 × 0.6 = 1.2 or less would qualify as an NR bar. An NR percentage that ranges between one-half and two-thirds of the ATR is recommended as the maximum value, as shown in Figure 1.11.

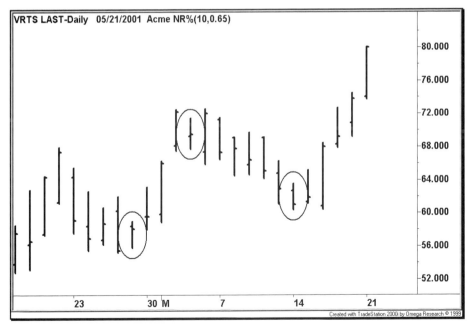

**Figure 1.11.** Narrow Range Bars

If a trading system places a stop at or around the previous bar's high or low, then the range of the bar dictates the size of the loss. Thus, an NR bar improves the risk/reward ratio of the trade because the loss is inherently limited to the narrow range. Further, a narrow range day implies a greater-than-even probability that a wide range (WR) day with a range greater than the ATR will occur the next day. A cluster of NR days means that the market is anticipating a major news event, such as a Fed meeting on interest rates or a key economic number.

### Average Directional Index (ADX)

The ADX is simply a measure of the strength of a trend and has been covered in depth by other authors [3, 4]. As a general rule, if the ADX is rising, then a stock is trending strongly – either up or down. The ADX is used in combination with the DMI for momentum trading systems. Although most systems use an absolute value of ADX to assess a strong trend (e.g., a minimum of 25 or 30), the ADX for a strong stock in a pullback will fall as low as 15. Thus, when screening for trading candidates, consider the ADX five or ten days ago along with the current reading.

A characteristic of the ADX is that a rising value indicates a strengthening trend. This is true, but a stock develops a strong trend well before the ADX reflects the movement of the stock. Geometric breakouts from a long or short base trigger signals much earlier. The stock in Figure 1.12 had a 30% move before the 14-day ADX even reached 30 in late September.

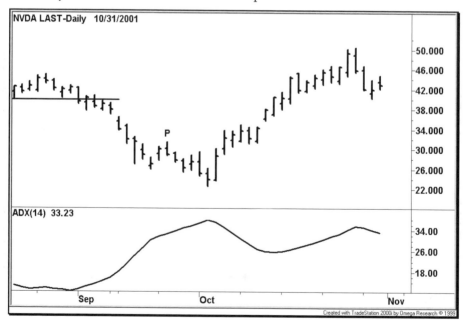

**Figure 1.12.** Average Directional Index

Each technical indicator has its niche, however. As shown in Figure 1.12, high ADX readings are useful for pullbacks (denoted by P) in very strong trends. A retracement of two or more bars is usually interrupted by a resumption of the prevailing long-term trend.

Returning to the example, a strong reversal begins in early October, and the ADX does not resume rising until well into the reversal. Thus, treat the ADX as a lagging indicator – the trader will benefit from shortening the study length from 14 to 7, especially for short sales.

### Directional Movement Index (DMI)

The DMI has 2 components: +DMI and -DMI. If +DMI is greater than -DMI, then the trend is up, and if the -DMI is greater than +DMI, then the trend is down. Figure 1.13 shows a crossover of the two lines under the 50-day moving average. Combined with a weakening ADX trend (the thick line), this crossover is typically a good shorting opportunity, and the same principle applies to long positions initiated above the 50-day moving average.

In Figure 1.13, the DMI lines widen near the end of the chart (beginning of March). When the spread between the two values is wide, a position should be covered. In this case, the down tick in -DMI corresponding with the up tick in +DMI is an opportunity to either cover a short position or go long.

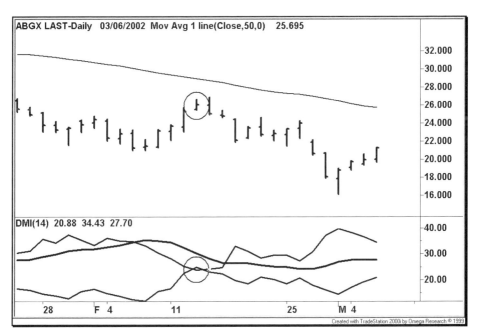

**Figure 1.13.** Directional Movement Index

## 1.5 Performance

This section establishes some guidelines on evaluating trading system performance using the TradeStation Performance Report. For a thorough evaluation of a trading system, refer to Stridsman's book *Trading Systems That Work* [30]. As the trader will discover, the key to any trading system is to analyze its *drawdown* in terms of losing streaks and the size of the average losing trade. Based on these data, we can calculate the appropriate amount of capital to risk per trade.

Table 1.8 shows a sample performance report. The Total Net Profit and Percent profitable numbers are alluring, but the important number is the Profit Factor: the number of dollars gained for each one lost. In this example, dividing the Gross Profit of $447,001.50 by the Gross Loss of $174,787.00 yields a profit factor of 2.56.

Reviewing some other ratios, the ratio of the average win to the average loss is $4,217.00 divided by $2,361.99 equals 1.79. The holding period ratio is the average number of bars in the winners (30) divided by the average number of bars in the losers (16), approximately 1.88.

**Table 1.8.** TradeStation Strategy Performance Report – A System QQQ-10 min

| | | | |
|---|---|---|---|
| Total Net Profit | $272,214.50 | Open position P/L | $0.00 |
| Gross Profit | $447,001.50 | Gross Loss | ($174,787.00) |
| Total # of trades | 180 | Percent profitable | 58.89% |
| Number winning trades | 106 | Number losing trades | 74 |
| Largest winning trade | $12,168.00 | Largest losing trade | ($5,280.00) |
| Average winning trade | $4,217.00 | Average losing trade | ($2,361.99) |
| Ratio avg win/avg loss | 1.79 | Avg trade (win & loss) | $1,512.30 |
| Max consec. Winners | 7 | Max consec. losers | 5 |
| Avg # bars in winners | 30 | Avg # bars in losers | 16 |
| Max intraday drawdown | ($21,993.00) | | |
| Profit Factor | 2.56 | Max # contracts held | 9,500 |

To assess the impact of drawdown, multiply the largest losing trade ($5,280.00) by the maximum consecutive losers (5) to get $26,400.00. The actual maximum drawdown (not shown in the table) was $19,720.00. The maximum intraday drawdown of $21,993.00 occurred when the system was short before a surprise interest rate cut, so we are fortunate to have this price shock in the results.

We look for month-to-month consistency with any trading system, as shown in Table 1.9. Day traders should expect consistent weekly profitability. A swing trader should expect occasional losing weeks because the combination of time frame and losing streak makes it almost impossible to avoid a losing week. For example, if the trader makes five trades a week and the maximum consecutive losers is four, then the odds of a losing week are highly probable. Compare the actual monthly performance with the expected monthly income in Table 1.3 to set reasonable profit goals.

**Table 1.9.** Monthly Analysis

| Period | Net Profit | % Gain | Profit Factor | # Trades | % Profitable |
|---|---|---|---|---|---|
| January | $14,532.00 | 9.04% | 2.21 | 13.50 | 48.15% |
| February | $8,994.25 | 4.00% | 1.79 | 12.50 | 56.00% |
| March | $18,932.75 | 9.21% | 7.10 | 8.00 | 75.00% |
| April | $19,467.50 | 10.16% | 2.21 | 19.00 | 57.89% |
| May | $24,333.00 | 11.53% | 3.04 | 17.00 | 64.71% |
| June | $18,020.50 | 7.66% | 3.30 | 13.00 | 76.92% |
| July | $22,304.50 | 8.80% | 6.79 | 16.00 | 68.75% |
| August | $27,699.00 | 10.05% | 3.88 | 16.00 | 68.75% |
| September | $5,841.00 | 1.93% | 1.59 | 10.00 | 50.00% |
| October | $10,592.00 | 3.43% | 1.57 | 13.00 | 46.15% |
| November | $9,011.00 | 7.65% | 1.64 | 11.50 | 60.87% |
| December | $20,508.50 | 12.79% | 3.27 | 15.50 | 64.52% |

As displayed in Figure 1.14, the *Equity Curve* (EC) is a graph of the cumulative profit of a set of trading systems. The vertical distance between each point on the chart represents the profit or loss of an individual trade. The EC is just like a price chart – it has trend and it has pullbacks (the distance from peak to trough is the drawdown). Technical indicators such as the moving average and ADX can be calculated for the curve to assess the strength of a trading system.

Analyze the Equity Curve from a three-month perspective because a trader should expect flat periods lasting up to thirty or sixty days for a system. The EC in Figure 1.14 has roughly the same net profit for each three-month period. Plot the EC every month to determine whether or not the system performance is deteriorating, e.g., it advances half as much over consecutive periods.

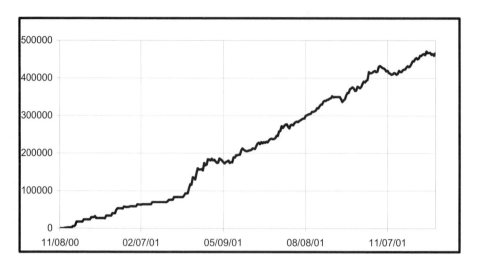

**Figure 1.14.** Equity Curve

Finally, measure the distance (in terms of number of trades) between successive equity peaks and troughs to approximate the cycle of the system. This cycle is a function of the number of winning and losing streaks made by the system.

## 1.5.1 A Tale of Two Stocks

### Ciena and Cigna

We finish the introduction with the tale of two stocks: Cigna and Ciena. Just one letter apart, the two stocks could not have been more opposite in personality, one a staid insurance company and the other a volatile optical stock. Since Cigna was listed on the New York Stock Exchange and Ciena on the Nasdaq, a bitter rivalry developed, so the two stocks requested a performance review from the Acme trading systems.

The performance reports in Tables 1.10 and 1.11 evaluate the unfiltered performance of the trading systems for both of the stocks. Clearly, any system that generates a profit factor of 0.65 is useless for trading but instructive. For Cigna, the systems fared poorly, with only five out of eighteen winning trades. In contrast, Ciena performance results were just the opposite—a profit factor of 4.49 with only three losing trades.

The whole point of this exercise is to demonstrate that a system or systems cannot be blindly applied to a universe of stocks. First, we need to identify the characteristics that differentiate these stocks through a learning process known as *data mining*.

**Table 1.10.** TradeStation Strategy Performance Report - Acme All Strategies CI-Daily

| | | | |
|---|---|---|---|
| Total Net Profit | ($6,644.60) | Open position P/L | $0.00 |
| Gross Profit | $12,378.40 | Gross Loss | ($19,023.00) |
| Total # of trades | 18 | Percent profitable | 27.78% |
| Number winning trades | 5 | Number losing trades | 13 |
| Largest winning trade | $4,995.00 | Largest losing trade | ($2,500.00) |
| Average winning trade | $2,475.68 | Average losing trade | ($1,463.31) |
| Ratio avg win/avg loss | 1.69 | Avg trade (win & loss) | ($369.14) |
| Max consec. Winners | 1 | Max consec. losers | 6 |
| Avg # bars in winners | 3 | Avg # bars in losers | 2 |
| Max intraday drawdown | ($11,528.00) | | |
| Profit Factor | .65 | Max # contracts held | 1,600 |

**Table 1.11.** TradeStation Strategy Performance Report - Acme All Strategies CIEN-Daily

| | | | |
|---|---|---|---|
| Total Net Profit | $17,814.10 | Open position P/L | $0.00 |
| Gross Profit | $22,917.30 | Gross Loss | ($5,103.20) |
| Total # of trades | 14 | Percent profitable | 78.57% |
| Number winning trades | 11 | Number losing trades | 3 |
| Largest winning trade | $4,343.70 | Largest losing trade | ($2,703.20) |
| Average winning trade | $2,083.39 | Average losing trade | ($1,701.07) |
| Ratio avg win/avg loss | 1.22 | Avg trade (win & loss) | $1,272.44 |
| Max consec. Winners | 9 | Max consec. losers | 1 |
| Avg # bars in winners | 3 | Avg # bars in losers | 2 |
| Max intraday drawdown | ($3,978.20) | | |
| Profit Factor | 4.49 | Max # contracts held | 1,500 |

First, we mine the trading filters to extract the characteristics that separate the trading stocks from the non-trading stocks. Then, we iterate through the characteristics to explain the difference in performance between two stocks. Clearly, we need to re-apply the trade filters every night to create a new stock universe; a trading stock can revert to a non-trading stock and vice versa.

The first distinguishing characteristic is volatility. As shown in Figures 1.15 and 1.16, the $HV_{30}$ for Cigna is 0.36 and the $HV_{30}$ for Ciena is 1.09. Cigna's HV does not meet the minimum threshold of 0.5 set by the indicator, although its HV is turning up, and it may soon become a trading candidate. The choice of a minimum threshold is a balance between discretion and automation, i.e., the higher the value, the fewer the number of charts to review; a lower value means the trader exercises more judgment during the stock selection process.

The trader should test each Acme system by stock sector. For example, the Acme N system is a momentum system that performs well on technology stocks but fares poorly on cyclical stocks. By testing each system per sector over distinct time frames, the trader will develop an appreciation for the cyclical symbiosis between sector volatility and the Acme systems, just another way to obtain an edge (see Chapter 8). The stock selection process is methodical; all stocks are funneled through market and sector filters to obtain the best trading candidates. Through experience and experimentation, the trader will learn how and when to apply the systems.

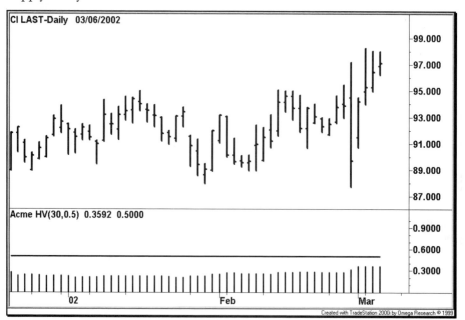

**Figure 1.15.** Low Volatility: Cigna

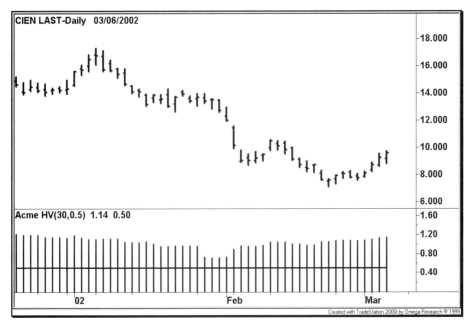

**Figure 1.16.** High Volatility: Ciena

# 2 Pair Trading

*We used to think that if we knew one,*
*We knew two, because one and one are two.*
*We are finding that we must learn*
*A great deal more about 'and'.*

Sir Arthur Eddington
*Mathematical Maxims and Minims*

*Pair trading* is a market-neutral strategy where a long position in one stock and a short position in another stock are initiated simultaneously. The profit principle of the trade is based on mean reversion, i.e., two stocks that normally trade in the same direction become temporarily uncorrelated and eventually will revert to the mean; this technique is also known as statistical arbitrage.

Most of the published work on pair trading pertains to positions held over several days [24] or as much as several months, e.g., a typical arbitrage where an acquiring company's stock is shorted and the target stock is bought. However, recent changes in margin requirements circa 2001 give the day trader access to as much as 4:1 intraday buying power, perfectly suited for intraday pair trading.

This chapter presents a complete strategy for trading stock pairs intraday, although the technique can be extended to positions of several days or more. First, a definition for the spread is presented along with a visual TradeStation indicator. Then, the spread bands are calculated to determine when a pair trade is initiated; a trade triggers only in the area outside the upper and lower bands. Finally, the complete entry and exit rules for the pair trading system are defined, followed by several examples.

The allure of pair trading is that it is a strategy with little risk. Further, the trader does not really care about the direction of the market and does not have to worry about nagging issues such as the S&P futures or the reaction to economic reports. However, no stock is immune to the risk of a trading halt or an earnings warning. Before trading begins each day, review each of the stocks for specific company news: upcoming earnings reports, conference calls, and upgrades and downgrades. Be aware that news will frequently create a spread opportunity, but a stock with major news may demand a reverse spread strategy.

## 2.1 The Spread

The *Spread* is the difference between two stock ratios sharing a common anchor point in time, for example, the closing price of today compared to the closing price of yesterday. For a stock pair A–B, if Stock A closed today at 21 and yesterday at 20, then its closing ratio is 21 ÷ 20 = 1.05. Similarly, if Stock B closed today at 42 and yesterday at 40, then its closing ratio is 42 ÷ 40 = 1.05. Thus, the spread is 1.05 minus 1.05 equals zero. Here, in this narrow instance, the stocks are moving in synchronization, i.e., they are *correlated*.

Consider the stock pair A–B again. If Stock A closed today at 20 and yesterday at 20, then its closing ratio is 20 ÷ 20 = 1.0. If Stock B closed today at 42 and yesterday at 40, then its closing ratio is 42 ÷ 40 = 1.05. Here, the spread is 1.0 minus 1.05 equals -.05, and Stock A is undervalued relative to Stock B. If the spread were a positive number, then Stock A would be overvalued relative to Stock B.

For a daily spread system, the anchor point could be the number of days ago, e.g., the close of today compared to the close five days ago. For an intraday system, we compare the last price on an intraday chart to either the closing price of yesterday or the opening price of today. The difference is whether or not the trader wants to factor gaps into the spread calculation. If so, then the closing price of yesterday is chosen.

$$Spread = (Last_A \div Close_A) - (Last_B \div Close_B) \qquad (3.1)$$

We calculate the Spread with Equation 3.1, using the variable *Last* to indicate a real-time price. Divide the last real-time trade price of Stock A by its closing price yesterday, and do the same for Stock B. Subtract the difference to obtain the current Spread.

The spread is displayed in a separate plot below the charts of the stock pair. As the charts update in real-time, the spread is plotted as a line within two channel lines known as *spread bands*. In Figure 2.1, the parallel line running across the top of the bottom panel is the upper spread band, and the bottom line is the lower spread band. The spread bands are computed at the beginning of each day using yesterday's historical volatilities and correlation (see below).

When the spread line touches the upper band, the stock in the top panel (Stock A) becomes overvalued relative to the stock in the lower panel (Stock B), a condition indicating that Stock A should be shorted and Stock B should be bought. When the spread touches the lower band, Stock A becomes undervalued relative to Stock B. In this case, Stock A should be bought and Stock B should be shorted at the same time.

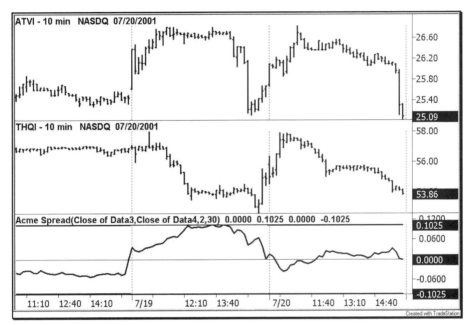

**Figure 2.1.** The Spread

## 2.2 Spread Bands

A *Spread Band* (SB) is a standard deviation-based unit of the normal probability curve. The SB factors in the combined volatility and correlation of a stock pair to derive an estimate of where a pair trade should be initiated. The trader then determines how many standard deviations are appropriate for any given pair. For example, if one standard deviation is selected, then when the spread hits the SB, the stock pair has a 68% chance of reverting to the mean. If two standard deviations are selected, then the pair has a 95% probability [29]. However, practice is different than theory – these calculations presume the absence of news and other external factors that affect stock prices.

First, we review the factors in the SB calculation. The Historical Volatility (HV) was discussed in Chapter 1, so the 30-day HV must be calculated for each stock in the pair: $HV_A$ and $HV_B$. The next factor in the Spread Band equation is the *Correlation Coefficient*, also known as *Coefficient R*. The R-value correlates the movement of one stock price with another. A correlation of +1 means that the two stocks move synchronously, while a correlation of -1 means that the two stocks move in opposite directions. R is the second factor in the SB equation.

The chart below (Figure 2.2) shows a daily chart of two correlated stocks with a current R$_{30}$ of 0.33, towards the low end of the established correlation range.

The Acme P System is based on highly correlated stock pairs with an R of at least +0.3. However, it is perfectly possible to reverse the signals to trade non-correlated pairs and use the area outside of the spread bands. Use an R-value of -0.3 or less for non-correlated stock pairs.

For further information on equity correlations, go to the Market Topology Web site at http://www.impactopia.com. At this site, a stock symbol query will return a list of stocks that are most correlated to a reference stock. The site provides equity maps for domestic and foreign market indices such as the S&P 500 showing the correlations among all of the stocks composing the index.

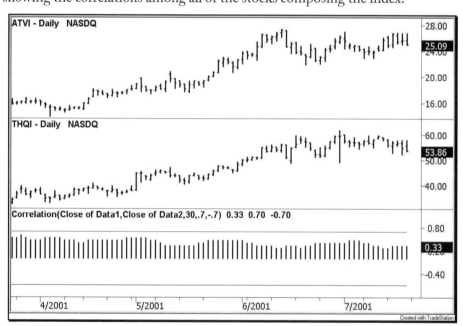

**Figure 2.2.** Correlation Coefficient

Now, we can calculate the Spread Bands for a stock pair for one trading day, as shown in Equation 3.2. The formula assumes 365 days in a year[1], so the square root of 1 ÷ 365 is taken to get the constant .0523, represented by $k$. The variable $SD$ represents the number of standard deviations. The variables $HV_A$ and $HV_B$ are the historic volatilities of Stock A and Stock B, respectively.

The relationship between the Spread Bands and R is an inverse relationship. As the correlation R increases, the bands narrow and vice versa. Consequently, the volatilities are multiplied by the factor (1- R).

---

[1] Some traders prefer using the number of trading days in a year (approximately 252) instead of the number of calendar days.

The formula for the Spread Band is as follows:

$$SB = k \times SD \times (HV_A + HV_B) \times (1 - R) \qquad (3.2)$$

Here is an example of two correlated video game software stocks. Our Stock A is Activision (ATVI:Nasdaq), and Stock B is THQ Incorporated (THQI:Nasdaq). The 30-day volatilities and correlation are as follows:

- $HV_{30}$ of ATVI is 0.643
- $HV_{30}$ of THQI is 0.822
- $R_{30}$ is 0.33

The Spread Band for a standard deviation for the ATVI–THQI Pair is:

$$0.0523 \times 1 \times (0.643 + 0.822) \times (1 - 0.33) = 0.0513$$

The final factor to consider is the number of standard deviations required for generating a pair-trading signal. We have selected two standard deviations as the default value because prices have at least a 95% chance of reverting to the mean, assuming a normal probability curve. Therefore, we multiply the Spread Band value (0.0513) by the number of standard deviations (2.0) to obtain the upper and lower Spread Band values, +0.1025 and -0.1025 (Figure 2.3).

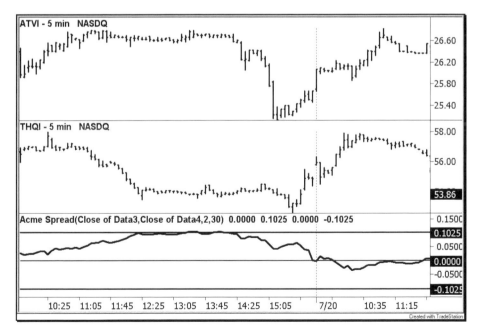

**Figure 2.3.** Spread Bands

## 2.3 Short Selling

Before defining the pair trading system, we review the practice of short selling. To effectively execute spreads, the trader must become adept at short selling. A short sale is the reverse of a long position: sell first and buy back later. Since short selling is a transaction where a security is first borrowed, the trader must check the broker's short list to ensure that either of the stocks in the pair can be borrowed before *legging* into the trade.

The ease of short selling depends upon the liquidity of the stock. Shorting Nasdaq stocks with penny spreads makes execution smoother for the pair trader. If the trader decides to leg into the long entry first, then executing the short side should be no problem with the liquid stock. Because of the uptick rule, however, the short leg should always be executed first. Shorting liquid NYSE stocks is just as easy, but if the stock is dropping fast, then the trader is not going to get an uptick; however, this problem can be solved through the practice of hedging (see Section 2.4).

### 2.3.1 NYSE Rules

Stocks on the NYSE can be sold short only on a *plus tick* or *zero-plus tick*. A plus tick is a trade price that is higher than the previous trade price. A zero-plus tick is a trade price equal to the previous trade price, but the previous trade price must have occurred on a plus tick. Table 2.1 is an example of an NYSE trade sequence, showing whether each trade occurred on a plus tick or minus tick.

**Table 2.1.** NYSE Short Sales Example

| Trade Price | Tick Type | Action |
|-------------|-----------------|----------|
| 30.00 | Plus Tick | Short |
| 29.95 | Minus Tick | No Short |
| 30.00 | Plus Tick | Short |
| 30.05 | Plus Tick | Short |
| 30.05 | Zero-Plus Tick | Short |
| 30.00 | Minus Tick | No Short |
| 30.00 | Zero-Minus Tick | No Short |
| 30.05 | Plus Tick | Short |

### 2.3.2 Nasdaq Rules

The Nasdaq uptick rule is different than the NYSE rule – it is based on the best bid price, not on the trade price. On the Nasdaq, one can sell short only on an *up bid* (denoted by an up arrow in a Level II window) and not on a *down bid* (denoted by a down arrow). Table 2.2 shows an example of when a Nasdaq stock can be shorted and when it cannot.

**Table 2.2.** Nasdaq Short Sales Example

| Trade Price | Best Bid | Tick Type | Action |
|:-----------:|:--------:|-----------|----------|
| 30.00 | 30.00 | Up Bid | Short |
| 29.95 | 29.95 | Down Bid | No Short |
| 30.00 | 29.95 | Down Bid | No Short |
| 30.05 | 30.00 | Up Bid | Short |
| 30.05 | 30.00 | Up Bid | Short |
| 30.00 | 29.95 | Down Bid | No Short |
| 30.05 | 29.95 | Down Bid | No Short |

## 2.4 Hedging

A *hedge* is two positions where a long position and a short position in the same security offset each other. The hedge can be composed of various instruments, e.g., a long stock position and a short options position. In the good old days circa 1995, a hedge could be created using two linked accounts. By establishing a long position in Account 1 and a short position in Account 2, a stock could be effectively sold short by just selling the long position in Account 1 and then buying it back to reestablish the hedge, thereby circumventing the short sale rule in the process. The trader was able to short a stock without an up bid or plus tick, as illustrated in Table 2.3.

Shortly thereafter, a rule was instituted that eliminated this loophole. The modern style of hedging is to combine a stock position with an option position to create a *conversion* [19]. A conversion is a long stock position combined with a synthetic short position (long put and short call). Thus, by selling the long position, the trader can go net short and then buy back the stock later to return to a hedged position. A conversion is a relatively complicated series of trades, but fortunately professional firms allow a trader to purchase a single-day conversion on the spot, commonly referred to as a *bullet*.

The introduction of single-stock futures presents another hedging alternative. A trader can simply short the stock futures contract, establish a long position simultaneously, and then execute sell-buy trade sequences to short the stock.

**Table 2.3.** Old-Style Hedging

| Account 1 | Account 2 | Action |
|-----------|-----------|--------|
| Buy CSCO |  | Establish the hedge |
|  | Sell Short CSCO | Establish the hedge |
| Sell CSCO |  | Short CSCO without up bid |
| Buy CSCO |  | Cover CSCO (close short) |
| Buy CSCO |  | Go long CSCO |
| Sell CSCO |  | Close long position |
| Sell CSCO |  | Go short again |

## 2.5 Pair Trading System (Acme P)

The Acme P system is a mechanical trading system for trading stock pairs. First, we calculate the volatility measures, and then define the entry and exit rules for each pair combination. We recommend using either a five-minute chart or even a three-minute chart for timely signals since the pair trades are entered on the close of the bar.

Although the system is designed for intraday pair trading, the system can be adapted to position trading because it works on any time frame. The system shown here uses the one-day *VolatilityConstant*. This constant can be multiplied by any number of days to adjust the Spread Bands to the proper width.

| Calculations |
|---|

1. Set the Standard Deviations (SD), default value is 2.0.
2. Obtain the 30-day Volatility of Stock A ($HV_A$).
3. Obtain the 30-day Volatility of Stock B ($HV_B$).
4. Calculate the 30-day Correlation of Stock A and Stock B ($R_{AB}$).
5. Calculate the Spread Band (SB).
6. Calculate the Spread (S).

### 2.5.1 Long A–Short B Rules

| Entry Rules |
| --- |

1. S crosses above −SB
2. **Sell Short** Stock B on Close.
3. **Buy** Stock A on Close.

| Exit Rules: Profit Target |
| --- |

1. S crosses above 0
2. **Sell** Stock A on Close.
3. **Cover** Stock B on Close.

| Exit Rules: Stop Loss |
| --- |

1. S < (SD * -SB)
2. **Sell** Stock A on Close.
3. **Cover** Stock B on Close.

Note how the entry rule waits for the Spread to cross over the lower Spread Band. If the spread falls below the lower SB, then the system waits for a reversal back above the SB. As an alternative, the aggressive trader may choose to let the Spread fall below the SB and then execute the pair trade as soon as the Spread ticks up, at which point the Spread may be well underneath the lower SB. If the signal occurs at the open, then the trader may choose to execute the trade immediately, and maintain a stop loss of two times the SB, the standard stop in the Acme P System.

### 2.5.2 Short A–Long B Rules

| Entry Rules |
| --- |

1. S crosses below SB.
2. **Sell** Short Stock A on Close.
3. **Buy** Stock B on Close.

Exit Rules: Profit Target

1. S crosses below 0
2. **Sell** Stock B on Close.
3. **Cover** Stock A on Close.

Exit Rules: Stop Loss

1. S > (SD * SB)
2. **Sell** Stock B on Close.
3. **Cover** Stock A on Close.

In the Acme P System shown in Example 2.1, the number of shares N is calculated from the daily data of Stock A, in this case Data3. Because each stock in the pair uses the Percent Volatility Model for position size, the pair is volatility-hedged. If a stock trading at 40 has an ATR of two and another stock at 20 has an ATR of two, then the position size for both stocks will be exactly the same. For this reason, gaps are an important part of pair trading. In this example, if both stocks gapped up one point, then the stock at 41 becomes undervalued relative to the stock at 21, and there is potential for a quick pair trade.

After position sizing, the HVs of both Stock A and Stock B are calculated from Data3 and Data4, respectively. The two stocks are then correlated, and the system can calculate the Spread Bands for the stock pair. First, the band for one standard deviation is calculated. Then, the system multiplies this band value by the number of standard deviations to obtain the Spread Band figure.

The upper Spread Band is the positive SB figure, and the lower Spread Band is the negative figure. Finally, the spread is calculated, and any crossover condition will trigger a pair signal.

As an alternative to the exit rules implemented in the code, the trader may wish for the Spread to traverse from one band all of the way to the other band instead of the crossing point at zero. In this case, the stop loss rule can be modified to allow for greater volatility in the Spread. Increase the *StandardDeviations* parameter for wider latitude.

The following code in Example 2.1 is an EasyLanguage rendition of the pair trading system. The system uses the number of standard deviations to determine the stop loss; however, a trader may wish to implement a separate stop for the system instead of depending on the number of standard deviations. The trader is also free to change the reference prices *Price1* and *Price2* for computing the spread. For example, *Price1* and *Price2* could reference the open of today versus the close of yesterday.

**Example 2.1.** Acme P System

```
{***********************************************************************
Acme P System: Pair Trading

Data1: Stock 1 Intraday
Data2: Stock 2 Intraday
Data3: Stock 1 Daily (hidden)
Data4: Stock 2 Daily (hidden)
***********************************************************************}

Inputs:
    Price1(Close of Data3),
    Price2(Close of Data4),
    StandardDeviations(1.5),
    Length(30),
    {Position Sizing Parameters}
    Equity(100000),
    RiskModel(3),
    RiskPercent(2.0),
    RiskATR(1.0),
    {Trade Logging}
    LogTrades(False),
    LogFile("Orders.txt");

Variables:
    N(0),
    HV1(0.0),
    HV2(0.0),
    CV(0.0),
    VolatilityBand(0.0),
    VolatilityConstant(0.0523),
    UpperBand(0.0),
    LowerBand(0.0),
    Spread(0.0);

If Date <> Date[1] Then Begin
    N = AcmeGetShares(Equity, RiskModel, RiskPercent, RiskATR)
    of Data3;
    HV1 = AcmeVolatility(Length) of Data3;
    HV2 = AcmeVolatility(Length) of Data4;
    CV = Correlation(Price1, Price2, Length);
    VolatilityBand = VolatilityConstant * (HV1 + HV2) * (1 - CV);
    UpperBand = StandardDeviations * VolatilityBand;
    LowerBand = StandardDeviations * (-VolatilityBand);
End;

Spread = (Close of Data1 / Price1) - (Close of Data2 / Price2);

If Spread crosses above LowerBand Then
    Buy("Acme P LE") N Shares This Bar on Close;

If Spread crosses above 0 Then
```

```
    ExitLong("Acme P LX +") This Bar on Close
Else If Spread <= StandardDeviations * LowerBand Then
    ExitLong("Acme P LX -") This Bar on Close;

If Spread crosses below UpperBand Then
    Sell("Acme P SE") N Shares This Bar on Close;

If Spread crosses below 0 Then
    ExitShort("Acme P SX +") This Bar on Close
Else If Spread >= StandardDeviations * UpperBand Then
    ExitShort("Acme P SX -") This Bar on Close;

{Log Trades for Spreadsheet Export}
Condition1 = AcmeLogTrades(LogTrades, LogFile, "P");
```

To see both legs of the pair trade executing simultaneously, the TradeStation workspace must be set up to have two charting windows stacked horizontally, one window configured as shown in Table 2.4 and the other configured as shown in Table 2.5.

**Table 2.4.** Pair Configuration for Chart Window 1

| Data1 | Stock A | Intraday |
|-------|---------|----------|
| Data2 | Stock B | Intraday |
| Data3 | Stock A | Daily |
| Data4 | Stock B | Daily |
| Data5 | Acme Spread | Indicator |

**Table 2.5.** Pair Configuration for Chart Window 2

| Data1 | Stock B | Intraday |
|-------|---------|----------|
| Data2 | Stock A | Intraday |
| Data3 | Stock B | Daily |
| Data4 | Stock A | Daily |
| Data5 | Acme Spread | Indicator |

With the windows configured in this manner, the trader will receive the long and short signals of the pair simultaneously. For a Long A–Short B pair, the long signal will trip in Chart Window 1, and the short signal will fire in Chart Window 2. For a Short A–Long B pair, the short signal will be displayed in Chart Window 1, and the long signal will appear in Chart Window 2.

## 2.6 Examples

The following examples illustrate how to trade the Acme P System. Each example uses an Equity value of $100,000, a Percent Volatility Model with a risk value of 2%, and the number of Standard Deviations is two. Because each leg uses the Percent Volatility Model, the number of shares is adjusted to each stock's ATR.

### 2.6.1 Activision–THQ Incorporated

Figure 2.4 is an example of a Short A–Long B entry. Stock A (ATVI) has become overvalued relative to Stock B (THQI) because the Spread has risen above the upper Spread Band. As soon as the Spread crosses back below the upper SB, we short 1400 shares of ATVI at a price of 26.70 at 1:40 pm and buy 600 shares of THQI at 54.10 (note that TradeStation does not show simultaneous signals in different plots, so the symbols have to be reversed to show the long signal in THQI – see Figure 2.5).

The Spread crosses **below** zero right at 9:35 am the next day, at which point the ATVI short trade is covered at 26.07 for a profit of 0.63 points. Simultaneously, we sell THQI at 55.96 for a profit of 1.86 points on the long side of the pair. Together, the pair trade nets a total profit of $1,998, not including slippage and commissions.

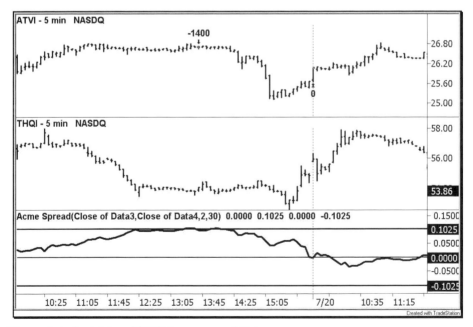

**Figure 2.4.** Activision–THQ Incorporated Pair

## 2.6.2 THQ–Activision

This is the reverse leg of the ATVI–THQI pair trade shown in Figure 2.4 and is a Long A–Short B Entry. Note the symmetry of the Spread Bands in the Acme Spread Indicator. Essentially, this spread is a mirror image of the spread shown in the previous example, but the SB value is the same (0.1025).

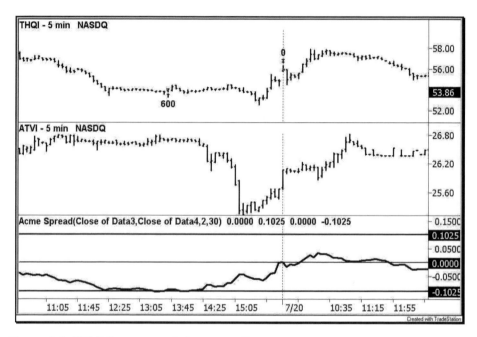

**Figure 2.5.** THQ Incorporated–Activision Pair

Tables 2.6 and 2.7 show the results of trading both legs of the ATVI–THQI pair from November 6th, 2000 through March 22nd, 2002. The average trade netted $285 for the ATVI leg and $462 for the THQI leg, totaling $747 for the stock pair. Net of commissions and slippage, the average trade for this account size would fall in the range of $500 to $600. This example is a typical scenario for a pair trade: one profitable leg and one unprofitable leg. The goal is to capitalize on the price difference with proper position sizing.

Some of the most effective pair trades occur when one stock in the pair gaps disproportionately to the other stock. For example, if two stocks with the same ATR but different prices gap up one point, e.g., the stock futures are up, then the gap creates a pricing disparity. If one stock closed at 30 and the other at 40, then the pair spread is (31 ÷ 30) 1.033 minus (41 ÷ 40) 1.025 equals +0.008. Hence, the former stock is overvalued relative to the latter, setting up a possible Short A–Long B pair trade.

**Table 2.6.** TradeStation Strategy Performance Report - Acme P System ATVI-5 min

| | | | |
|---|---|---|---|
| Total Net Profit | $9,114.00 | Open position P/L | $0.00 |
| Gross Profit | $22,392.00 | Gross Loss | ($13,278.00) |
| Total # of trades | 32 | Percent profitable | 59.38% |
| Number winning trades | 19 | Number losing trades | 13 |
| Largest winning trade | $3,159.00 | Largest losing trade | ($2,880.00) |
| Average winning trade | $1,178.53 | Average losing trade | ($1,021.38) |
| Ratio avg win/avg loss | 1.15 | Avg trade (win & loss) | $284.81 |
| Max consec. Winners | 4 | Max consec. losers | 3 |
| Avg # bars in winners | 50 | Avg # bars in losers | 61 |
| Max intraday drawdown | ($5,149.00) | | |
| Profit Factor | 1.69 | Max # contracts held | 3,600 |

**Table 2.7.** TradeStation Strategy Performance Report - Acme P System THQI-5 min

| | | | |
|---|---|---|---|
| Total Net Profit | $14,797.00 | Open position P/L | $0.00 |
| Gross Profit | $27,628.00 | Gross Loss | ($12,831.00) |
| Total # of trades | 32 | Percent profitable | 62.50% |
| Number winning trades | 20 | Number losing trades | 12 |
| Largest winning trade | $3,360.00 | Largest losing trade | ($3,500.00) |
| Average winning trade | $1,381.40 | Average losing trade | ($1,069.25) |
| Ratio avg win/avg loss | 1.29 | Avg trade (win & loss) | $462.41 |
| Max consec. Winners | 5 | Max consec. losers | 3 |
| Avg # bars in winners | 45 | Avg # bars in losers | 71 |
| Max intraday drawdown | ($3,971.00) | | |
| Profit Factor | 2.15 | Max # contracts held | 2,600 |

### 2.6.3 Apache–Anadarko

The New York Stock Exchange is an excellent vehicle for trading correlated pairs, especially among the oil service companies. The APA–APC pair usually has a correlation above 0.9 and exhibits smooth multi-day swings between the spread bands.

In Figure 2.6, APA becomes relatively expensive to APC as the spread nicks the upper spread band. This is an example of a Short A–Long B Entry. As soon as the Spread crosses back below the upper SB, we short 1400 shares of APA at a price of 57.98 at 1:00 pm and buy 1400 shares of APC at 58.00. Two hours later at 3:00 pm, the spread crosses below zero; the APA short is covered at 57.48 for a profit of $700, and the APC long is sold at 58.10 for a profit of $140. In this case, the total spread profit is $840, with one leg of the pair making most of the profit.

Be skeptical of exceedingly narrow Spread Bands for stock pairs with high correlations. This is probably an indication that the correlation period is too small. Use 30 days at a minimum – we recommend at least 90 days to factor in the quarterly earnings cycle. The problem with narrow Spread Bands is that they are sensitive to small changes in the stock price, and too many signals will be generated. Moreover, if the stocks do not have high ATRs, then overcoming the slippage and commissions will be difficult.

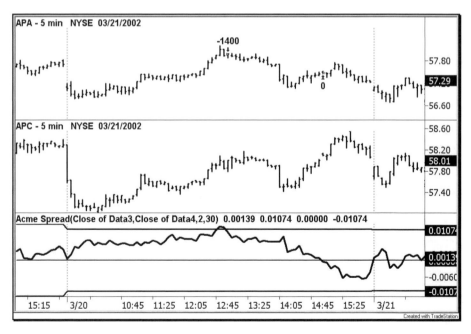

**Figure 2.6.** Apache–Anadarko Pair

### 2.6.4 Allstate–Progressive

An advanced pair trading strategy uses a correlated pair of a leader and a laggard in a specific stock sector. One of the stocks is a growth stock, and the other stock is a value stock or blue chip stock with little volatility. Typically, the bellwether stock starts moving before the other, and the lag in price action creates a spread opportunity. Here, two insurance companies have been chosen, conservative Allstate (ALL:NYSE) and momentum favorite Progressive (PGR:NYSE).

In Figure 2.7, ALL starts declining at 11:45 am and by 1:00 pm has become undervalued relative to PGR. When the spread crosses above the lower SB, a long ALL signal is generated, and thus PGR is a short; the spread is covered at the end of the day. For the period 11/06/2000 through 03/01/2002, each leg of this spread had profit factors of 2.32 and 3.24, respectively. With so many traders on the information highway, it pays to go off-road and play a niche strategy.

When scanning for stock pairs, look for the behavior demonstrated in the chart below. While Allstate was declining, Progressive managed to stay up for several hours before falling. Essentially, we are looking for a phase shift between two stocks, so we recommend keeping a quote table of all pairs to quickly judge which pairs are showing price discrepancies.

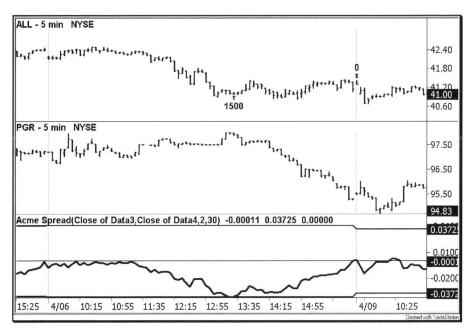

**Figure 2.7.** Allstate–Progressive Pair

## 2.6.5 Emulex–QLogic

Figure 2.8 is an illustration of how a news item creates opportunity. On January 23rd, 2002, QLogic Corporation reported earnings after the closing bell, but then commented on "limited visibility". We were tracking the Emulex–QLogic pair, so the following day Emulex stayed well above the upper SB all day long. At 3:50 pm, a spike in QLGC carried the spread below the SB, where 700 shares of EMLX were shorted. Simultaneously, a long position was taken in QLogic. Just two bars later on the following morning, the spread dropped below zero, and the spread was covered.

A trader might question why QLogic would rise so suddenly. The answer is that pricing disparities are created near and at the closing bell, as well as at the opening bell. Because of the artificiality of the moves, these times provide the best quick pair trading opportunities. Do not think about why the trade happened; just take it because logic does not apply here. The logical trader probably got caught leaning the wrong way.

Some of the most interesting pairs are composed of stocks that belong to a major market index such as the Nasdaq 100 or S&P 500. With the growth in index funds and *exchange-traded funds* (ETFs), money managers are obligated to buy or sell the component stocks that compose the index. In the absence of any news, an index stock cannot get too far out of whack before index buying or selling brings the stock back into line.

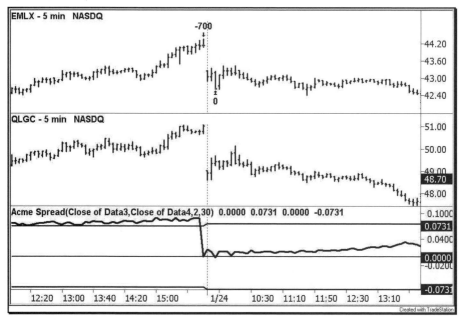

**Figure 2.8.** Emulex–QLogic Pair

### 2.6.6 RF Micro Devices–TriQuint Semiconductor

In the spirit of price anomalies, we want to exploit the morning reversals with pairs. When two stocks start moving in opposite directions, the spread chart will form a spike[2]. The trader may be thinking that if one stock in the pair goes up but the other does not, then that would be a perfect opportunity to short the rising stock and buy the other. In the absence of news, this may be a good idea, but remember that the stocks are moving this way for a reason, and you will probably not know why.

In Figure 2.9, RFMD has moved up, but TQNT has not. The spread spikes above the SB and crosses below the line two bars later. This scenario illustrates the importance of waiting for a spread to reverse across the SB. If the spread does not reverse, then the trader may consider a reverse spread strategy in the event of significant news.

Another way to confirm an "out of bounds" pair trade is to wait for either stock to reverse its trend on a break of the high or the low. In the chart below, although the spread is above the upper SB, the trader may wait to short RFMD until it breaks the low of the previous bar, which it did not do until the fifth bar of the session. Similarly, he or she may wait to buy TQNT until it breaks above the previous high, exceeded on the sixth bar. Finally, the trader may want both conditions to occur before taking the pair trade.

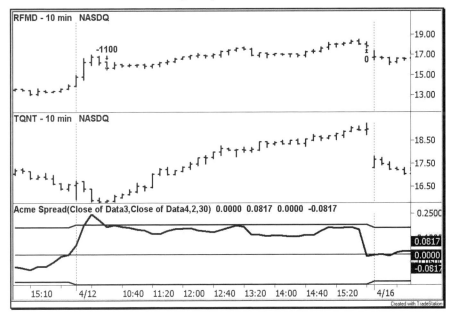

**Figure 2.9.** RF Micro Devices–TriQuint Semiconductor Pair

---

[2] Biotechnology stocks often move in opposing directions. These stocks are extremely news-sensitive because of their dependence on the success of one or two drugs.

## 2.7 Pair Trading Strategies

We keep an Excel spreadsheet of at least fifty correlated pairs for the Acme P System. Of course, the stock market has an almost infinite number of possible pairs, but trading this strategy requires both liquidity and volatility, making most of them infeasible. Filter out those stocks with little volume and low ATRs. The key is to find two competing stocks in the same industry satisfying these criteria. Following are some examples:

- ❑ Abgenix (**ABGX:Nasdaq**)–Medarex (**MEDX:Nasdaq**)
- ❑ Arch Coal (**ACI:NYSE**)–Massey Energy (**MEE:NYSE**)
- ❑ Allstate (**ALL:NYSE**)–Progressive (**PGR:NYSE**)
- ❑ Apache (**APA:NYSE**)–Anadarko Petroleum (**APC:NYSE**)
- ❑ Activision (**ATVI:Nasdaq**)–THQ Incorporated (**THQI:Nasdaq**)
- ❑ Altera (**ALTR:Nasdaq**)–Xilinx (**XLNX:Nasdaq**)
- ❑ BJ's Wholesale Club (**BJ:NYSE**)–Costco (**COST:NYSE**)
- ❑ Ballard Power (**BLDP:Nasdaq**)–FuelCell Energy (**FCEL:Nasdaq**)
- ❑ Citigroup (**C:NYSE**)–J.P. Morgan Chase (**JPM:NYSE**)
- ❑ Caterpillar (**CAT:NYSE**)–Ingersoll-Rand (**IR:NYSE**)
- ❑ Carnival (**CCL:NYSE**)–Royal Caribbean (**RCL:NYSE**)
- ❑ Capital One (**COF:NYSE**)–Household International (**HI:NYSE**)
- ❑ Calpine (**CPN:NYSE**)–Dynegy (**DYN:NYSE**)
- ❑ Centex (**CTX:NYSE**)–Lennar (**LEN:NYSE**)
- ❑ Quest Diagnostics (**DGX:NYSE**)–Laboratory Corporation (**LH:NYSE**)
- ❑ DuPont Photomasks (**DPMI:Nasdaq**)–Photronics (**PLAB:Nasdaq**)
- ❑ EMC (**EMC:NYSE**)–Network Appliance (**NTAP:Nasdaq**)
- ❑ Emulex (**EMLX:Nasdaq**)–QLogic (**QLGC:Nasdaq**)
- ❑ Goldman Sachs (**GS:NYSE**)–Morgan Stanley (**MWD:NYSE**)
- ❑ Home Depot (**HD:NYSE**)–Lowe's Companies (**LOW:NYSE**)
- ❑ Human Genome Sciences (**HGSI:Nasdaq**)–Millennium Pharmaceuticals (**MLNM:Nasdaq**)
- ❑ Starwood Hotels (**HOT:NYSE**)–Marriott (**MAR:NYSE**)
- ❑ Internet Security Systems (**ISSX:Nasdaq**)–VeriSign (**VRSN:Nasdaq**)
- ❑ Jabil Circuit (**JBL:NYSE**)–Sanmina (**SANM:Nasdaq**)
- ❑ Jones Apparel (**JNY:NYSE**)–Liz Claiborne (**LIZ:NYSE**)
- ❑ Mercury Interactive (**MERQ:Nasdaq**)–Micromuse (**MUSE:Nasdaq**)
- ❑ PeopleSoft (**PSFT:Nasdaq**)–Siebel Systems (**SEBL:Nasdaq**)

❑ RF Micro Devices (**RFMD:Nasdaq**)–TriQuint Semiconductor (**TQNT:Nasdaq**)

❑ UnitedHealth Group (**UNH:NYSE**)–WellPoint Health (**WLP:NYSE**)

### 2.7.1 Tips and Techniques

1. When legging into a pair trade, initiate the short trade first to make sure you can get an uptick, unless you have a forward conversion or bullet that allows you to short without an uptick.

2. There are several alternatives for closing out a pair trade. Some traders prefer to close out all trades at the end of the trading day. Others prefer to let the spread go to the opposite spread band over a period of two to three days.

3. If one of the stocks in the pair trade has significant news, then the pair trade may not be feasible because the spread may widen dramatically; however, the system rules preclude entering a trade until the spread starts reverting to the mean.

4. Find stock pairs that fit the "leader–laggard" criterion within a specific industry niche. Do not settle on a general sector; look for stocks with products that directly compete with each other, e.g., two companies with a similar cancer drug.

5. For intraday pair trading, use as small a time frame as possible. The window of opportunity can be small, so three-minute and five-minute charts should be used. Another option is to change the Acme Spread indicator to alert the trader whenever either of the SBs is touched.

6. When assessing a potential stock pair, research its technical characteristics. The stocks should be bouncing around within the bands, not flat-lining. Look for spikes in the form of the letter "V". In contrast, some stock pairs are so correlated that they are not worth trading.

7. News is not necessarily bad for a pair trade–it can create opportunity. Unless the news is significant, the pair trade is a good option; otherwise, the reverse spread may be a better trade. Psychologically, this is a difficult type of trade but gets easier with experience.

8. We prefer morning trades around 10:30 am and afternoon trades around 2:30 pm because these times tend to be intraday reversal points in the market. If the spread is still widening after 3 pm, then traders are probably caught the wrong way, and the spread will probably not reverse in time.

9.  Compare the performance of the system using today's open versus
    yesterday's close. Some stocks exhibit a tendency towards unusual
    gaps, and this usually improves pair trading performance.

10. To adapt the Acme P system to position pair trading, add a parameter
    that specifies the number of days to carry the position. Then, multiply
    this number by the Spread Band value to widen the bands. Finally,
    change the Price1 and Price2 parameters to reference the closing
    prices of N days ago.

11. We monitor all pairs with a set of TradeStation workspaces, six chart
    pairs per workspace. Note that running multiple workspaces with
    multiple charts requires extensive computing power; we recommend a
    dual processor machine.

# 3 Pattern Trading

*Paranoia is the belief*
*in a hidden order*
*behind the visible.*

Anonymous

Computer technology has changed the zeitgeist of the market into a real-time information machine, sending multiple data sources flooding into a trader's computer. Currently, raw data feeds supply primitive quote information. The next generation of data feeds will feed patterns into the computer, mining data on the fly to identify technical patterns that match the trader's criteria.

A pattern combination system identifies charts with two or more patterns with a similar bias – bullish or bearish. If a chart shows both bullish and bearish qualities, then the bias is neutral. Essentially, the system catalogs all known bar patterns and then identifies combinations of them. Furthermore, the system is extensible. A trader can add as many patterns as possible, building the pattern catalog. For example, Dunnigan developed a swing-trading catalog of patterns that could be implemented in a pattern combination system [9].

The system is not limited to any particular style of chart. Every candlestick pattern has an analog that can be encoded in a normal bar chart [22, 23]. So, a Harami can be combined with a Gann pullback [18]. The exciting aspect of the Acme M system presented here is that the trader is free to invent his or her own patterns and plug them in. Design the pattern, code the pattern function, and call it from the Market Patterns model. As an illustration, we designed a sample bar pattern called a *Cobra* because of its resemblance to a striking snake, with a head at the top and a tail at the bottom.

Non-technical information about a stock can also be encoded in a pattern. For example, a stock may have a quarterly earnings pattern cycle [13]; it may simply be the date five days before the company's earnings report. This earnings date may coincide with a pullback pattern, so fundamental information can be combined with technical information to create a trading signal.

One issue facing the trader is the lack of access to a universal database. The trader should have a real-time interface to fundamental data such as the stock float or its EPS growth. We envision the day when Internet-wide public feeds transmit all kinds of information in real-time: earnings reports, baseball scores, weather forecasts, etc.

## 3.1 Market Patterns

The *Market Patterns* indicator is a series of letters that identify specific bar patterns. Gartley inspired this idea because he made liberal use of the letters of the alphabet to identify market pivots [15]. For our purposes, a single letter denotes each pattern. For bullish patterns, a letter is placed on top of the bar. For bearish patterns, the letter is placed below the bar. The list of Acme patterns is shown in Table 3.1:

**Table 3.1.** Acme Market Patterns

| Pattern | Identifier |
|---|---|
| Cobra | C |
| Hook | H |
| Inside Day 2 | I |
| Tail | L |
| Harami | M |
| Pullback | P |
| Test | T |
| V Zone | V |

### 3.1.1 Cobra (C)

A *Cobra* is a narrow range bar named for its resemblance to the snake, i.e., the open and close finish at opposite extremes of the bar. For a bullish Cobra, the open must be in the bottom of the range, and the close must be in the top of the range. For a bearish Cobra, the open must be in the top of the range, and the close must be in the bottom of the range.

Figure 3.1 shows two bullish Cobras with the letter C above each bar. Typically, the Cobra precedes a large-range day. The pattern is essentially a narrow range day showing strength. The letter N denotes a narrow range day; it is not an independent pattern per se but is noted when other patterns are present (see Section 3.2 on Pattern Qualifiers).

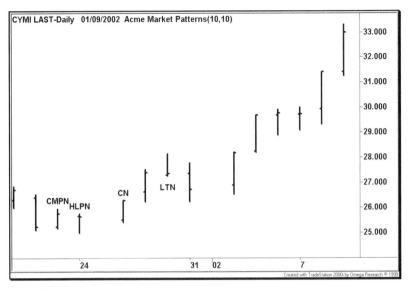

**Figure 3.1.** Cobra

### 3.1.2 Hook (H)

A *Hook* is a retracement bar that appears to reverse the retracement trend but then closes in the direction of the retracement. Figure 3.2 is an example of a bearish Hook with the letter H below the bar: a series of pullback days, then the stock gaps up at the open but closes down on the day, continuing the pullback. Essentially, the buyers here were "hooked" on the day's open.

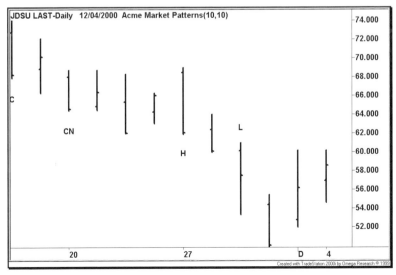

**Figure 3.2.** Hook

### 3.1.3 Inside Day 2 (I)

An *Inside Day 2* bar is an *inside day*[1] followed by another inside day. By definition, it is a narrow range day without any directional bias, thus the reason for
annotating both the top and bottom of the bar with the letter I. A trade would
normally be taken in the direction of the breakout, as in Figure 3.3 below. Note
that an inside day is not necessarily a narrow range day. If an outside day has a
very large range, then the inside day's range may still be greater than the ATR.

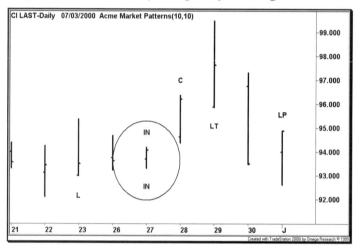

**Figure 3.3.** Inside Day 2

### 3.1.4 Tail (L)

A *Tail* is a bar where the open and close are in the same half-bar. If both the
close and open are in the upper half of the range, then that is a bullish tail[2]. If
both the close and open are in the lower half of the range, then that is a bearish
tail[3]. Figure 3.4 shows two bullish tails with the letter L above each bar; each tail
is also a narrow range bar.

The *AcmeRangePercent* function calculates where a price falls as a percentage
of the range (between 0 and 100) for a single bar or for a number of bars; this
number is the *Range Percentage* (RP). For a single bar, the low of the bar has an
RP of 0, and the high of the bar has an RP of 100. For a range of bars, the
lowest low of the range has an RP of 0, and the highest high of the range has
an RP of 100.

---

[1] An inside day is a bar where the high is lower than the previous high and the low is greater
than the previous low, i.e., the current bar fits inside the previous bar.

[2] In candlestick charting, a similar pattern is known as a Hammer, but it is more restrictive.

[3] The Candlestick approximation of this pattern is a Shooting Star, but the Shooting Star is
more range-restrictive.

The RP is also used as an input parameter to specify where the open and close must appear on a given bar. For example, an RP of 80 means that the open and close must be in the upper or lower 20% of the bar. The trader can adjust the RP for certain patterns, e.g., 80 for more restrictive or 60 for less restrictive. If the trader wants shaven heads [22], then the RP can be set even higher. Ultimately, the choice is a tradeoff between discretion and automation.

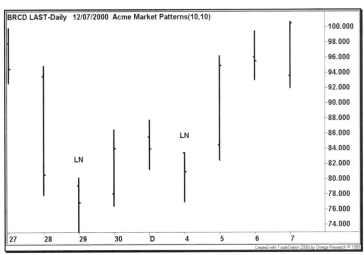

**Figure 3.4.** Tail

The EasyLanguage code for identifying a tail is shown below in Example 3.1. Each pattern function assigns the following codes to return the pattern status:

- ❑  0 = Pattern Not Found
- ❑  1 = Bullish Pattern Found
- ❑  2 = Bearish Pattern Found

**Example 3.1.** Function *AcmeTail*

```
{****************************************************************
AcmeTail: Search for a Tail Pattern
****************************************************************}

Inputs:
    Percent(Numeric),
    RangeLength(Numeric);

Variables:
    RP(0.0),
    RP25(0.25),
    RP50(0.50);
```

```
AcmeTail = 0;
RP = (AcmeRangePercent(Open, 1) + AcmeRangePercent(Close, 1)) / 2;

Condition1 = RP >= (1 - Percent);
Condition2 = AcmeRangePercent(Close, 1) >= (1 - RP25);
If (Condition1 or Condition2) and
AcmeRangePercent(Low, RangeLength) <= Percent and
AcmeRangePercent(Open, 1) > RP50 and
AcmeRangePercent(Close, 1) > RP50 Then
    AcmeTail = 1;

Condition1 = RP <= Percent;
Condition2 = AcmeRangePercent(Close, 1) <= RP25;
If (Condition1 or Condition2) and
AcmeRangePercent(High, RangeLength) >= (1 - Percent) and
AcmeRangePercent(Open, 1) < RP50 and
AcmeRangePercent(Close, 1) < RP50 Then
    AcmeTail = 2;
```

## 3.1.5 Harami (M)

A *Harami* is a classic candlestick pattern. It is a two-bar pattern where an inside
bar follows a wide range bar, and the inside bar closes in the opposite direction.
A Harami by itself does not indicate a change in trend, but it can signal a reversal when combined with other market patterns. Figure 3.5 is a chart with both a
bearish Harami (the close is greater than the open in the wide range bar followed by the close below the open in the inside bar) and a bullish Harami (the
close is less than the open in the wide range bar, and the close is above the open
in the second inside bar):

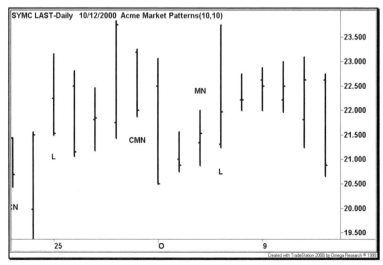

**Figure 3.5.** Harami

The function *AcmeHarami* implements an extended Harami pattern for up to
three bars, that is, if the wide range bar is followed by a series of inside bars, then
the pattern is in effect until price breaks out of the original wide range bar.

### 3.1.6 Pullback (P)

A *Pullback* is the traditional Gann pullback pattern. A bullish pullback occurs
when the trend is up, and price makes a certain number of lower lows or a combination of lower lows and inside days [4]. A bearish pullback occurs when the
trend is down, and price makes a certain number of higher highs or a combination of higher highs and inside days. Figure 3.6 shows an example of a bearish
Pullback with the letter P below the bar.

The function *AcmePullback* defines a pullback in other ways, too. Either a
bullish Tail or a bullish Cobra can mark the bottom of a retracement in an up
trend. Similarly, a bearish Tail or Cobra can mark the top of a retracement in a
downtrend. The EasyLanguage code for the *AcmePullback* function is shown in
Example 3.2:

**Example 3.2.** Function *AcmePullback*

```
{*******************************************************************
AcmePullback: Search for a Gann Pullback Pattern
*******************************************************************}

Inputs:
    ADXLimit(Numeric),
    Length(Numeric);

Variables:
    PullbackBars(3),
    Percent(0.35),
    RangeLength(5),
    RangeFactor(0.7);

AcmePullback = 0;

Condition1 = AcmeRetraceDown(PullbackBars) = True;
Condition2 = AcmeTail(Percent, RangeLength) = 1;
Condition3 = AcmeCobra(Percent, RangeFactor) = 1;

If ADX(Length) >= ADXLimit and
DMIPlus(Length) > DMIMinus(Length) and
AcmeRangePercent(Close, RangeLength) <= Percent and
(Condition1 or Condition2 or Condition3) Then
    AcmePullback = 1;

Condition1 = AcmeRetraceUp(PullbackBars) = True;
```

```
Condition2 = AcmeTail(Percent, RangeLength) = 2;
Condition3 = AcmeCobra(Percent, RangeFactor) = 2;

If ADX(Length) >= ADXLimit and
DMIMinus(Length) > DMIPlus(Length) and
AcmeRangePercent(Close, RangeLength) >= (1 - Percent) and
(Condition1 or Condition2 or Condition3) Then
   AcmePullback = 2;
```

The *AcmePullback* function is divided into two code fragments: the first section looks for a bullish pullback, and the second section looks for a bearish pullback. A bullish pullback must satisfy the following minimum criteria:

1. The ADX over *Length* must be greater than or equal to the *ADXLimit*.
2. The +DMI must be greater than -DMI, indicating an up trend.
3. The Range Percentage (RP) of the close must be 35% or less over the past *RangeLength* bars.
4. The bar pattern must be a bullish three-bar Pullback, Tail, or Cobra.

The minimum criteria for a bearish pullback are reversed for items 2, 3, and 4. The -DMI must be greater than +DMI, and the RP must be at least 65%.

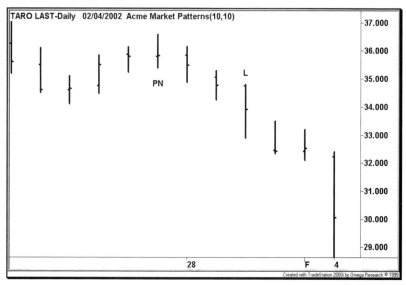

**Figure 3.6.** Pullback

### 3.1.7 Test (T)

A *Test* is a bar that breaks previous support or resistance and then rebounds in the other direction. In a bullish Test, the Test bar breaks below a previous low (cannot be the low of one bar ago) and closes in the top half of its range. In a bearish Test, the Test bar exceeds a previous high (cannot be the high one bar ago) and closes in the bottom half of its range. In Figure 3.7 below, the highest high is a bearish Test marked by the letter T. It breaks the previous high of four bars ago but closes near the bottom of its range.

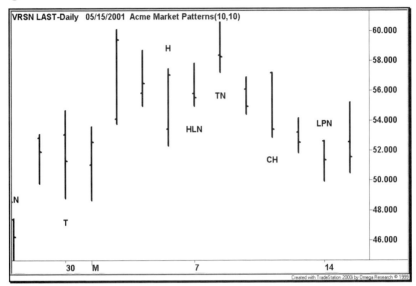

**Figure 3.7.** Test

## 3.1.8 V Zone (V)

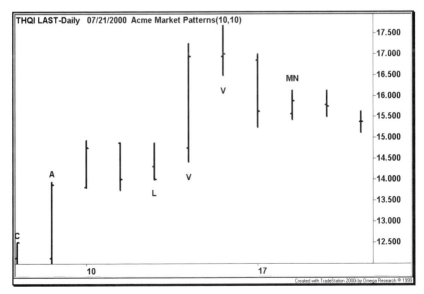

**Figure 3.8.** V Zone

The *V Zone* is another Acme-designed pattern. It is a pattern based on a break of weekly support or resistance. The V Zone is named for its resemblance to the letter "V" on the chart for a bullish pattern and an inverted "V" for a bearish pattern (see Figure 3.8). The V Zone is the only pattern that takes the weekend into effect because a stock that closes on its low for the week will tend to break that low the following week. Over the weekend, people in such a long position think about how poorly their position is faring and have two days to build up emotional capital in their position. These emotions trigger panic the following week if the stock continues its downward momentum. The EasyLanguage code for calculating the V Low price is shown in Example 3.3:

**Example 3.3.** Function *AcmeVLow*

```
{*****************************************************************
AcmeVLow: Find the V Low Price
****************************************************************}

Inputs:
   VolatilityFactor(Numeric),
   Length(Numeric);

AcmeVLow = 0.0;
If LowW(1) > 0 and
Volatility(Length) > 0 Then
   AcmeVLow = LowW(1) - (VolatilityFactor * Volatility(Length));
```

The formula for calculating the V Low Zone is simple: determine the low of the previous week using the *LowW* EasyLanguage function, and then subtract a multiple (*VolatilityFactor*) of the ATR from the weekly low. Similarly, for the V High Zone, calculate the high of the previous week with the *HighW* function, and add the multiple of the ATR.

## 3.2 Pattern Qualifiers

A *Pattern Qualifier* (PQ) is a characteristic of a bar, not a bar pattern per se; however, it qualifies for the pattern count in the Acme M System. For example, if two patterns are found, and the bar is an NR bar, then the pattern count is equal to three.

### 3.2.1 Narrow Range (N)

The first qualifier is the Narrow Range (N) qualifier, denoted by the letter N on the chart. It is not placed on the chart unless other bar patterns accompany it, and it is marked only with the bias of the bar pattern, i.e., it is placed on only one end of the bar. For example, in Figure 3.9, the N qualifier is appended to a bullish Tail (L) and a Test (T), forming the "LTN" sequence.

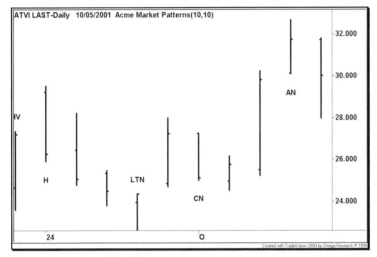

**Figure 3.9.** Narrow Range Qualifier

### 3.2.2 Average (A)

The second qualifier is the Average Pattern Qualifier, denoted by the letter A. The Average PQ marks a bar that is sitting on the 50-bar moving average. It alerts the trader to this critical moving average by placing an A above and below the bar. Unlike the Narrow Range qualifier, the Average PQ implies no bias when a stock is trading at its 50-bar moving average (see Figure 3.10).

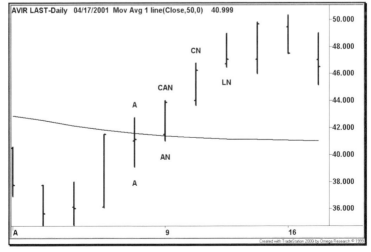

**Figure 3.10.** Average Qualifier

Although the Average PQ is 50 bars by default, the trader can implement PQs for other critical moving averages such as the 200-bar moving average. The key to pattern trading is to recognize those patterns that are important to technical analysts to supplement the patterns that the trader discovers on his or her own. For example, a Fibonacci Pattern Qualifier could be designed to mark a swing retracement from a pivot bar of a given strength.

## 3.3 Pattern Trading System (Acme M)

With the patterns and qualifiers defined, we now implement a pattern trading system known as the Acme M System. It simply counts the number of bullish or bearish patterns on any given bar. If the number of patterns is greater than the minimum number of patterns specified by the system, and the swing trading criteria are satisfied, then a signal is generated.

The swing trading criteria are two-fold. First, the bar must be a swing high or low over a certain range of bars. Second, the swing high or low must fall in a certain range percentage over that same range. Currently, the default value for the reference range is five bars, and the default value for the Range Percentage is 40%. Note that the Acme M System avoids gaps that are not in the direction of the trade. For example, if the high of the current bar is less than the low of the previous bar (gap down), then a long trade will not be taken.

### 3.3.1 Long Signal

| Calculations |
| --- |

1. Total the number of Bullish Patterns and Pattern Qualifiers.
2. Calculate the Lowest Low of the previous 4 bars ($LL_4$).
3. Calculate the Range Percentage of the High of the current bar relative to the range of the previous 4 bars ($RP_{H4}$).
4. Calculate the ATR for the last 14 bars ($ATR_{14}$).

| Entry Rules |
| --- |

1. Number of Bullish Patterns >= 3
2. Low < $LL_4$
3. $RP_{H4}$ <= 40%
4. **Buy** the next bar at or above the High + (EntryFactor * $ATR_{14}$)

Exit Rules: Profit Target

1. **Sell** half of the position at or above the High + (ProfitFactor * $ATR_{14}$)
2. **Sell** half of the position at or above the High of ProfitBars ago + (2 * ProfitFactor * $ATR_{14}$)

Exit Rules: Stop Loss

1. **Sell** all shares at or below the Lowest Low for StopBars − (ExitFactor * $ATR_{14}$)

### 3.3.2 Short Signal

Calculations

1. Total the number of Bearish Patterns and Pattern Qualifiers.
2. Calculate the Highest High of the previous 4 bars ($HH_4$).
3. Calculate the Range Percentage of the Low of the current bar relative to the range of the previous 4 bars ($RP_{L4}$).

Entry Rules

1. Number of Bearish Patterns >= 3
2. High > $HH_4$
3. $RP_{L4}$ >= 60%
4. **Sell Short** the next bar at or below the Low - (EntryFactor * $ATR_{14}$)

Exit Rules: Profit Target

1. **Cover** half of the position at or below the Low − (ProfitFactor * $ATR_{14}$)
2. **Cover** half of the position at or below the Low of ProfitBars ago − (2 * ProfitFactor * $ATR_{14}$)

Exit Rules: Stop Loss

1. **Cover** all shares at or above the Highest High for StopBars + (ExitFactor * $ATR_{14}$)

The Acme M code is divided into five general sections:

- Trade Filtering
- Market Pattern Identification
- Pattern Qualifier Identification
- Position Sizing
- Signal Generation

The Acme M system uses two trade filters: Minimum Price and Minimum ATR. The filters can be applied individually or together. For example, filter out all stocks with a price less than $20 and an ATR of less than one. To use just one filter, set the other filter to zero. For example, set the Minimum Price to zero, and set the ATR to a number such as 1.5.

If the stock passes the filtering process, then the eight market patterns are tested in sequence. Two strings are created that track the bullish and bearish patterns for each bar. If the Acme pattern function returns 1, then the pattern is bullish, and the corresponding letter is appended to the *LongString* variable. If the Acme function returns 2, then the pattern is bearish, and the letter is added to the *ShortString* variable.

After pattern identification, the bar is tested for pattern qualifiers. First, the *AcmeOnAverage* function is called to determine whether or not the bar is on the 50-day moving average. If so, then the letter A is added to both the LongString and ShortString. Then, all of the narrow range patterns are tested. If any narrow range pattern is found, then the letter N is appended to the appropriate string, depending on whether or not a bar pattern has already been found. For example, if a bullish Test pattern has been found, and the bar is an NR bar, then the letter sequence "TN" will be contained in the LongString variable. If a bearish Test pattern has been found, then the letter sequence "TN" will be contained in the ShortString variable.

Now, with the patterns and qualifiers identified, the system compares the number of patterns in each string with the minimum number specified as an input parameter, *MinimumPatterns*. If the LongString has a length greater than the minimum, then a potential long entry has been identified. If the ShortString has a length greater than the minimum, then a short entry has been identified.

Finally, the system tests the following entry conditions before validating the signal:

- Swing condition,
- Range percentage condition, and
- Gap condition.

The EasyLanguage code for the Acme M System is shown in Example 3.4.

**Example 3.4.** Acme M System

```
{******************************************************************
Acme M System: Look for multiple combinations of market patterns

1. Cobra (C)
2. Hook (H)
3. Inside Day 2 (I)
4. Tail (L)
5. Harami (M)
6. 1-2-3 Pullback (P)
7. Test (T)
8. V Zone (V)

Qualifiers

1. Moving Average (A)
2. Narrow Range (N)

******************************************************************}

Inputs:
    {M Parameters}
    MinimumPatterns(3),
    {Filter Parameters}
    FiltersOn(True),
    FilterLength(14),
    MinimumPrice(15),
    MinimumATR(1.0),
    {Position Parameters}
    Equity(100000),
    RiskModel(3),
    RiskPercent(2.0),
    RiskATR(1.0),
    EntryFactor(0.10),
    DrawTargets(True);

Variables:
    N(0),
    ATR(0.0),
    ATRLength(20),
    TradeFilter(True),
    BuyStop(0.0),
    ShortStop(0.0),
    {M Variables}
    PatternString(""),
    LongString(""),
    ShortString(""),
    ReturnValue(0),
    ALength(50),
    ACondition(False),
```

```
        CPercent(0.25),
        CRangeFactor(0.8),
        HLength(1),
        HPercent(0.2),
        LPercent(0.3),
        LLength(7),
        PADX(25),
        PLength(14),
        VFactor(1.5),
        NRFactor(0.7),
        NLength1(5),
        NLength2(10),
        NLength3(4),
        MRange(5),
        MRangePercent(0.4),
        HighText(0),
        LowText(0);

ATR = Average(Range, ATRLength);
BuyStop = High + (EntryFactor * ATR);
ShortStop = Low - (EntryFactor * ATR);

{Run trade filters}

If FiltersOn Then
    TradeFilter = Close > MinimumPrice and ATR >= MinimumATR;

If TradeFilter Then Begin

    PatternString = "";
    LongString = "";
    ShortString = "";

    ReturnValue = AcmeCobra(CPercent, CRangeFactor);
    If ReturnValue > 0 Then Begin
        PatternString = "C";
        If ReturnValue = 1 Then
            LongString = LongString + PatternString
        Else
            ShortString = ShortString + PatternString;
    End;

    ReturnValue = AcmeHook(HLength, HPercent);
    If ReturnValue > 0 Then Begin
        PatternString = "H";
        If ReturnValue = 1 Then
            LongString = LongString + PatternString
        Else
            ShortString = ShortString + PatternString;
    End;

    If AcmeInsideDay2 Then Begin
        PatternString = "I";
```

```
    LongString = LongString + PatternString;
    ShortString = ShortString + PatternString;
End;

ReturnValue = AcmeTail(LPercent, LLength);
If ReturnValue > 0 Then Begin
    PatternString = "L";
    If ReturnValue = 1 Then
        LongString = LongString + PatternString
    Else
        ShortString = ShortString + PatternString;
End;

ReturnValue = AcmeHarami;
If ReturnValue > 0 Then Begin
    PatternString = "M";
    If ReturnValue = 1 Then
        LongString = LongString + PatternString
    Else
        ShortString = ShortString + PatternString;
End;

ReturnValue = AcmePullback(PADX, PLength);
If ReturnValue > 0 Then Begin
    PatternString = "P";
    If ReturnValue = 1 Then
        LongString = LongString + PatternString
    Else
        ShortString = ShortString + PatternString;
End;

ReturnValue = AcmeTest;
If ReturnValue > 0 Then Begin
    PatternString = "T";
    If ReturnValue = 1 Then
        LongString = LongString + PatternString
    Else
        ShortString = ShortString + PatternString;
End;

If High >= AcmeVHigh(VFactor, FilterLength) Then
    ShortString = ShortString + "V";

If Low <= AcmeVLow(VFactor, FilterLength) Then
    LongString = LongString + "V";

{Pattern Qualifiers}

ACondition = AcmeOnAverage(ALength);
If ACondition Then Begin
    PatternString = "A";
    LongString = LongString + PatternString;
```

```
        ShortString = ShortString + PatternString;
    End;

    Condition1 = AcmeNarrowRange(NLength1, 1) and
    AcmeNarrowRange(NLength1, 0)[1];

    Condition2 = Low > Low[1] and High < High[1] and
    Low[1] > Low[2] and High[1] < High[2];

    Condition3 = AcmeNarrowRange(NLength2, 0);
    Condition4 = AcmeInsideDayNR(NLength3, 0);
    Condition5 = Range <= NRFactor * ATR;

    If (Condition1 or Condition2 or Condition3 or
    Condition4 or Condition5) Then Begin
        PatternString = "N";
        If StrLen(LongString) > 0 Then
            LongString = LongString + PatternString;
        If StrLen(ShortString) > 0 Then
            ShortString = ShortString + PatternString;
    End;

    {Calculate shares based on risk model}
    N = AcmeGetShares(Equity, RiskModel, RiskPercent, RiskATR);

    {Multiple Pattern Buy Signal}

    If StrLen(LongString) >= MinimumPatterns and
    Low < Lowest(Low, MRange - 1)[1] and
    AcmeRangePercent(High, MRange) <= MRangePercent and
    High > Low[1] Then Begin
        {Draw Entry Targets on the Chart}
        If DrawTargets Then
            Condition1 = AcmeEntryTargets("M", BuyStop, 0, 0, 0);
        Buy("Acme LE M") N Shares Next Bar on BuyStop Stop;
    End;

    {Multiple Pattern Sell Signal}

    If StrLen(ShortString) >= MinimumPatterns and
    High > Highest(High, MRange - 1)[1] and
    AcmeRangePercent(Low, MRange) >= (1 - MRangePercent) and
    Low < High[1] Then Begin
        {Draw Entry Targets on the Chart}
        If DrawTargets Then
            Condition1 = AcmeEntryTargets("M", 0, 0, ShortStop, 0);
        Sell("Acme SE M") N Shares Next Bar on ShortStop Stop;
    End;
End;
```

## 3.4 Examples

The following charts are examples of trades generated by the Acme M System. Each example uses Equity of $100,000 and the Percent Volatility Model with a risk of 2%. For stocks, trade filtering is turned on, and for indices, trade filtering is turned off. We do not apply trade filtering to the indices because they have lower ADX readings.

### 3.4.1 Abgenix

The chart in Figure 3.11 shows an Acme M long entry on August 20th, 2001. The number of bullish patterns is equal to four:

- ❏ A Hook (H) where a short would have been triggered but the bar reversed,
- ❏ A Tail (L) where the open and close are in the high end of the range,
- ❏ A successful Test (T) of the previous low two bars earlier, and
- ❏ The bar is a narrow range (N) bar.

The original position size of the entry was 800 shares. Half of the position (400 shares) was closed two days later, and the rest of the position was sold on the third and fifth days after entry.

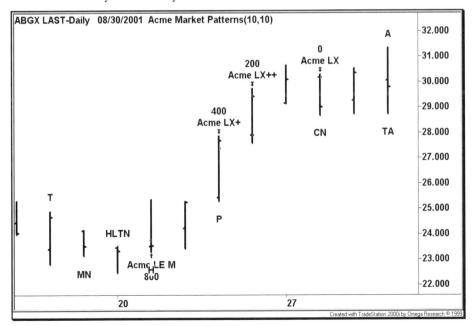

**Figure 3.11.** Abgenix Pattern

## 3.4.2 PMC-Sierra

The chart in Figure 3.12 shows an Acme M short entry on January 25th, 2001, with the number of bearish patterns equal to three:

- ❏ A Hook (H) down after a three-bar pullback, and
- ❏ A Tail (L) where the open and close are near the low of the range, and
- ❏ An unsuccessful Test (T) of the previous high three bars earlier.

The original position size of the entry was 200 shares. Both halves of the position (100 shares apiece) were covered on the following day for almost 40 points. These abrupt reversals of fortune tend to occur before an earnings release. Bad news just happens to leak out, a wonderfully human aspect of the business.

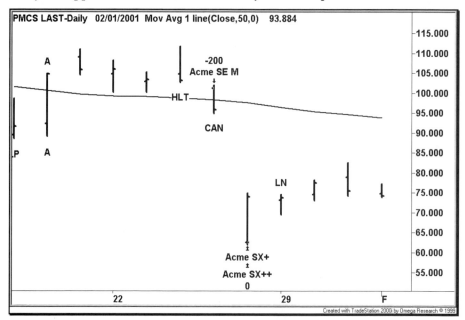

**Figure 3.12.** PMC-Sierra Pattern

Note how the stock went in the CAN after the initial short entry was triggered. On the subsequent bar, the stock moved below its 50-day moving average, and closed near the low of the day. This chart exemplifies a confluence of bearish patterns and only increases the probability of a winning trade. The trader may choose to make the Acme M system less restrictive by removing the swing criteria and just focusing on these pattern clusters. Again, the trader makes the choice of which stocks will be eliminated by the scans and how many need to be reviewed by eye. As will be demonstrated in Chapter 9, the human eye and brain are not always better judges of charts than the computer.

### 3.4.3 Check Point Software

The chart in Figure 3.13 shows an Acme M long entry after a double hook. First, some longs were sucked in at a tick above the high on the 13th, and then some shorts were entrapped a tick below the low on the 14th (not a good idea on a wide range bar). After the trade was triggered, the ATR factor prevented the trade from getting stopped out at the previous day's low on the 18th.

Currently, the better methodology seems to be fading the swing traders around the lows and highs, i.e., there appear to be more hooks, proving that just as a particular style of trading becomes popular among the masses, the less likely it will work in the future. Consequently, the ATR factor on entries eliminates many of these types of trades.

The Acme software defines mechanical trade exits for its systems; research has shown that two alternative systematic methods work equally well:

❑ Exit the long position when the close is below the open, and exit a short position when the close is greater than the open. This technique works after a swing of several days because a trend reversal may be forthcoming, beating traders who operate around highs and lows.

❑ Do not use profit targets after a holding period of four or five days. If the trade is still going in your direction, then the market is having a rare extended rally or decline, and the swing should be ridden out.

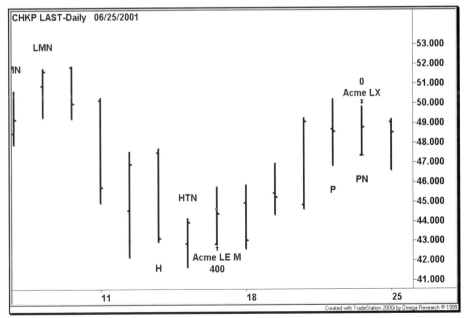

**Figure 3.13.** Check Point Software Pattern

### 3.4.4 New York Futures Exchange

The NYFE chart in Figure 3.14 shows an LE M signal. First, note how the stock has bounced off a double bottom and is forming a triple top. Second, the chart has formed a big "W", similar to the crisscrossed palm trees in *It's a Mad, Mad, Mad, Mad World*[4]. This bullish pattern portended a major market rally in early March 2002.

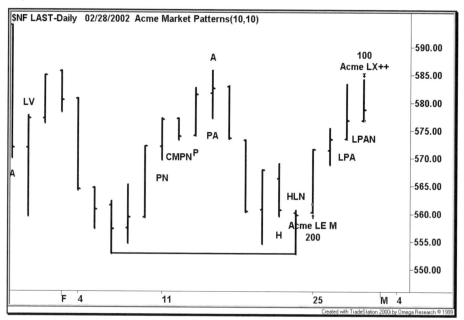

**Figure 3.14.** NYFE Index Pattern

In Chapter 5, we discuss geometric formations such as triangles, double bottoms and triple tops. The purpose of covering these patterns is to convey as much information as possible on the chart. In the example above, the double bottom from early to late February provided supporting evidence for the long trade entry. For the trade exit, the approach to a triple top was a clue that the up trend may still have been in effect, and the position could have been held longer to see if the index could break out above the triple top.

Stridsman uses the term "indicator piling" to express the danger of using similar indicators that give the trader a false impression of a sure winner [30]. Further, Bollinger stresses the need for independent variables such as volume to confirm trades [1]. When designing or implementing a pattern catalog, strive for a diversity of patterns, each with a unique concept.

---

[4] A 1963 comedy about a trans-California treasure hunt, starring Jimmy Durante, Milton Berle, Jonathan Winters, Sid Caesar, Ethel Merman, and Spencer Tracy

### 3.4.5 Comverse Technology

The chart shown in Figure 3.15 exemplifies the "CAN do" spirit: a Cobra above the moving average precedes a 15% move in four days.

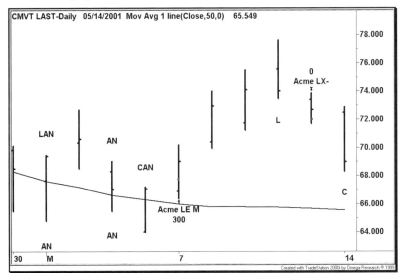

**Figure 3.15.** Comverse Technology Pattern

### 3.4.6 Nasdaq Composite Index

The chart in Figure 3.16 is not just for accountants.

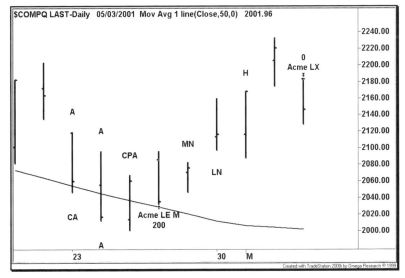

**Figure 3.16.** Nasdaq Composite Index Pattern

### 3.4.7 Computer Associates

Look for stocks bucking the market trend, as the Computer Associates chart illustrates in Figure 3.17. Before the gap down, rumors were swirling about the company's accounting practices during the Enron scandal. Two days later after the trade entry, several major newspapers reported that the company was under investigation by the SEC.

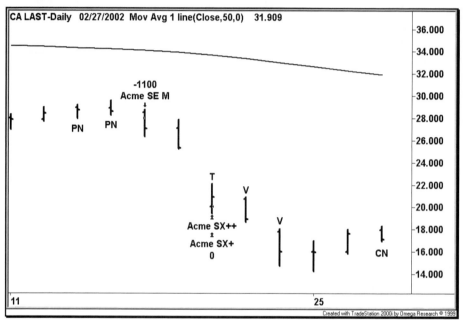

**Figure 3.17.** Computer Associates Pattern

# 4 Float Trading

*Ideas must work through the brains*
*and the arms of good and brave men,*
*or they are no better than dreams.*

Ralph Waldo Emerson

If anyone ever asks you why the Internet stocks soared as high as they did in the late 1990's, tell them it was the "low floats". This was a group of stocks with good earnings and revenue momentum, but more importantly, the demand outstripped the supply of shares. Because the companies had only recently gone public, few shares were available for trading (the *float*); some companies issued only three million shares, the equivalent of 300 investors owning 10000 shares apiece. Compare this number of shares with established companies such as General Electric, as shown in Table 4.1.

**Table 4.1.** Company Float Values

| Stock Symbol | Float |
|---|---|
| GE | 9.84 billion shares |
| CIEN | 301.0 million shares |
| PDLI | 35.5 million shares |
| THQI | 17.9 million shares |
| COCO | 7.8 million shares |

As the prices of Internet stocks soared, fueled by the short sellers who were repeatedly forced to buy in their shares, the companies declared stock splits. These splits increased the number of shares, thereby increasing the float. After two or three splits, eventually these companies had floats of fifty to a hundred million shares. With prices in the hundreds, these companies attained market caps greater than the largest companies in America, in some cases exceeding ten billion dollars. When the growth slowed, the next phase was inevitable. Suddenly, money managers were holding millions of shares in Internet companies that did not make any money, setting the stage for 95%-plus declines in valuation.

Although momentum traders were cognizant of the float and its impact on stock movement, the work by Woods is the first serious attempt to develop a new class of technical indicators based on the float [38]. Using the float of a stock is an attempt to measure the movement of stock price based on supply and demand, but one cannot use the float number per se, so one must ask the following questions:

1.  Where does one start adding up trade volume to determine when the float has "turned over"?

2.  How often does the float turn over, and what is the relationship between turnover and price movement?

3.  What happens once the float has turned over, and how are the critical turning points identified?

A *float turnover* is the number of bars needed for a stock's cumulative trading volume to exceed its float. Pick any bar, and start adding the daily volume to an accumulator, working forward or backwards in time. When the accumulator value exceeds the float of the stock, then the float is said to have turned over during that time period. For example, if Ciena trades an average of 10 million shares per day and its float is ~300 million shares, then Ciena's float turnover is 300 million divided by 10 million equals 30 days. If the chart interval is weekly, then Ciena's float turnover is six weeks. Stocks with huge floats such as GE and MSFT should be analyzed on a weekly or even a monthly basis, so these stocks require a longer-term trading horizon.

To understand how float can be incorporated into a trading model, consider the movement of stock prices. Stock prices generally trend only 20% of the time and spend the rest of the time trading in narrow ranges. Thus, a natural point to monitor the float is while a *base* is being formed. A horizontal channel line above or below a bar sequence defines a base while the float is being tracked. Using these channels, there are two points at which we start counting volume: at the beginning of a base and at a breakout from the base either to the upside or downside (the longer the base the better). As a result, a *float breakout* works like a traditional channel breakout.

So how does one trade the float model? When a base of a certain length is established, we initialize the volume accumulator. If the float turns over during the formation of the base, then we infer that the float changed hands and that the stock may be poised to break out; however, a stock that attracts day traders may require a higher multiplier of the float (e.g., $1.5\times$) to account for the short-term trading turnover.

Second, when a breakout occurs, the float accumulator is reset, and a position is theoretically held until the float turns over once again, or at least reaches a likely target area to exit a position. Consequently, the trader can choose to exit a trade using the float turnover technique or a traditional swing technique.

Before describing the details of the Acme F System, we adapt some of the technical charting indicators that are described in Woods's book *The Precision Profit Float Indicator* [38]. The modified indicators serve as decision support for trading the Acme F System.

## 4.1 Float Box

The *Float Box*[1] is a series of five parallel lines, consisting of two outer solid lines and three inner dashed lines, as shown in Figure 4.1. The Float Box represents one complete float turnover going back in time from the current date. Starting with the last bar and moving left, add up the total volume for each bar until the accumulated volume exceeds the stock's float value—this final point marks the beginning of the Float Box.

**Figure 4.1.** Float Box

---

[1] The Float Box is an adaptation of the Cumulative-Volume "Float" Indicator [38].

The upper line is drawn across the highest high of the turnover range, and the lower line is drawn across the lowest low of the turnover range. The three inner dashed lines represent Fibonacci retracement levels of 38%, 50%, and 62%. The Float Box indicator input parameter *FloatFactor* can be changed to adjust the float turnover multiple, e.g., 1.5 or 2.0.

## 4.2 Float Channel

The *Float Channel*[2] is a series of two lines resembling moving averages. Each point on the upper channel line represents the highest high of a float turnover range at that bar in time. Each point on the lower line represents the lowest low of the turnover range up until and including that bar.

By tracking the highest high and lowest low of the turnover range at any given bar, the Float Channel is just another type of price envelope. Further, the Float Channel is a dynamic version of the Float Box. If we plotted the Float Box at every bar and connected the right endpoints of all the Float Boxes, the Float Channel would be formed. Essentially, the Float Channel adjusts to new high and low values as the float turns over.

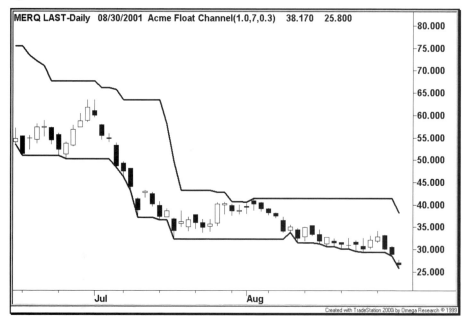

**Figure 4.2.** Float Channel

---

[2] The Float Channel is a facsimile of the Cumulative-Volume "Channel" Indicator [38].

Another way to trade the float model is to use the float channel to buy or short stocks that touch the float channel lines [38]. If a stock is in a strong downtrend and price touches the upper channel, then that is a short signal. If a stock is in an uptrend and price touches the lower channel, then that is a long signal. Note the areas in Figure 4.2 where the channel lines are parallel. These lines define the support and resistance bases.

## 4.3 Float Percentage

The *Float Percentage*[3] is a histogram that shows the increase in float turnover starting from a high or low base. The Float Percentage adds up the volume starting from a breakout or breakdown from a base and calculates this value as a percentage of the float. As the float percentage approaches 100%, the trader is alerted to the condition when the float is close to turning over. Note that the length of the base is adjustable in the Acme code. Reducing the length of the base will increase the number of histograms, and increasing the base length will reduce the number.

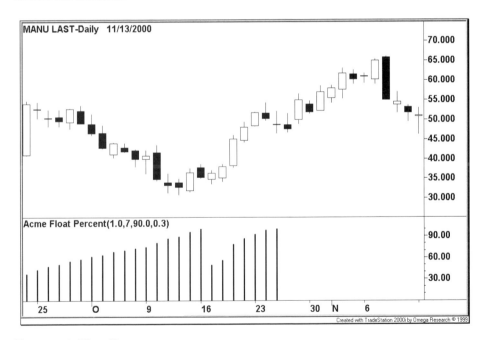

**Figure 4.3.** Float Percentage

---

[3] The Float Percentage is a variation of the Cumulative-Volume "Percentage" Indicator [38].

In Figure 4.3, the float percentage climbs above 80% towards the end of a deep correction in Manugistics (**MANU:Nasdaq**), signaling a possible trend change. At this point, the Float Percentage indicator will alert the trader when the float is about to turn over. The default minimum threshold for a Float Percentage alert is 80% and can be adjusted by the trader.

When a float turnover coincides with a swing low, a short position should be covered. The risk in covering later is that once the float becomes absorbed, this can be a prelude to dramatic price spikes. Similarly, a long position should be sold when a float turnover coincides with a swing high.

## 4.4 Float Trading System (Acme F)

The Acme F System is actually two separate systems, a Breakout system (FB) and a Pullback system (FP), although both systems trade with the prevailing trend. The Breakout system is a channel breakout system that requires a base of a given length to be established before a signal is generated. A base is formed if the current value of the float channel line is close to the previous value of the float channel line for a certain number of bars, thereby forming a nearly parallel segment. Two base counts are maintained, one for the upper float channel line and another for the lower float channel line.

The Breakout system requires consolidation near the base. For a long signal, the high of the current bar must be within one ATR of the upper float channel, an indication that the stock is about to break out. For a short signal, the low of the current bar must be within one ATR of the lower float channel, an indication that the stock is about to break down.

Finally, the Breakout system uses the *table* pattern. A table is a consolidation pattern where the highs or lows of a range of bars are close to each other. The Acme FB system defines a three-bar table; it calculates the difference between the highest high and the lowest high of the table range for long signals and thus the difference between the highest low and lowest low for short signals. This difference must be less than a certain percentage of the ATR (*TableFactor*) to qualify as a valid signal.

The Pullback system operates between the float channel lines. If a stock is in an uptrend, then the system goes long on a near-tag of the lower float channel line. If a stock is in a downtrend, then the system goes short near the upper float channel line. Watch for a float turnover that coincides with the signal.

The performance of the Acme F system depends on the float turnover cycle of the individual stock. If the float turns over on average every thirty days, then the *FilterLength* parameter should be set to thirty for consistency (the default value for *FilterLength* is thirty days). The float value is obtained automatically from the *AcmeGetFloat* lookup function (refer to Chapter 11), as shown in the following calculations.

**Calculations**

1. Get the float of the stock using the function *AcmeGetFloat*.
2. Compute the Average True Range for the past 30 days ($ATR_{30}$).
3. Calculate the 50-day moving average ($MA_{50}$).
4. Compute the upper Float Channel ($FC_{Upper}$) based on the float.
5. Compute the lower Float Channel ($FC_{Lower}$) based on the float.

### 4.4.1 Breakout System (Acme FB)

*Long Signal*

**Calculations**

1. Calculate the base count of the upper float channel ($BC_{Upper}$).
2. Calculate the TableDelta = TableFactor * $ATR_{30}$ (default TableFactor = 0.35).
3. Determine the Highest High of the last 3 bars ($HH_3$).
4. Determine the Lowest High of the last 3 bars ($LH_3$).

**Entry Rules**

1. $BC_{Upper} >= 7$
2. High > $FC_{Upper} - ATR_{30}$
3. $HH_3 - LH_3 <= $ TableDelta
4. Close > $MA_{50}$
5. **Buy** the next bar at or above the High + (EntryFactor * $ATR_{30}$)

**Exit Rules: Profit Target**

1. **Sell** half of the position at or above the High + (ProfitFactor * $ATR_{30}$)
2. **Sell** half of the position at or above the High of ProfitBars ago + (2 * ProfitFactor * $ATR_{30}$)

**Exit Rules: Stop Loss**

1. **Sell** all shares at or below the Lowest Low for StopBars – (ExitFactor * $ATR_{30}$)

*Short Signal*

Calculations

1. Calculate the base count of the lower float channel ($BC_{Lower}$).
2. Calculate the TableDelta = TableFactor * $ATR_{30}$ (default TableFactor = 0.35).
3. Determine the Highest Low of the last 3 bars ($HL_3$).
4. Determine the Lowest Low of the last 3 bars ($LL_3$).

Entry Rules

1. $BC_{Lower}$ >= 7
2. Low < $FC_{Lower}$ + $ATR_{30}$
3. $HL_3$ - $LL_3$ <= TableDelta
4. Close < $MA_{50}$
5. **Sell Short** the next bar at or below the Low – (EntryFactor * $ATR_{30}$)

Exit Rules: Profit Target

1. **Cover** half of the position at or above the Low – (ProfitFactor * $ATR_{30}$)
2. **Cover** half of the position at or above the Low of ProfitBars ago – (2 * ProfitFactor * $ATR_{30}$)

Exit Rules: Stop Loss

1. **Cover** all shares at or below the Highest High for StopBars + (ExitFactor * $ATR_{30}$)

### 4.4.2 Pullback System (Acme FP)

Here are the long and short signals for the Pullback System. The Exit Rules are the same because both systems use the Acme Trade Manager signal for profit targets and stop losses.

*Long Signal*

Calculations

1. Calculate the +DMI for the *FilterLength* of 30 days.
2. Calculate the -DMI for the same period.

## Entry Rules

1. Low $< FC_{Lower} + ATR_{30}$
2. $+DMI > -DMI$
3. Close $> MA_{50}$
4. **Buy** the next bar at or above the High + (EntryFactor * $ATR_{30}$)

## Exit Rules: Profit Target

1. **Sell** half of the position at or above the High + (ProfitFactor * $ATR_{30}$)
2. **Sell** half of the position at or above the High of ProfitBars ago + (2 * ProfitFactor * $ATR_{30}$)

## Exit Rules: Stop Loss

1. **Sell** all shares at or below the Lowest Low for StopBars – (ExitFactor * $ATR_{30}$)

### Short Signal

## Calculations

1. Calculate the +DMI for the *FilterLength* of 30 days.
2. Calculate the -DMI for the same period.

## Entry Rules

1. High $> FC_{Upper} - ATR_{30}$
2. $-DMI > +DMI$
3. Close $< MA_{50}$
4. **Sell Short** the next bar at or below the Low – (EntryFactor * $ATR_{30}$)

## Exit Rules: Profit Target

1. **Cover** half of the position at or above the Low – (ProfitFactor * $ATR_{30}$)
2. **Cover** half of the position at or above the Low of ProfitBars ago – (2 * ProfitFactor * $ATR_{30}$)

## Exit Rules: Stop Loss

1. **Cover** all shares at or below the Highest High for StopBars + (ExitFactor * $ATR_{30}$)

The Acme F System relies on a known and current value of the float for a given stock (ETFs do not have floats). TradeStation does not transmit the float value in real-time, so we have provided the *AcmeGetFloat* function in Chapter 11 for adding a symbol with its associated float value. The symbol must be added alphabetically within the *AcmeGetFloat* function, and the function must be verified before it takes effect.

To find a stock's float and update the TradeStation code, do the following:

1. Go to the Yahoo Finance Web site at http://finance.yahoo.com/.
2. Enter the stock symbol and click on the *Get* button.
3. Click on *Profile*.
4. Scroll down to the bottom of the page.
5. On the left-hand side, *Float* is the last field under *Share-Related Items*.
6. Enter the float value (in millions) in the *AcmeGetFloat* function.
7. Verify the *AcmeGetFloat* function.

The code for the Acme F System is shown below in Example 4.1.

**Example 4.1.** Acme F System

```
{********************************************************************
Acme F System: Look for float breakouts and pullbacks
********************************************************************}
Inputs:
    {F Parameters}
    FloatFactor(1.0),
    BaseBars(7),
    BaseFactor(0.25),
    TableBars(3),
    TableFactor(0.35),
    {Filter Parameters}
    FiltersOn(True),
    FilterLength(30),
    MinimumPrice(15),
    {Position Parameters}
    Equity(100000),
    RiskModel(3),
    RiskPercent(2.0),
    RiskATR(1.0),
    EntryFactor(0.3),
    DrawTargets(True);

Variables:
    N(0),
    ATR(0.0),
```

```
    ATRLength(20),
    MA(0.0),
    MALength(50),
    TradeFilter(True),
    BuyStop(0.0),
    ShortStop(0.0),
    {F Variables}
    TheFloat(0.0),
    FloatHigh1(0.0),
    FloatHigh2(0.0),
    HighBaseCount(1),
    FloatLow1(0.0),
    FloatLow2(0.0),
    LowBaseCount(1),
    BaseDelta(0.0),
    TableDelta(0.0);

If TheFloat = 0.0 Then
Begin
    {Compute the number of base bars based on float turnover}

    TheFloat = FloatFactor * AcmeGetFloat(GetSymbolName);

End Else If TheFloat > 0.0 Then
Begin
    {Initialize variables}

    ATR = Average(Range, ATRLength);
    MA = Average(Close, MALength);
    FloatHigh1 = AcmeFloatChannelHigh(TheFloat);
    FloatLow1 = AcmeFloatChannelLow(TheFloat);

    {Run trade filters}

    If FiltersOn Then
        TradeFilter = Close >= MinimumPrice;

    If TradeFilter Then Begin

        {Calculate shares based on risk model}
        N = AcmeGetShares(Equity, RiskModel, RiskPercent, RiskATR);

        {Entry Signals}

        BuyStop = High + (EntryFactor * ATR);
        ShortStop = Low - (EntryFactor * ATR);
        BaseDelta = BaseFactor * ATR;
        TableDelta = TableFactor * ATR;

        If HighBaseCount >= BaseBars and
        High > (FloatHigh1 - ATR) and
        Highest(High, TableBars) - Lowest(High, TableBars) <=
        TableDelta and
```

```
    Close > MA Then Begin
        {Draw Entry Targets on the Chart}
        If DrawTargets Then
            Condition1 = AcmeEntryTargets("F", BuyStop, 0, 0, 0);
        Buy("Acme LE FB") N Shares Next Bar at BuyStop Stop;
    End;

    If LowBaseCount >= BaseBars and
    Low < (FloatLow1 + ATR) and
    Highest(Low, TableBars) - Lowest(Low, TableBars) <=
    TableDelta and
    Close < MA Then Begin
        {Draw Entry Targets on the Chart}
        If DrawTargets Then
            Condition1 = AcmeEntryTargets("F", 0, 0, ShortStop, 0);
        Sell("Acme SE FB") N Shares Next Bar at ShortStop Stop;
    End;

    If Low <= (FloatLow1 + ATR) and
    DMIPlus(FilterLength) > DMIMinus(FilterLength) and
    Close > MA Then Begin
        {Draw Entry Targets on the Chart}
        If DrawTargets Then
            Condition1 = AcmeEntryTargets("F", BuyStop, 0, 0, 0);
        Buy("Acme LE FP") N Shares Next Bar on BuyStop Stop;
    End;

    If High >= (FloatHigh1 - ATR) and
    DMIMinus(FilterLength) > DMIPlus(FilterLength) and
    Close < MA Then Begin
        {Draw Entry Targets on the Chart}
        If DrawTargets Then
            Condition1 = AcmeEntryTargets("F", 0, 0, ShortStop, 0);
        Sell("Acme SE FP") N Shares Next Bar on ShortStop Stop;
    End;
End;

{Calculate running base count and changing float channel values}

If AbsValue(FloatHigh1 - FloatHigh2) <= BaseDelta Then
    HighBaseCount = HighBaseCount + 1
Else
    HighBaseCount = 1;
FloatHigh2 = FloatHigh1;

If AbsValue(FloatLow1 - FloatLow2) <= BaseDelta Then
    LowBaseCount = LowBaseCount + 1
Else
    LowBaseCount = 1;
FloatLow2 = FloatLow1;
End;
```

## 4.5 Examples

The following charts are examples of trades generated by the Acme F System, with both Acme FB and Acme FP signals. Each example uses starting Equity of $100,000 and the Percent Volatility Model with a risk of 2%. Trade filtering is turned on. Because of the longer float cycle, profit targets have been turned off.

### 4.5.1 THQ Incorporated

Figure 4.4 shows several examples of an Acme FB long entry. After the initial failed breakout, the stock THQ (THQI:Nasdaq) broke above the upper Float Channel after forming a long base. Fourteen days later, it formed another base and broke to new highs again. After the second long entry, the Float Percentage reached 100%, shortly before the stock began a correction.

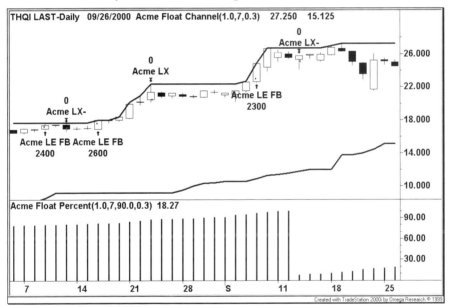

**Figure 4.4.** THQ Incorporated

When stocks form bases, examine the magnitude of float that was turned over during the formation of the base. If the total volume is greater than one float turnover, then that stock is a better trading candidate than a base formed on low volume. The best trading candidates will show a Float Percentage of 80% or higher coinciding with a breakout of a long base. Note that the float turnover rate of a stock influences the length of the base. A stock with high volume and a low float does not get the chance to form a reasonable base, so the base may be no longer than three or four bars.

### 4.5.2 Juniper Networks

For the Acme FP short entries in Figure 4.5, Juniper broke down twice from
low bases. In the first instance, the float turned over in only six trading sessions.
After the float turned over, the stock did not go down much further. In the second instance, the trade could have been stopped out on the third day when the
stock gapped up. Since the stock was in a downtrend, we waited out the gap on
the open to see if it held before covering the short position.

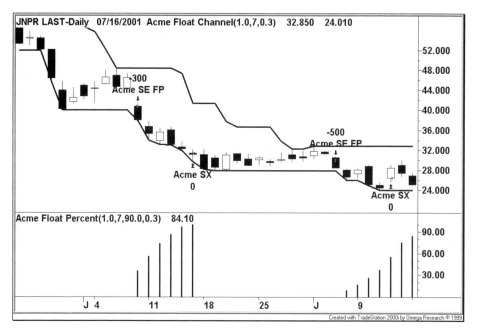

**Figure 4.5.** Juniper Networks

When a long base is being formed, an FP signal may precede an FB signal. In
this example, the price continued downward and broke below the extended base
of the lower float channel the same day; however, in both cases the price did not
form a table near the lower float channel, therefore an FB signal would not have
triggered. Essentially, both float systems work in concert. The trader gets an
opportunity to enter on a pullback (FP) or waits until the stock consolidates
near the base and breaks out (FB). If both conditions occur, then the trader will
get the FP signal first, followed by the FB signal usually one or two days later.

In cases where multiple signals occur within one or two days, we simply treat
each signal separately, even if it means doubling a position in the same stock. A
second signal serves as confirmation for the first signal; we are more confident
with a second entry in the same stock rather than an isolated entry in a different
stock; the concept of multiplicity applies here, too.

### 4.5.3 Ariba

The Acme FP short entry in Figure 4.6 bounces off the upper float channel. This is a strongly trending stock, emulating an Acme M or N swing entry. Although the FP system relies strictly on DMI, the trader is free to add an ADX filter for FP entries only. Using the ADX filter on FB entries only eliminates good trades because when a stock forms a base, the ADX is bound to be low.

For non-trending stocks, the float channels serve as support and resistance – be wary of taking breakouts in trading range stocks. In the example, after the short entry was covered, there was a break below a fourteen-bar base. The FB system did not go short on this breakout because the stock did not form a table near the lower float channel. Further, the stock had already declined over 30% in seven days. In these situations, a test usually occurs, followed by a rebound for a few days before a new trend is established.

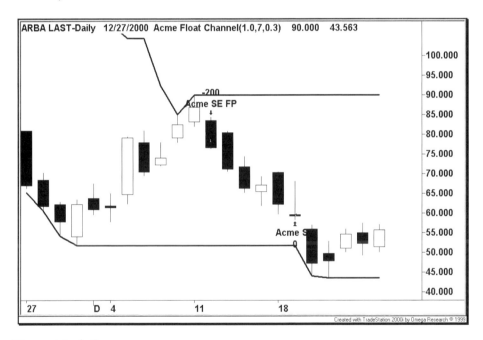

**Figure 4.6.** Ariba

With experience, the trader learns that stocks have symmetric consolidations after protracted moves. A stock that advances or declines 10% in four or five days usually requires the same amount of time to digest the move. The general market tends to follow a similar cycle, alternating an NR day with a WR day, or an NR2 day followed by two WR days, etc. Recently, the market had six NR days followed by six WR days, not the swing trader's optimal pattern.

### 4.5.4 Ciena

Figure 4.7 is an example of an FB short entry. Ciena was in a downtrend and its high touched the upper float channel on August 2nd, 2001. Six days later, it approached the lower float channel. After gapping down and closing near the high of the day, the stock formed a 180 pattern [4], completing a three-day table in the process. The FB short entry triggered the following day.

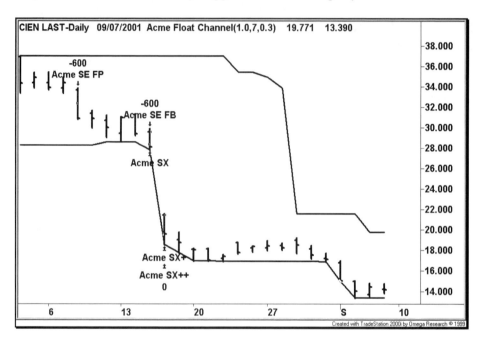

**Figure 4.7.** Ciena

This chart is another illustration of pattern convergence. Although the chart above does not show all of the Acme indicators, we highly recommend the practice. When the trader sees all of the indicators working in concert, his or her eyes are opened to all of the possibilities, leaving little to chance. We prefer this technique to interpreting some vague head-and-shoulder formation.

   The ultimate goal is to encode as much technical and fundamental information as possible and annotate the chart with it: the letters and lines approach. Too many times to count, we have chosen between multiple signals only to miss a critical piece of information that distinguished one of the signals among the many others. Through the process of observation, the trader can simply encode the new piece of information and use the chart as an artist's palette, each color representing a unique characteristic of the stock. By automating the stock selection process as much as possible, the trader is free to focus on new techniques.

### 4.5.5 Check Point Software

Figure 4.8 shows an example of float turnover for CHKP in late November 2000, as shown by the Float Percentage histogram reaching 100% after breaking below a long base. Although this technique is not encoded in the Acme F System, an alternative way of playing float turnover is to let a stock break out, then wait for it to reach 100% turnover while it is trending. Once the float turns over, take a counter-trend trade on an exhaustion move, using either the Acme M or Acme V systems as confirmation. In the example below, a long position taken at the 100% turnover mark would have netted over 30 points in five days. Because of the volatility, this may be a strategy better suited for options.

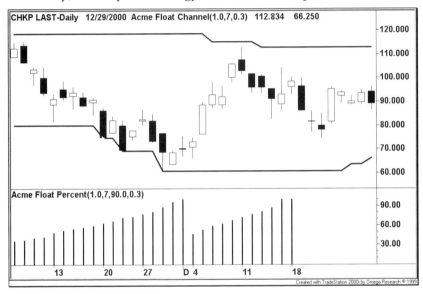

**Figure 4.8.** Check Point Software

Now, examine the second Float Percentage histogram in Figure 4.8 – it is not a mirror image of the stock price like the first one. This FP started at zero in late November (the first histogram overlaps it) when CHKP broke below the lower float channel. The stock bottomed and reversed, approaching the upper float channel in early December. At this point, the FP reading was 70%, with price near resistance at 110 established in early November.

Moreover, the stock had formed a V-bottom pattern, encompassing a fifty-point move. In this case, the trader does not wait for a full turnover to exit the trade because of the disparity in volume between the down leg and up leg of the "V". Over 60% of the float changed hands during the down leg, but only 30% of the float turned over on the up leg. Clearly, the stock had rebounded on some hot air, outpacing itself.

### 4.5.6 FLIR Systems

The chart in Figure 4.9 appears to be the picture-perfect chart. Three times in the month of October, the stock attempted to break out above the upper float channel. The stock consolidated for five days in early November, and finally it broke out above the channel. After one day of going slightly higher, the trade was stopped out for a loss and then fell into a waterfall over the next five days. Clearly, if the apparently perfect trade does not follow through, then take the loss and fade the original trade. Consider how many people got into this trade waiting for it to break out.

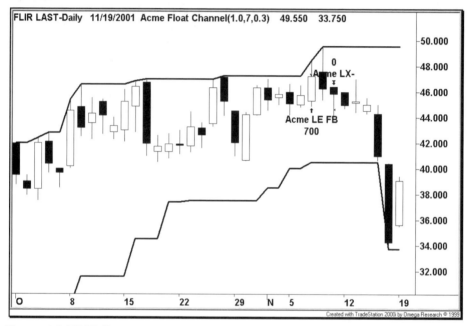

**Figure 4.9.** FLIR Systems

## 4.6 Float Trading Strategies

1. When the trade entry coincides with a Float Percentage greater than 90%, the probability of success increases dramatically. Use the Alert feature of the Float Percentage indicator to find charts completing a float turnover.

2. For Acme FB long and short entries, use the Double Bottom and Double Top indicators to assess the trade entry. If the stock price has traversed from the top of the channel to the bottom of the channel and then back up again, the breakout may be false and there may be a Test

pattern first. In this case, buy a pullback near the upper channel and sell short on a retracement up from the lower channel.

3. Because TradeStation generates its Performance Report for one instrument at a time, we have included trade logging with the function *AcmeLogTrade*. When trade logging is turned on, each trade is written to a common text file that can be imported into a Microsoft Excel spreadsheet. By running the TradeStation 2000*i* Workspace Assistant on a portfolio, every trade will be recorded for each symbol stored in the GlobalServer.

4. The current float value is valid only as far back as the most recent split date. Unless the software automatically adjusts the float for stock splits, interpreting the float turnover will be meaningless for pre-split data. For example, if a stock has a float of 10 million shares and a 2:1 stock split occurred on January 1$^{st}$, then the pre-split amount was 5 million shares. When analyzing historical data, adjust the float value to its pre-split level.

# 5 Geometric Trading

*Inspiration is needed in geometry,*
*just as much as in poetry.*

Aleksandr Pushkin, *Likhtenshtein*

Geometric analysis is the interpretation of lines on charts, ranging from a single line segment to a Gann square with intersecting angles [18]. Horizontal lines are drawn at support and resistance levels: *double bottoms* and *double tops*, and *triple bottoms* and *triple tops*. Lines also enclose patterns such as *rectangles* and *triangles*. Much has been written about these chart patterns [2, 11, 15, 25, 26]. Here, we present a simple but effective daily and intraday trading system based on a unique definition of a rectangle. Further, we explore variations of other geometric patterns, e.g., the encapsulated triangle.

Geometric chart patterns are notoriously hard to trade because every trader in the world is looking for them. The days of the clean breakout are long gone, so the trader must use techniques such as double confirmation, as demonstrated in our definition of encapsulated triangles. Trading off of the traditional chart patterns is dangerous to one's portfolio because in the mind's eye one can detect a head-and-shoulders pattern in a blanket of cumulus clouds.

The Rectangle Trading System (Acme R) simply computes the ratio of a consolidation range to a trending range. This system can be traded on any time frame, and it is equally useful on an intraday time frame because many stocks consolidate during the middle of the day and then continue in the direction of the morning trend until the closing bell, or they reverse around 2:30 pm EST. The system does not need any trading filters – the only requirement is that the stock has some degree of volatility.

The R system works well in conjunction with other systems. For example, suppose an opening range breakout system goes long or short sixty minutes after the opening bell, holding the position until the end of the day. The breakout system triggers a short entry, and the stock falls until mid-day, where it consolidates in a tight range. If the stock reverses in the afternoon, then the breakout system would give back more of the profit using a traditional stop strategy than with the Acme R system. A breakout system that exits a trade on a move out of a rectangle gives back a profit equal only to the height of the rectangle.

## 5.1 Rectangle

The *Rectangle* is two solid parallel lines that bound the high and low of a trading range (Figure 5.1). The dimensions of the rectangle are its length (in bars), its height (high minus low), and its aspect ratio: its height divided by the height of a preceding range known as the *reference range*. In order to qualify as a rectangle, the aspect ratio must be less than or equal to a maximum aspect ratio. Further, the height of the rectangle must be less than a specified multiple of the ATR, or *RangeFactor*.

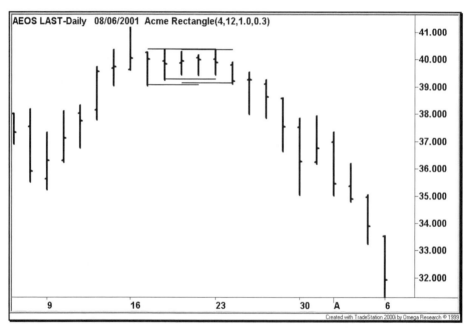

**Figure 5.1.** Rectangle

For example, suppose our rectangles are four bars in length. The highest high of the current range is 42, and the lowest low of this range is 40. Therefore, the rectangle's height is 42 − 40 = 2. The length of the reference range is twelve, so next we calculate the height of the range *preceding* the rectangle. The highest high of the reference range is 43, and the lowest low of the reference range is 35, so the reference range height is 43 − 35 = 8.

Now, we must qualify the current range as a rectangle. We specify a maximum aspect ratio of 0.3, i.e., the rectangle's height must be 30% of the reference range's height. First, divide the rectangle height (2) by the reference range height (8) to get the aspect ratio of $2 \div 8 = 0.25$, which qualifies this range as a rectangle (< 0.3). Next, we confirm the rectangle using a RangeFactor of 1.0. The rectangle's height can be no greater than the stock's ATR multiplied by the RangeFactor. If the ATR of the stock is 1.9, then the current range does not qualify as a rectangle because the height (2) is not less than the RangeFactor (1.0) multiplied by the ATR (1.9). If the ATR is 2.1, then the current range qualifies as a rectangle because the height (2) is less than the RangeFactor (1.0) multiplied by the ATR (2.1).

The EasyLanguage function code in Example 5.1 determines whether or not a specified range is a rectangle:

**Example 5.1.** Function *AcmeRectangular*

```
{******************************************************************
AcmeRectangular: Determine whether the region is a rectangle
******************************************************************}

Inputs:
    RectangleLength(Numeric),
    RangeLength(Numeric),
    RangeFactor(Numeric),
    RangeRatio(Numeric);

Variables:
    ATR(0.0),
    VLength(30),
    RectangleHigh(0.0),
    RectangleLow(0.0),
    RectangleHeight(0.0),
    RangeHigh(0.0),
    RangeLow(0.0),
    RangeHeight(0.0);

AcmeRectangular = False;
ATR = Average(Range, VLength);

RectangleHigh = Highest(High, RectangleLength);
RectangleLow = Lowest(Low, RectangleLength);
RectangleHeight = RectangleHigh - RectangleLow;

RangeHigh = Highest(High, RangeLength)[RectangleLength];
RangeLow = Lowest(Low, RangeLength)[RectangleLength];
RangeHeight = RangeHigh - RangeLow;

If RectangleHeight > 0 and RangeHeight > 0 Then
    If (RectangleHeight / RangeHeight) <= RangeRatio and
    RectangleHeight <= RangeFactor * ATR Then
        AcmeRectangular = True;
```

The code for the Boolean function is divided into two sections. After computing the ATR, we calculate the height of both the rectangle and the reference range. Then, we test both of our conditions: whether or not the rectangle height divided by the reference range height is less than the maximum *RangeRatio* and whether the rectangle height is less than or equal to the *RangeFactor* multiplied by the ATR. If both conditions are true, then a rectangle has been found. An indicator calling this function can test every bar for the existence of a rectangle. Some code for drawing rectangles is shown in Example 5.2.

**Example 5.2.** Indicator *Acme Rectangle*

```
{*******************************************************************
Acme Rectangle: Draw a rectangle
*******************************************************************}

Inputs:
    RectangleLength(4),
    RangeLength(12),
    RangeFactor(1.0),
    RangeRatioLimit(0.3);

Variables:
    RectangleHigh(0.0),
    RectangleLow(0.0),
    UpperLine(-1),
    LowerLine(-1);

RectangleHigh = Highest(High, RectangleLength);
RectangleLow = Lowest(Low, RectangleLength);
If AcmeRectangular(RectangleLength, RangeLength, RangeFactor,
RangeRatioLimit) Then Begin
    UpperLine = TL_New(Date[RectangleLength-1],
    Time[RectangleLength-1], RectangleHigh,
    Date[0], Time[0], RectangleHigh);
    If UpperLine >= 0 Then Begin
        If GetBackGroundColor = Black Then
            TL_SetColor(UpperLine, Yellow)
        Else
            TL_SetColor(UpperLine, Black);
        TL_SetSize(UpperLine, 1);
    End;
    LowerLine = TL_New(Date[RectangleLength-1],
    Time[RectangleLength-1], RectangleLow,
    Date[0], Time[0], RectangleLow);
    If LowerLine >= 0 Then Begin
        If GetBackGroundColor = Black Then
            TL_SetColor(LowerLine, Yellow)
        Else
            TL_SetColor(LowerLine, Black);
        TL_SetSize(LowerLine, 1);
```

```
    End;
End;
```

The code in Example 5.2 is a template for other geometric patterns in the sense that the current bar is tested for the pattern, and if the pattern exists, then the lines are drawn. Here, the indicator calls the *AcmeRectangular* function, which returns true or false. If true, then two trend lines are drawn, one across the top of the rectangle (the high of the bar range) and one across the bottom of the rectangle (the low of the bar range).

## 5.2 Rectangle Trading System (Acme R)

The Acme R system is simple. If a rectangle is identified, then a stop order is placed on either side of the rectangle. As with all other Acme systems, the parameters can be adjusted to fit the trader's selection criteria. The brackets [] reference historical bars, e.g., [4] means four bars ago.

| Calculations |
| --- |

1. Calculate the Average True Range for the past 30 bars ($ATR_{30}$).
2. Get the Highest High of the last 4 bars ($HH_4$).
3. Get the Lowest Low of the last 4 bars ($LL_4$).
4. Get the Highest High of the 12 bars preceding $HH_4$ ($HH_{12}[4]$).
5. Get the Lowest Low of the 12 bars preceding $LL_4$ ($LL_{12}[4]$).

### 5.2.1 Long Signal

| Entry Rules |
| --- |

1. $(HH_4 - LL_4) / (HH_{12}[4] - LL_{12}[4])$ <= 0.3
2. $(HH_4 - LL_4)$ <= 1.0 * $ATR_{30}$
3. **Buy** the next bar at or above $HH_4$ + (EntryFactor * $ATR_{30}$)

| Exit Rules: Profit Target |
| --- |

1. **Sell** half of the position at or above the High + (ProfitFactor * $ATR_{30}$)
2. **Sell** half of the position at or above the High of ProfitBars ago + (2 * ProfitFactor * $ATR_{30}$)

---

**Exit Rules: Stop Loss**

1. **Sell** all shares at or below the Lowest Low for StopBars – (ExitFactor * $ATR_{30}$)

### 5.2.2 Short Signal

**Entry Rules**

1. $(HH_4 - LL_4) / (HH_{12} - LL_{12}) <= 0.3$
2. $(HH_4 - LL_4) <= 1.0 * ATR_{30}$
3. **Sell Short** the next bar at or below $LL_4 - $ (EntryFactor * $ATR_{30}$)

**Exit Rules: Profit Target**

1. **Cover** half of the position at or below the Low – (ProfitFactor * $ATR_{30}$)
2. **Cover** half of the position at or below the Low of ProfitBars ago – (2 * ProfitFactor * $ATR_{30}$)

**Exit Rules: Stop Loss**

1. **Cover** all shares at or above the Highest High for StopBars + (ExitFactor * $ATR_{30}$)

The EasyLanguage code for the Acme R System is shown in Example 5.3:

**Example 5.3.** Acme R System

```
{****************************************************************
Acme R System: Look for Rectangle Breakouts
****************************************************************}

Inputs:
    {R Parameters}
    RectangleLength(4),
    RectangleRange(12),
    RectangleFactor(1.0),
    RectangleRatio(0.3),
    {Filter Parameters}
    FiltersOn(True),
    FilterLength(14),
    MinimumATR(1.0),
    {Position Parameters}
```

```
    Equity(100000),
    RiskModel(3),
    RiskPercent(2.0),
    RiskATR(1.0),
    EntryFactor(0.25),
    DrawTargets(True);

Variables:
    N(0),
    ATR(0.0),
    ATRLength(20),
    TradeFilter(True),
    BuyStop(0.0),
    ShortStop(0.0),
    {R Variables}
    InRectangle(False),
    RectangleHigh(0.0),
    RectangleLow(0.0);

ATR = Volatility(ATRLength);

RectangleHigh = Highest(High, RectangleLength);
RectangleLow = Lowest(Low, RectangleLength);

BuyStop = RectangleHigh + (EntryFactor * ATR);
ShortStop = RectangleLow - (EntryFactor * ATR);

If FiltersOn Then
    TradeFilter = ATR >= MinimumATR;

If TradeFilter Then Begin

    {Calculate shares based on risk model}
    N = AcmeGetShares(Equity, RiskModel, RiskPercent, RiskATR);

    {Determine whether or not we are in a rectangle}
    InRectangle = AcmeRectangular(RectangleLength, RectangleRange,
    RectangleFactor, RectangleRatio);

    If InRectangle Then Begin
        {Draw Entry Targets on the Chart}
        If DrawTargets Then
            Condition1 = AcmeEntryTargets("R", BuyStop, 0, 0, 0);
        Buy("Acme LE R") N Shares Next Bar on BuyStop Stop;
        {Draw Entry Targets on the Chart}
        If DrawTargets Then
            Condition1 = AcmeEntryTargets("R", 0, 0, ShortStop, 0);
        Sell("Acme SE R") N Shares Next Bar on ShortStop Stop;
    End;
End;
```

## 5.3 Examples

The following charts are examples of trades generated by the Acme R System. Each example uses Equity of $100,000 and the Percent Volatility Model with a risk of 2%.

### 5.3.1 AirGate PCS

The chart in Figure 5.2 is an illustration of an Acme R short entry. Once the low of the rectangle at 57.50 was broken, a short trade was entered, and the price fell five points in a period of two days. Both the single-bar and multi-bar profit targets triggered on the same day. Half of the position was covered near 55, and the rest was covered in the low 54's. The point of this example is to demonstrate the market's general pattern of extended consolidation periods followed by explosive moves (note the double rectangles).

The stock bounced off of its 50-day moving average on August 17th. The moving average is an area of natural support for a stock with a rising trend, so this area of the chart would also have been an excellent time to cover the entire position.

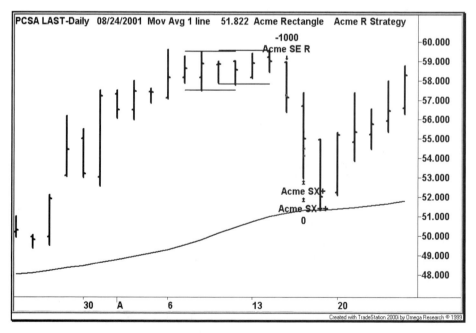

**Figure 5.2.** AirGate PCS Rectangle

### 5.3.2 Rambus

Figure 5.3 is an example of an intraday rectangle for Rambus (RMBS:Nasdaq) on August 28th, 2001. One might assume that a stock that gaps up on the day would consolidate and resume its rise later in the afternoon. Our testing shows that a stock in consolidation is just as likely to break in the opposite direction, regardless of the opening gap bias.

With rectangles, it is important to stay neutral on the eventual direction of the stock. If you are playing rectangles intraday, then monitor the charts of the associated market and sector indices to determine whether or not the stock moves synchronously with the indices. For example, with Rambus, one would monitor the PHLX Semiconductor Sector Index (SOX) along with the Nasdaq Composite Index.

Although the Acme R system includes a volatility filter, the R system is self-checking because the definition of a rectangle requires a large range preceding it in order to satisfy the aspect ratio requirement. For intraday trading, the rectangle will almost always occur in the middle of the day after the morning trend has developed. Then, later in the afternoon, the stock will continue either in the direction of the morning trend or reverse completely. So, we split the trading day into three segments and use the rectangle to represent the middle segment as a reversal tool.

**Figure 5.3.** Rambus Rectangle

### 5.3.3 Electro-Optical Engineering

This is our favorite rectangle of all time, as shown in Figure 5.4. We emphasize the point about not using trend filters for rectangles because stocks tend to move up above rectangles at bottoms and explode down out of rectangles at tops (refer to Figure 5.2). Here, the rectangle was under the $MA_{50}$ at the breakout.

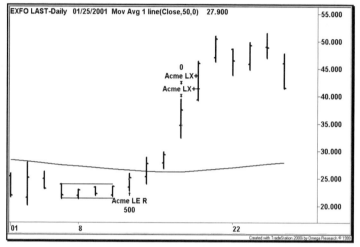

**Figure 5.4.** Electro-Optical Engineering Rectangle

### 5.3.4 Stericycle

Figure 5.5 is an example of *multiplicity* – multiple rectangles and multiple signals all coming together to form a powerful move.

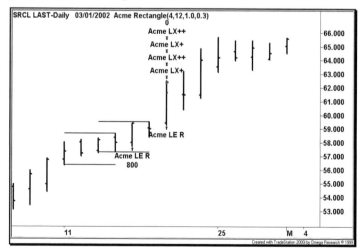

**Figure 5.5.** Multiplicity

## 5.4 Double Bottom

Much of the technical analysis literature places geometric patterns into either bullish or bearish categories. For example, the *double bottom* is considered to be a bullish formation. Our stance is that a double bottom is bullish only if it works. The problem with bottoms and tops is that by the time they can be recognized, the good trade may have already occurred. If a stock has established a low several bars ago, then every bar thereafter approaching that low is a potential double bottom. The question for the trader is: How must the price action develop to prove that in fact a double bottom has occurred, and how soon can a long trade be entered? If the price breaks below the previous low, then should the trader go short on that breakdown?

The answer is that the trader requires a bullish bar pattern to trigger a long entry. When price tests a previous low, then that is a possibly bullish Test pattern. Since a Test bar must close near the high of its range, this is the first sign that a double bottom has probably been established, and only then can a long entry be considered. The pattern does not have to strictly be a Test pattern, but simply a bar that closes near the high.

In Figure 5.6, look at the last bar of the double bottom. The line can only be drawn once the low of the day has been established, and that is not known until the end of the day (although confidence increases as the end of the day approaches). If one thinks of the optimal entry under intraday conditions, then the trader must be alerted to the condition that a double bottom is possibly being formed based on the current low of the day, i.e., the double bottom line can be drawn in real-time throughout the day and redrawn as the low of the day changes, as long as the low stays within the parameters of what constitutes a double bottom.

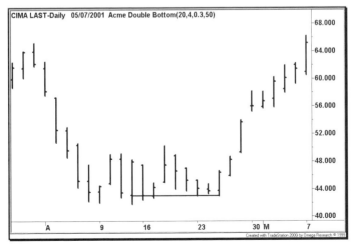

**Figure 5.6.** Double Bottom

The best intraday solution is to enter a trade when a stock *goes green*, at which point the long entry is triggered. The risk/reward ratio of this trade is good because the stop can be placed at the low of the day, and then the position can be held until the end of the day. If the stock closes up on the day or even near the high, then the trader has effectively anticipated the double bottom, and the nightly scans will recognize the double bottom with a bar that closed strongly on the day. In turn, other traders will take long positions on the following day when the high is exceeded.

Figure 5.6 is an example of a single double bottom (one line). In the next few examples, we show how consecutive instances of the same pattern (multiple lines) alert the trader to impending moves. Further, we apply the concept of an ATR factor to construct bottom and top formations where the pivot points are not perfectly connected.

## 5.5 Double Top

The chart in Figure 5.7 shows a *Double Top* formation of three parallel lines with the same origin. Notice how two of the lines do not touch the exact high of the origin of the double top because we use the same principle that has been applied throughout the book: a range factor or a percentage of the ATR. For all bottoms and tops, the Acme software uses a *RangeFactor* of 0.3, or 30% of the ATR. Thus, if a high is within the tolerance of a previous high, then the formation qualifies as a double top.

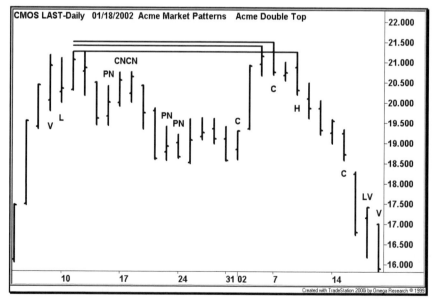

**Figure 5.7.** Double Top

For example, suppose the current high is 21.5 and the high of the previous high pivot bar is 21.25, a difference of 0.25 points. If the ATR of the stock is 0.9, then the allowable difference is 0.3 x 0.9 = 0.27 points. Consequently, this high qualifies as a double top.

At this point, the concept of multiplicity cannot be emphasized enough. The first double top in Figure 5.7 is an NR bar. The second double top is a bearish Cobra, signified by the close at the low of the day. At this point, the trader may not even wait for the short trigger with two consecutive double tops. Finally, the third double top is a Hook that breaks the low of the previous day. This serves as another confirmation for a short entry. The EasyLanguage code for detecting a Double Top is shown in Example 5.4.

**Example 5.4.** Function *AcmeDoubleTop*

```
{*****************************************************************
AcmeDoubleTop: Find a double top formation
*****************************************************************}

Inputs:
    LookbackBars(Numeric),
    Strength(Numeric),
    RangeFactor(Numeric);

Variables:
    RangeDelta(0.0),
    HighPivot(0.0),
    LowPivot(0.0),
    HighMinimum(7);

AcmeDoubleTop = -1;
RangeDelta = RangeFactor * Volatility(LookbackBars);
HighPivot = PivotHighVSBar(1, High, Strength, Strength, LookbackBars);
LowPivot = PivotLowVSBar(1, Low, Strength, Strength, LookbackBars);

If HighPivot <> -1 and
LowPivot <> -1 and
HighPivot >= HighMinimum and
AbsValue(High - High[HighPivot]) <= RangeDelta and
AbsValue(High - Highest(High, HighPivot)) <= RangeDelta and
HighPivot > LowPivot Then
    AcmeDoubleTop = HighPivot;
```

The code for finding bottoms and tops is based on the concept of a *pivot* bar, also known as a *swing* bar. Each pivot bar has a characteristic known as *strength*, a reference to the number of bars on either side of the bar. For a high pivot, the strength refers to the number of bars on either side that are lower than the pivot price. For a low pivot, the strength refers to the number of bars that are higher than the pivot price. Further, each pivot can have a separate left strength and right strength. If a high pivot bar has a left strength of three and a right strength of two, then the three highs to the left and the two highs to the right are lower than the pivot bar high. Typically, the left strength is equal to the right strength for symmetry. The default strength for the Acme indicators is four.

The *AcmeDoubleTop* function has a chart window to look for high and low pivots, scoped by the parameter *LookbackBars*. It first locates a high pivot and a low pivot. If both are found, then the function goes on to test other conditions to qualify the pattern as a double top. First, the origin of the double top must be at least seven bars away (this parameter can be adjusted). Second, the difference between the high of the current bar and the high of the origin of the top must be less than a certain percentage of the ATR; by definition, either of these values must be the highest high of the range. Finally, the high pivot must be greater than the low pivot.

## 5.6 Triple Bottom

The difference between the double bottom and *triple bottom* is that the former is drawn across two pivots and the latter across three pivots. Figure 5.8 is an example of a double triple bottom. Note the difference between an intraday entry on the second triple bottom and an entry the following day. The stock closed near 39 on the day of the second triple bottom, nearly three points above the low of 36, making a second day entry a low-probability trade. On that second day, the stock gapped open at 39, tested 40, and closed at the low of the day near 38.

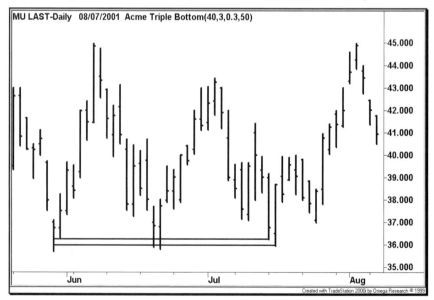

**Figure 5.8.** Triple Bottom

## 5.7 Triple Top

The *Triple Top* has cachet. A stock attempts to break out for the third time, and all of the bulls get lathered up about its big breakout potential. As with any other simple pattern, its success rate is not as high as one might be led to believe. If the pattern were that easy to trade, then there would be a Web site named www.tripletop.com, and every trader would flock to it.

In Figure 5.9, notice how many times in early June the index tried to break above the triple top–once, then three bars later twice, the next bar, and the next bar. A buy stop a tick above the high would have been stopped out twice, while an ATR factor would have prevented both trades.

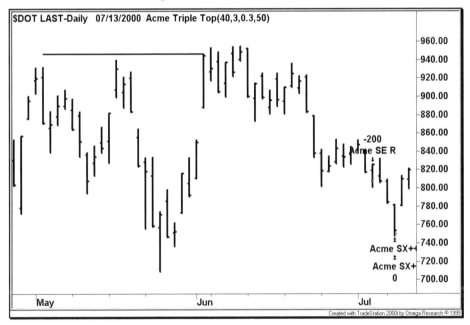

**Figure 5.9.** Triple Top

## 5.8 Triangle

A *Triangle* is a consolidation pattern with a narrowing range. A trend line sloping down connects the highs, and a trend line sloping up connects the lows. As with other geometric patterns, we devised a new way of looking at a triangle with multiplicity. The formation is called a *Stealth Triangle* because of its resemblance to the B-2 Spirit[1], a multi-role bomber.

---

[1] The Stealth Bomber flies under the radar because of its special coatings, composition, and flying-wing design.

Figure 5.10 shows an example of a stealth triangle. First, the most recent pairs of pivot highs and pivot lows are located based on a minimum *Strength* within a range specified by *Length*. Then, an imaginary trend line is projected across each pair of pivots to the current bar. If the high of the current bar is less than the value of the projected trend line for the high pivot pair, then the first condition for a triangle pattern is satisfied. Similarly, if the low of the current bar is greater than the value of the projected trend line for the low pivot pair, then the second condition is satisfied. Finally, the *slope* of each trend line must be less than the maximum specified slope to avoid acute triangles. We scan for obtuse triangles that resemble shims[2], as shown in Figure 5.10.

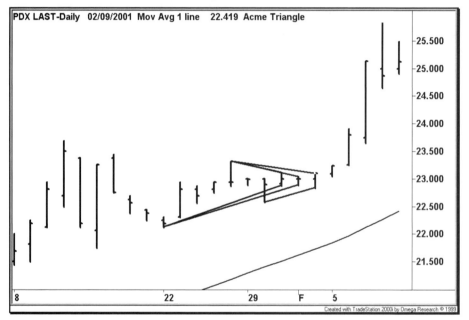

**Figure 5.10.** Stealth Triangle

To trade a triangle, we wait for the stealth formation and then enter a trade on a break of the highest or lowest bar of the nesting triangles. In each of the triangle examples in Figures 5.11 and 5.12, the slope of the moving average is a guide to trade direction. Trade triangles in the direction of the trend, checking whether or not the triangle is above or below the moving average.

Like the rectangle, the triangle is a short-term formation for day trading, although it does not have as much reversal value as a rectangle. The triangle is more biased towards the prevailing trend, giving the trader a chance to enter on a consolidation pattern.

---

[2] A shim is a thin piece of wood that resembles and functions as a wedge.

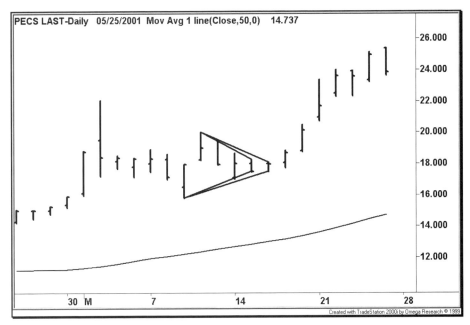

**Figure 5.11.** PECS Stealth Triangle

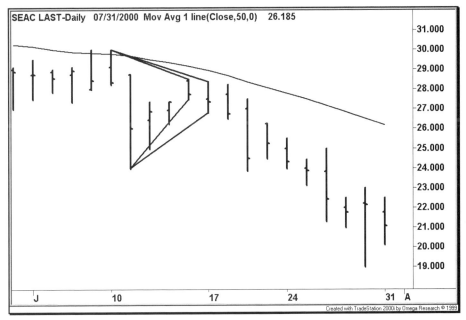

**Figure 5.12.** SEAC Stealth Triangle

# 6 Volatility Trading

*There are some things*
*You learn best in calm,*
*and some in storm.*

Willa Cather

Most human beings are conditioned from childhood that if we can buy something at a cheaper price, then it must be a great deal, and we feel good about the purchase. Since stocks trade in prices, we take the mental leap and assume that a cheaper stock is a bargain, expecting those good feelings in return for a higher stock price. When the stock continues lower, more shares are purchased because the price is an even better bargain, and the buyer is wondering what these sellers must be thinking. This "buy the dip" strategy worked well during the bull market of the 1990's but fell apart in the early 2000's.

As with any strategy, the efficacy of a system depends on where and when it is applied, as shown by the bottom-fishing example. The Acme V system is self-checking because it takes a long position only within the context of what it defines as bullish conditions. For example, the system requires the stock to be trading above its 50-day moving average – a simple yet effective filter.

The Acme V System is the most unorthodox system of all. Even with the moving average filter, it still breaks most of the rules because it is a counter-trend system for volatile stocks. It is the only Acme system that does not take short positions because it has a few other tricks under its sleeve, and one of those tricks is the so-called *Tuesday Turnaround* effect [16].

The key to the system is the weekend because Saturday and Sunday do matter. Before the weekend, a given stock or index has established its weekly low and high. If this stock or index finishes the week near its weekly low, then this weakness creates weekend anxiety for the buyers. When trading resumes the following week, the stock will continue its descent, triggering a further sell-off in the stock. While the panicked investors bail out of the stock, the V system steps in, absent of any news that is causing the decline. This is where the professional traders drink from the pool of liquidity and hunt in the land of volatility, where the trader without a plan is prey.

The V System is a strategy especially suited for options because of the extreme volatility. Buying a stock in the *V Zone* is dangerous because there may be no apparent reason for the decline, especially if it is bucking the market and sector trend. This strategy works best during general market declines and is tailored to the sector indices. When a sector signal is generated, find the best-performing stocks in that sector, and buy a basket of them.

This system does **not** work well for industrial and financial stocks. Because of their cyclical nature and tendency to trend, these stocks tend not to have mid-week reversals. In contrast, the strategy works well for both biotechnology and technology stocks.

## 6.1 Linear Regression

The basis for the V system is a statistical method known as *linear regression* [20]. Linear regression analyzes past data to project future values using *least squares fitting*, computing a formula for a line drawn through these data. For a stock chart, the regression line can reference any bar price in the formula: open, high, low, or close.

Since we are attempting to pick a bottom, we use the low prices, so the regression line is drawn through the lows of the data, as shown in Figure 6.1. The rectangle contains the projection of the previous four lows to Low 5. We select a regression length of five bars because the V system works on the weekly cycle.

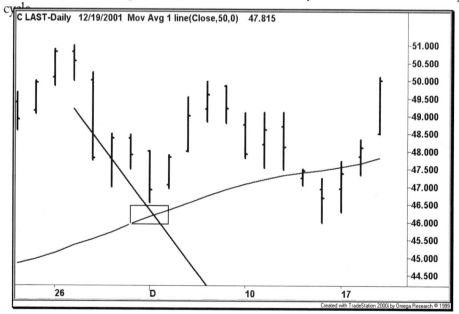

**Figure 6.1.** Linear Regression Line, Point 1

Proceeding to the next bar, we calculate the linear regression for the previous four bars to project a line towards Low 5, highlighted by the rectangle on the chart in Figure 6.2. Now, compare the slope of the regression line in Figure 6.1 with the line in Figure 6.2. The former slope is at a steeper downward angle, while the latter is more horizontal. This is the basis of the V system. As soon as the slope starts to flatten out, we want to consider a long entry.

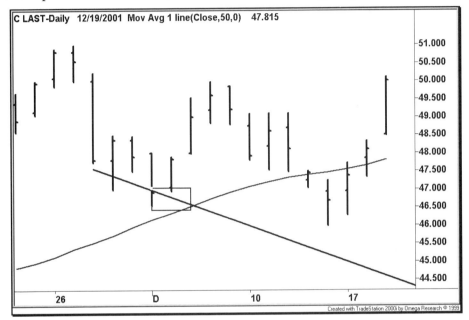

**Figure 6.2.** Linear Regression Line, Point 2

The easiest way to detect the changing slope is to connect the dots for each linear regression projection. The result is the *linear regression curve* shown in Figure 6.3. Note how the curve descends and then ticks up at the point where the long entry is taken.

The astute trader will speculate about how the V system went long when the slope of the regression curve was down on the previous bar, given that the value of the curve is not known until the end of the trading day. The answer is that the linear regression value is projected one bar into the future, giving us a statistical jump on the other traders (refer to the discussion on real-time trade entry versus end-of-day entry in Chapter 5). Instead of participating in just a follow-through day, the trader is able to capitalize on the first day as well.

Unlike the other systems, the V system enters on a stop order above the previous day's close instead of the high, i.e., when the stock goes green plus the ATR percentage. In the following section, we discuss the other conditions that make the V system more robust.

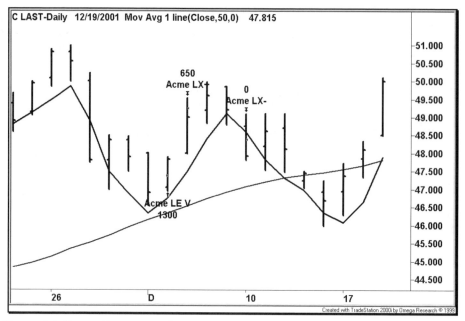

**Figure 6.3.** Linear Regression Curve

## 6.2 Volatility Trading System (Acme V)

Since V bottoms are tricky, the system has strict requirements for entry. The system takes entries only on Tuesdays or Wednesdays. In the past several years, Monday has been a relatively bullish day as well [16], so the trader may wish to change the code to accommodate Mondays. A stock that has not reversed by late Wednesday or Thursday will tend to close on the low of the week

The second condition is that the stock must be above its 50-day moving average. We are trying to simulate bullish conditions and to filter out all stocks and indices trading below their 50-day moving average. During the prolonged bull market, we did not need this filter but learned quickly once the market turned down in the spring of 2000.

The third condition is that the low of the current bar is greater than the projected low of the regression curve. When a stock is falling sharply, it tends to outpace the regression curve, i.e., the lows are below the curve. As soon as the projected low is above the curve, then this condition is satisfied.

The other entry conditions are that the high of the current bar must be the lowest high of the regression range, the current bar's range must be less than a given percentage of the ATR, and the high of the current bar must be greater than yesterday's low (no gap down).

---

Calculations

---

1. Calculate the Average True Range for the past 20 bars ($ATR_{20}$).
2. Calculate the Moving Average for the past 50 bars ($MA_{50}$).
3. Calculate the Linear Regression value of the projected low from the last 5 bars ($LR_5$).
4. Get the Lowest High of the previous 4 bars ($LH_4$).

## 6.2.1 Long Signal

---

Entry Rules

---

1. Today is Monday or Tuesday
2. High < $LH_4$
3. Range < RangeFactor * $ATR_{20}$
4. Low > $LR_5$
5. Low > $MA_{50}$
6. High > Yesterday's Low
7. Buy the next bar at or above the Close + (EntryFactor * $ATR_{20}$)

---

Exit Rules: Profit Target

---

1. **Sell** half of the position at or above the High + (ProfitFactor * $ATR_{20}$)
2. **Sell** half of the position at or above the High of ProfitBars ago + (2 * ProfitFactor * $ATR_{20}$)

---

Exit Rules: Stop Loss

---

1. **Sell** all shares at or below the Lowest Low for StopBars − (ExitFactor * $ATR_{20}$)

## 6.2.2 Short Signal

The V System does not have a corresponding short entry. The design of this strategy is "an exercise left to the reader." Our recommendation is that the short entry be symmetric to the long entry. Use the linear regression of the high and a stock below its 50-day moving average.

The EasyLanguage code for the Acme V System is shown in Example 6.1. Since the stop order is being triggered above the close, and not above the high as in the other systems, the *ExitFactor* may be set higher.

**Example 6.1.** Acme V System

```
{******************************************************************
Acme V System: Anticipate a "V" Bottom based on Linear Regression
******************************************************************}

Inputs:
    {V Parameters}
    VolatilityFactor(2.0),
    RegressionBars(5),
    RangeFactor(1.0),
    {Position Parameters}
    Equity(100000),
    RiskModel(3),
    RiskPercent(2.0),
    RiskATR(1.0),
    EntryFactor(0.25),
    DrawTargets(True);

Variables:
    N(0),
    ATR(0.0),
    ATRLength(20),
    MA(0.0),
    MALength(50),
    LRValue(0.0);

ATR = Volatility(ATRLength);
MA = Average(Close, MALength);
LRValue = LinearRegValue(Low, RegressionBars, -1);

{Entry Signal}

If (DayOfWeek(Date) = 1 or DayOfWeek(Date) = 2) Then Begin

    {Calculate shares based on risk model}
    N = AcmeGetShares(Equity, RiskModel, RiskPercent, RiskATR);

    If High < Lowest(High, RegressionBars - 1)[1] and
    Range <= RangeFactor * ATR and
    Low > LRValue and
    Low > MA and
    High > Low[1] Then Begin
        {Draw Entry Targets on the Chart}
        If DrawTargets Then
            Condition1 = AcmeEntryTargets("V",
            Close + (EntryFactor * ATR), 0, 0, 0);
        Buy("Acme LE V") N Shares Next Bar on
        Close + (EntryFactor * ATR) Stop;
    End;
End;
```

## 6.3 Examples

The following charts are examples of trades generated by the Acme V System. Each example uses Equity of $100,000 and the Percent Volatility Model with a risk of 2%.

### 6.3.1 Microsemi Corporation

Figure 6.4 shows an entry right at the 50-day moving average. Note the difference between entering at the moving average on the same day versus entering the next day on a breakout above the high – a difference of almost two points.

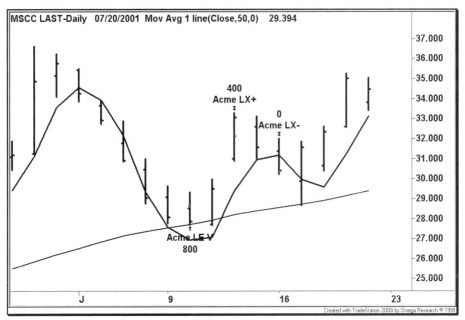

**Figure 6.4.** Microsemi Corporation Volatility

Given the performance of the market from early 2000 to early 2002, with the Nasdaq declining over 60%, we tested the performance of the V system over this period since it is a long-only system. Over one thousand stocks from various sectors were back-tested using daily data from the TradeStation historical database. The results are shown in Table 6.1.

The profit factor for the test period is 1.75. Although the winning percentage is under 50%, the average winner was nearly twice the amount of the average loser. The next step is to test the V system near the 50-day moving average to see if results are improved by using a support level.

**Table 6.1.** Acme V System Performance from March 2000 – March 2002

| | |
|---|---|
| % Winners | 47.2% |
| Winners | 1491 |
| Avg Win | $2,609.83 |
| Losers | 1669 |
| Avg Loss | -$1,333.79 |
| Profit Factor | 1.75 |

Table 6.2 shows the results of confining entries to prices within half the ATR of the 50-day moving average. The profit factor decreased from 1.75 to 1.20, with a winning percentage of only 39%. Now, confess that you expected the profit factor to be higher because of support at the moving average. Intuitively, such a conclusion is logical, but in trading one learns quickly that the logical choice is not the best choice.

Let's explore the reasons for the disparity in results. Return to the beginning of the chapter and read the first page. Assume the trader has a choice between a V signal that is five points above the moving average and another signal that is one point above the moving average. Considering the number of points above the moving average, describe the key factors that differentiate these two trades. Clearly, there are two distinguishing factors, and they are both psychological. In the trader's mind, the second trade is both "cheaper" (comfort factor #1) and also conformist (comfort factor #2 because the literature tells the trader to buy when a stock approaches the 50-day moving average). The reality is that a stock that has been trading above a key moving average and then proceeds to test that average will strike fear among the long holders and inspire short entries as well. Our modus operandi is: Support is meant to be broken.

**Table 6.2.** Acme V System Performance near 50-day MA from March 2000 – March 2002

| | |
|---|---|
| % Winners | 39.2% |
| Winners | 131 |
| Avg Win | $2,463.57 |
| Losers | 203 |
| Avg Loss | -$1,322.13 |
| Profit Factor | 1.20 |

### 6.3.2 Veritas Software

The V system enters near the low of the day, as shown in Figure 6.5. This is the only way to put the odds in your favor when a stock is in a downtrend. Entering on a high stop gives too much of the profit away. In general, the V system is an excellent system for intraday range trading. The trader can enter when the stock goes green and either close the position at the end of the day with a profit or get stopped out close to the low.

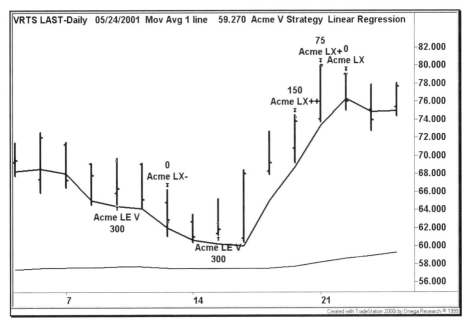

**Figure 6.5.** Veritas Software Volatility

### 6.3.3 webMethods

Figure 6.6 shows two examples of V entries well above the fifty-day moving average. The advantage of the V system over traditional ADX/DMI combination systems is that the ADX and DMI can filter out trades even if a stock is trading above its moving average. Further, the DMI is deceptive because when a stock is in a long, shallow downtrend, the DMI ratio will flip from positive to negative, even though the long-term trend is up.

Do not eliminate stocks priced below $20 per share. Both of the entries in Figure 6.6 occurred in the $15-$16 range, and at the time, webMethods had an ATR of ~1.3. Most of the industrial and cyclical stocks trade at much higher prices with lower ATRs. We remind you to drink from the fountain of liquidity.

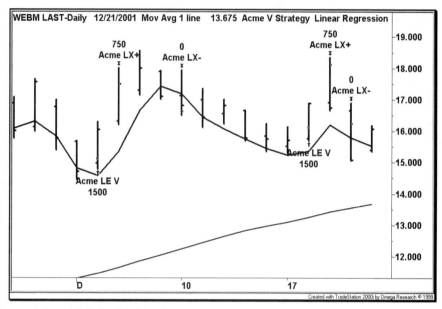

**Figure 6.6.** webMethods Volatility

### 6.3.4 SeaChange

The second Acme V entry in Figure 6.7 is a losing trade that followed a choppy downtrend. Entries after inside days are slightly more difficult but risk-limited.

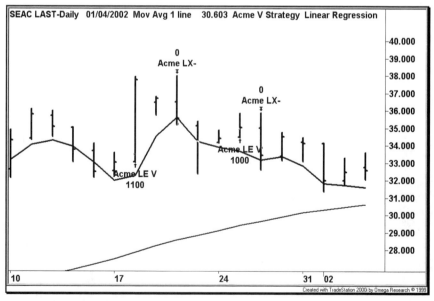

**Figure 6.7.** SeaChange Volatility

### 6.3.5 Biotechnology Index

Run the V system on all of the indices to get a sense of where the sectors are trading. For the entry in Figure 6.8, we buy either the Biotechnology HOLDR (BBH:Amex) or a basket of biotechnology stocks in the Nasdaq 100 such as Amgen (AMGN:Nasdaq), Biogen (BGEN:Nasdaq), and Protein Design Labs (PDLI:Nasdaq). The advantage of using the sector indices to trigger trades is that they trend smoother than individual stocks, and the average holding period is longer. The disadvantage of trading a basket of stocks is that it is a difficult combination of maintaining multiple positions and picking stocks that may not trade synchronously with the index. Instead, we prefer high-cap stocks that are components of the BBH.

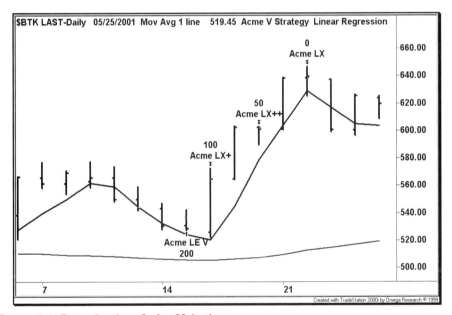

**Figure 6.8.** Biotechnology Index Volatility

### 6.3.6 Computer Associates

The chart in Figure 6.9 shows a V entry in Computer Associates (CA:NYSE). The problem with this entry is the gap down that occurred two days earlier. Our reaction to this chart is that the V system code should be changed to look for down gaps over the entire linear regression range. If there are any gaps over the range, then the trade is nullified.

Ultimately, the trader's goal is to eliminate mistakes, which means not taking trades such as the one in Figure 6.9. What may seem as minor observations directly affect the bottom line, and so these observations will become ingrained with practice and experience.

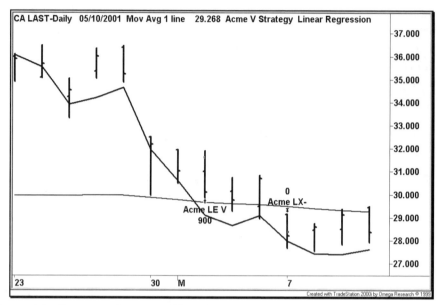

**Figure 6.9.** Computer Associates Volatility

# 7 Range Trading

*A speculator is a man*
*Who observes the future,*
*and acts before it occurs.*

Bernard Baruch

In his book *The Science of Hitting*, Ted Williams describes how he calculated that the strike zone was approximately seven balls wide and eleven balls high. The result was a matrix of baseballs, and he calculated his batting average for each ball in the matrix[1]. While the ordinary batter decided between ball and strike, Williams refined the strike into seventy-seven separate categories [37].

Williams also determined that once a batter started swinging at pitches just several inches outside of the strike zone, the strike zone expanded from 4.2 square feet to 5.8 square feet, an increase of almost 37 percent. Once a pitcher learned a batter would swing at bad pitches, then that's all the batter would get, and the batter was destined to be a .250 hitter.

Now, imagine if the "Splendid Splinter" applied his analysis to the stock market and turned his attention to the *range*. He would sort all of the ranges into their various sizes and then determine his batting average, or profit factor, for each range. He would conclude that when the range is narrow (in the strike zone), his profit factor is higher. In contrast, when the range is wide (out of the strike zone), his profit factor is lower.

The average trader analyzes a trade as either a winner or a loser—a ball or a strike. The professional trader analyzes a trade from its risk/reward ratio [13]. If the trader uses range to determine stops, then the risk numerator is the range itself (the higher the range, the higher the risk), and the reward denominator is the profit target. For example, if a long entry is triggered at the high of the bar, and the range is 1.5 times the ATR, then the trader is probably swinging out of the strike zone.

---

[1] Ted Williams batted .400 in the center of the strike zone, achieving a .344 lifetime batting average (some consider this baseball's greatest record). His worst pitch was low and outside, where he batted .230.

## 7.1 Range Ratio

The Acme N System is based on a simple concept called the *Range Ratio*. We want a ratio value less than one because a day with a low Range Ratio (RR) is generally followed by a wide range (WR) day under volatile market conditions. To calculate the RR, divide the current day's range by the Average True Range (ATR) over a certain reference range to estimate today's volatility. For example, if the ATR of Juniper Networks for the past seven days is 2.5, and today's range is 2.0, then the Range Ratio is 2.0 ÷ 2.5, or 0.8.

The Range Ratio has two inputs: *Length1* and *Length2*. The default values are one and seven, referred to as RR 1:7. The first range does not have to be the range of just the current bar; it can span a number of bars, so one can experiment with other ratio values such as 2:10 or 3:12. The Acme N system uses a default threshold of 0.7; once the RR falls below this value, the system trades a breakout in the direction of the trend.

The Range Ratio indicator is a separate plot that tracks the ratio of the ATR of one range of bars to the ATR of another range of bars. When the ratio is less than a certain percentage, the chart is in consolidation and is poised to break out. When the ratio is greater than a certain percentage, then the next bar will probably be a narrow range (NR) bar. In Figure 7.1, each time the ratio is less than 0.7 or 70%, the next day is a wide range day.

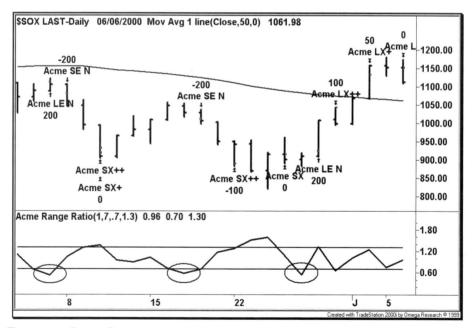

**Figure 7.1.** Range Ratio

## 7.2 Range Patterns

The Acme N system integrates the Range Ratio with other narrow range patterns developed by Cooper and Crabel [4, 6]. Further, we have developed other variations, such as two $NR_5$ days in a row and an NR% bar. All of these other NR patterns are part of the Acme Range Patterns, as shown in Table 7.1.

**Table 7.1.** Range Patterns

| Pattern | Description |
|---------|-------------|
| ID2 | Two Consecutive Inside Days |
| $IDNR_n$ | Inside Day with the Narrowest Range of the last n bars |
| $NR2_n$ | Two Consecutive Narrowest Range bars over n bars |
| $NR_n$ | Narrowest Range of the last n bars |
| $NR\%_x$ | Range is x% of the Average True Range |

### 7.2.1 Inside Day 2 (ID2)

The Inside Day 2 pattern (ID2) is two consecutive Inside Days (ID)[2], as shown in Figure 7.2. It is the same as Cooper's Boomer pattern [4].

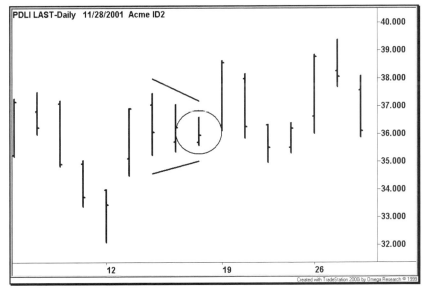

**Figure 7.2.** ID2 Example

---

[2] Dunnigan's equivalent of the Inside Day is the Inside Range, which he denoted as IR.

### 7.2.2 Inside Day–Narrow Range 4 (IDNR₄)

The Inside Day–Narrow Range 4 pattern (IDNR₄) is an inside day with the narrowest range of the past four days [3], as shown in Figure 7.3.

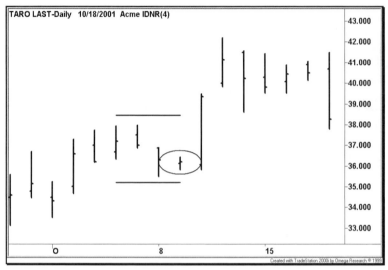

**Figure 7.3.** IDNR₄ Example

### 7.2.3 Narrow Range 2 (NR2)

The Narrow Range 2 pattern (NR2) is two consecutive NR bars over a given range. Figure 7.4 shows a chart with two consecutive NR₅ days (NR2₅).

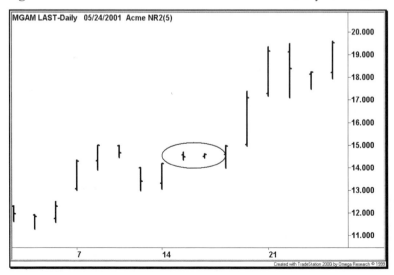

**Figure 7.4.** NR2₅ Example

### 7.2.4 Narrow Range 10 ($NR_{10}$)

The Narrow Range 10 pattern ($NR_{10}$) is the narrowest range of the last ten days, as shown in Figure 7.5.

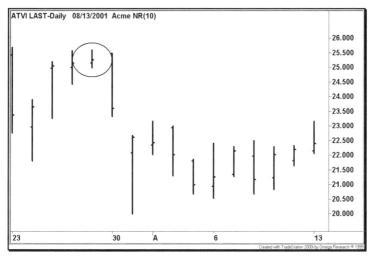

**Figure 7.5.** $NR_{10}$ Example

### 7.2.5 Narrow Range % (NR%)

The Narrow Range % pattern (NR%) is based upon a percentage of the ATR. Dunnigan defines an NR in the context of an Upswing or Downswing, where an NR bar is any bar with a range less than half of the widest range bar in the swing [9]. Four examples of an $NR\%_{50}$ bar are shown in Figure 7.6.

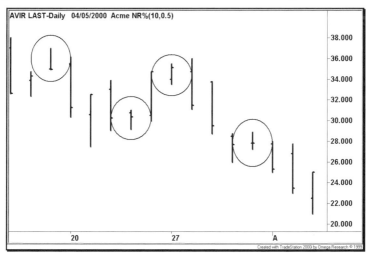

**Figure 7.6.** $NR\%_{50}$ Example

## 7.3 Range Trading System (Acme N)

With all of the patterns defined, we can now implement a range trading system known as the Acme N System. The Acme N System is based on a combination of Cooper's short-term swing techniques [4]; Crabel's narrow range patterns [6] and the Acme Range Ratio. The N system is a traditional momentum system because it uses the ADX and pullbacks – the difference is that trades are entered only on breaks of NR bars.

The Acme N system requires one of the following five criteria to establish the existence of a "Narrow Range Condition":

1. Two consecutive NR bars (NR2 pattern), or
2. Two consecutive ID bars (ID2 pattern), or
3. Narrowest range of the last n bars (NR pattern), or
4. Inside day and narrow range bar (IDNR pattern), or
5. The Range Ratio (RR) is less than a certain percentage.

Once a low-volatility condition has been established, the range of the current bar must be less than a certain percentage of the ATR, i.e., it is an NR% bar of 70% or less (this is the *RangePercent* parameter).

The trader should choose the option of using traditional technical filters for a momentum system. Historical testing has shown that the higher each of these values is set, the better the performance of the system. The N system uses the following filters:

❑ Minimum Price
❑ Minimum ADX
❑ Minimum HV

We now define the rules of the system, including the filters. First, we enumerate the narrow range conditions.

---

Narrow Range Condition

---

1. Is the current bar an $NR_5$ bar and the previous bar an $NR_5$ bar?
2. Is the current bar an ID bar and the previous bar an ID bar?
3. Is the current bar an $NR_{10}$ bar?
4. Is the current bar an ID bar and an $NR_4$ bar?
5. Calculate the Range Ratio (RR) for the current bar divided by the range of the last 7 bars (RR 1:7). Is the RR 1:7 less than 0.7?

If any of the above range conditions are true, then the Narrow Range Condition is satisfied. Finally, the Range Percentage is applied to the bar to qualify it as a potential Acme N trade entry.

### 7.3.1 Long Signal

| Calculations |
| --- |

1. Calculate the ATR for the past 20 bars ($ATR_{20}$).
2. Multiply the Range Percentage (RP) of the current bar by $ATR_{20}$.
3. Calculate the ADX for the filter length ($ADX_{14}$).
4. Calculate the 50-bar moving average ($MA_{50}$).
5. Calculate the historic volatility for the filter length ($HV_{14}$).

| Entry Rules |
| --- |

1. Narrow Range Condition = True
2. Range <= RP * $ATR_{20}$
3. Close > 20
4. $ADX_{14}$ >= 18
5. $HV_{14}$ >= 0.5
6. Retracement Bars >= 2
7. Median Price > $MA_{50}$
8. **Buy** the next bar at or above the High + (EntryFactor * $ATR_{20}$)

| Exit Rules: Profit Target |
| --- |

1. **Sell** half of the position at or above the High + (ProfitFactor * $ATR_{20}$)
2. **Sell** half of the position at or above the High of ProfitBars ago + (2 * ProfitFactor * $ATR_{20}$)

| Exit Rules: Stop Loss |
| --- |

1. **Sell** all shares at or below the Lowest Low for StopBars − (ExitFactor * $ATR_{20}$)

## 7.3.2 Short Signal

| Calculations |
| --- |

1.  Calculate the ATR for the past 20 bars ($ATR_{20}$).
2.  Multiply the Range Percentage (RP) of the current bar by $ATR_{20}$.
3.  Calculate the ADX for the filter length ($ADX_{14}$).
4.  Calculate the 50-bar moving average ($MA_{50}$).
5.  Calculate the historic volatility for the filter length ($HV_{14}$).

| Entry Rules |
| --- |

1.  Narrow Range Condition = True
2.  Range <= RP * $ATR_{20}$
3.  Close > 20
4.  $ADX_{14}$ >= 18
5.  $HV_{14}$ >= 0.5
6.  Retracement Bars >= 2
7.  Median Price < $MA_{50}$
8.  **Sell Short** the next bar at or below the Low – (EntryFactor * $ATR_{20}$)

| Exit Rules: Profit Target |
| --- |

1.  **Cover** half of the position at or below the Low – (ProfitFactor * $ATR_{20}$)
2.  **Cover** half of the position at or below the Low of ProfitBars ago – (2 * ProfitFactor * $ATR_{20}$)

| Exit Rules: Stop Loss |
| --- |

1.  **Cover** all shares at or above the Highest High for StopBars + (ExitFactor * $ATR_{20}$)

The EasyLanguage code for the Acme N System is shown in Example 7.1:

**Example 7.1.** Acme N System

```
{****************************************************************
Acme N System: Use the Range Ratio to find Narrow Range Patterns
****************************************************************}

Inputs:
    {N Parameters}
    RatioLength1(1),
```

```
    RatioLength2(7),
    RangePercent(0.7),
    MaxRangeRatio(0.7),
    RetraceBars(2),
    {Filter Parameters}
    FiltersOn(True),
    FilterLength(14),
    MinimumPrice(20),
    MinimumADX(18),
    MinimumHV(0.5),
    {Position Parameters}
    Equity(100000),
    RiskModel(3),
    RiskPercent(2.0),
    RiskATR(1.0),
    EntryFactor(0.10),
    DrawTargets(True);

Variables:
    N(0),
    ATR(0.0),
    ATRLength(20),
    MA(0.0),
    MALength(50),
    TradeFilter(True),
    BuyStop(0.0),
    ShortStop(0.0),
    {N Variables}
    NLength1(5),
    NLength2(10),
    NLength3(4),
    LowVolatility(False);

ATR = Volatility(ATRLength);
MA = Average(Close, MALength);

{Set Entry and Exit Stops}
BuyStop = High + (EntryFactor * ATR);
ShortStop = Low - (EntryFactor * ATR);

{Acme N Setup}
Condition1 = AcmeNarrowRange(NLength1, 1) and
AcmeNarrowRange(NLength1, 0)[1];
Condition2 = Low > Low[1] and High < High[1] and Low[1] > Low[2] and
High[1] < High[2];
Condition3 = AcmeNarrowRange(NLength2, 0);
Condition4 = AcmeInsideDayNR(NLength3, 0);
Condition5 = AcmeRangeRatio(RatioLength1, RatioLength2) <= MaxRangeRatio;
LowVolatility = Condition1 or Condition2 or Condition3 or Condition4 or
Condition5;

{Run trade filters}
If FiltersOn Then
```

```
    TradeFilter = Close > MinimumPrice and
    ADX(FilterLength) >= MinimumADX and
    AcmeVolatility(FilterLength) >= MinimumHV;

If LowVolatility and
Range <= RangePercent * ATR and
TradeFilter Then Begin
    N = AcmeGetShares(Equity, RiskModel, RiskPercent, RiskATR);

    TradeFilter = True;
    If FiltersOn Then
        TradeFilter = MedianPrice > MA;

    If TradeFilter and
    AcmeRetraceDown(RetraceBars) and
    TradeFilter Then Begin
        {Draw Entry Targets on the Chart}
        If DrawTargets Then
            Condition1 = AcmeEntryTargets("N", BuyStop, 0, 0, 0);
        Buy("Acme LE N") N Shares Next Bar at BuyStop Stop;
    End;

    TradeFilter = True;
    If FiltersOn Then
        TradeFilter = MedianPrice < MA;

    If TradeFilter and
    AcmeRetraceUp(RetraceBars) and
    TradeFilter Then Begin
        {Draw Entry Targets on the Chart}
        If DrawTargets Then
            Condition1 = AcmeEntryTargets("N", 0, 0, ShortStop, 0);
        Sell("Acme SE N") N Shares Next Bar at ShortStop Stop;
    End;
End;
```

After performing some price calculations at the beginning of the code, the N system calls all of the Acme functions for determining narrow range conditions. The *AcmeNarrowRange* function is designed to locate any narrow range bar using the *Index*. For example, it can determine whether the current bar is an NR bar for the last ten bars, or whether the bar seven days ago was an NR bar.

With the catalog of Acme trading patterns defined, the trader can see how much computing power is required for each bar. The TradeStation indicators (lines and letters) are provided so the trader can recognize all possible patterns that are encoded within a single bar. Multiply this horsepower by the number of stocks, and one recalls the chained captives in Ben-Hur[3] straining their oars at ramming speed.

---

[3] *Ben-Hur* (1959) from MGM starring Charlton Heston, directed by William Wyler.

## 7.4 Examples

The following charts are examples of trades generated by the Acme N System. Each example uses Equity of $100,000 and the Percent Volatility Model with a risk of 2%. For stocks, trade filtering is turned on. For indices, trade filtering is turned off because of their lower ADX readings.

### 7.4.1 Nasdaq Composite Index

This chart shows the Nasdaq Composite Index with the Range Ratio falling below 0.7 four times (circled in Figure 7.7). The chart shows two long entries and two short entries in a relatively choppy market. The DMI would have eliminated most of these trades. The problem is that the DMI is typically based on a 14-bar study period. By the time it catches up to the trend, the trend has already changed. A volatile stock or market index is characterized by several sudden trend changes within much shorter periods.

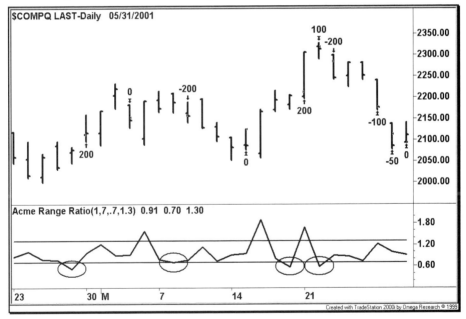

**Figure 7.7.** Nasdaq Composite Index

The Acme N System simply enters trades on consolidation days or retracement days. Many traders wait for pullbacks, but the chart in Figure 7.7 illustrates how a trade can be entered even in the midst of a swing.

Table 7.2 shows the unfiltered Acme N system performance report for the Nasdaq Composite Index from mid-1994 to early 2002. When the filters are applied, the number of trades is cut in half, but the profit factor improves from 2.01 to 2.91, while the Total Net Profit is reduced by just 21%.

**Table 7.2.** TradeStation Performance Acme N Strategy COMPX-Daily (5/2/1994-3/1/2002)

| | | | |
|---|---|---|---|
| Total Net Profit | $884,875.50 | Open position P/L | $0.00 |
| Gross Profit | $1,757,161.50 | Gross Loss | ($872,286.00) |
| | | | |
| Total # of trades | 291 | Percent profitable | 56.01% |
| Number winning trades | 163 | Number losing trades | 128 |
| | | | |
| Largest winning trade | $93,797.00 | Largest losing trade | ($62,296.00) |
| Average winning trade | $10,780.13 | Average losing trade | ($6,814.73) |
| Ratio avg win/avg loss | 1.58 | Avg trade (win & loss) | $3,040.81 |
| | | | |
| Max consec. Winners | 12 | Max consec. losers | 6 |
| Avg # bars in winners | 3 | Avg # bars in losers | 1 |
| | | | |
| Max intraday drawdown | ($90,726.00) | | |
| Profit Factor | 2.01 | Max # contracts held | 300 |

**Table 7.3.** TradeStation Performance Acme N Strategy COMPX-Daily with Filter

| | | | |
|---|---|---|---|
| Total Net Profit | $699,612.63 | Open position P/L | $0.00 |
| Gross Profit | $1,065,632.63 | Gross Loss | ($366,020.00) |
| | | | |
| Total # of trades | 140 | Percent profitable | 65.00% |
| Number winning trades | 91 | Number losing trades | 49 |
| | | | |
| Largest winning trade | $93,797.00 | Largest losing trade | ($62,296.00) |
| Average winning trade | $11,710.25 | Average losing trade | ($7,469.80) |
| Ratio avg win/avg loss | 1.57 | Avg trade (win & loss) | $4,997.23 |
| | | | |
| Max consec. Winners | 9 | Max consec. losers | 3 |
| Avg # bars in winners | 3 | Avg # bars in losers | 2 |
| | | | |
| Max intraday drawdown | ($62,296.00) | | |
| Profit Factor | 2.91 | Max # contracts held | 300 |

These performance reports have problems, however, because they are based on indices that cannot directly be traded. The stock that closely tracks the Nasdaq Composite Index is the Nasdaq-100 Index Tracking Stock (**QQQ:Amex**). Although the QQQ did not start trading until 1999, its profit factor matches the performance of the indices, as shown in Table 7.4.

**Table 7.4.** TradeStation Performance - Acme N Strategy QQQ-Daily (3/10/1999-3/1/2002)

| | | | |
|---|---|---|---|
| Total Net Profit | $24,536.30 | Open position P/L | $0.00 |
| Gross Profit | $49,854.55 | Gross Loss | ($25,318.25) |
| | | | |
| Total # of trades | 50 | Percent profitable | 54.00% |
| Number winning trades | 27 | Number losing trades | 23 |
| | | | |
| Largest winning trade | $4,238.20 | Largest losing trade | ($2,500.00) |
| Average winning trade | $1,846.46 | Average losing trade | ($1,100.79) |
| Ratio avg win/avg loss | 1.68 | Avg trade (win & loss) | $490.73 |
| | | | |
| Max consec. Winners | 3 | Max consec. losers | 4 |
| Avg # bars in winners | 4 | Avg # bars in losers | 2 |
| | | | |
| Max intraday drawdown | ($6,162.50) | | |
| Profit Factor | 1.97 | Max # contracts held | 1,500 |

## 7.4.2 Securities Broker/Dealer Index

The chart in Figure 7.8 displays some Acme N long signals for the Securities Broker/Dealer Index (XBD). As with other sector indices, the XBD does not have a direct proxy. One possibility is the *Exchange Traded Fund*, or ETF. The ETF is just a stock that is composed of a group of stocks in a specific sector. The problem with the ETFs is that most are not yet liquid enough for short-term trading, and the spreads are wide enough such that the Acme N system does not perform well on some of these stocks (see Chapter 8).

Another alternative is a *basket* of stocks. Select three or four representative stocks, and buy or sell them when the Acme N signal fires on the sector index. The advantage of this approach is that the trader can select a few volatile stocks that are much more liquid than the ETF. The disadvantage is that one or two of the stocks may not trade in line with the index. The best approach is to select stocks that most closely track the sector–those with the highest weightings in the index.

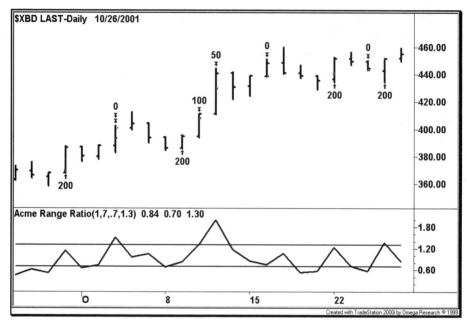

**Figure 7.8.** Securities Broker/Dealer Index

The performance report in Table 7.5 shows the unfiltered performance for the
Securities Broker/Dealer index for the past four years.

**Table 7.5.** TradeStation Performance Acme N Strategy XBD.X-Daily (3/24/1998-3/1/2002)

| | | | |
|---|---|---|---|
| Total Net Profit | $57,799.00 | Open position P/L | $0.00 |
| Gross Profit | $72,391.00 | Gross Loss | ($14,592.00) |
| Total # of trades | 26 | Percent profitable | 69.23% |
| Number winning trades | 18 | Number losing trades | 8 |
| Largest winning trade | $8,446.50 | Largest losing trade | ($4,060.00) |
| Average winning trade | $4,021.72 | Average losing trade | ($1,824.00) |
| Ratio avg win/avg loss | 2.20 | Avg trade (win & loss) | $2,223.04 |
| Max consec. Winners | 7 | Max consec. losers | 4 |
| Avg # bars in winners | 3 | Avg # bars in losers | 2 |
| Max intraday drawdown | ($9,976.00) | | |
| Profit Factor | 4.96 | Max # contracts held | 200 |
| Account size required | $9,976.00 | Return on account | 579.38% |

### 7.4.3 Analog Devices

Here is an example of three Acme N entries, as shown in Figure 7.9. Examine the price patterns preceding the occurrence of the narrow range bar. For the first entry, the stock consolidated for at least three days before the signal. The second entry was an extended pullback, and the third entry was a three-bar retracement. Look for rectangles and tables preceding the narrow range bar because this type of entry has a better risk/reward ratio.

The longer the Range Ratio is below the threshold, the more explosive the move. Study the contour of the RR curve when the Range Ratio dips below the threshold. Either the ratio spikes, or it forms a long, shallow bottom. While the Range Ratio is below the threshold, the stock is storing potential energy for a protracted move.

The three entries in Figure 7.9 illustrate why profit targets are essential in today's trading environment. All three stocks hit their optimum profit after only two days. By waiting for the extreme of the previous bar to be exceeded, the trader may be giving up as much as one-third to one-half of the profit while having to hold the position another day. When deciding whether or not to use profit targets, the profit factor is not the only deciding factor. The profit factor should be divided by the average holding period to calculate the optimum time to exit the trade.

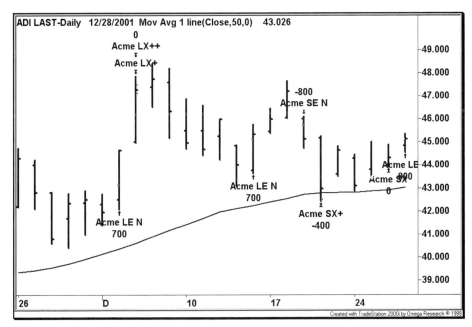

**Figure 7.9.** Analog Devices

### 7.4.4 Taro Pharmaceutical

Figure 7.10 is an example of three Acme N long entries over a period of one month. This system works best on strongly trending stocks with the following characteristics, some of them taken from Investors Business Daily (IBD):

- ❑ IBD Relative Price Strength Rating (RS) > 90
- ❑ IBD Earnings Per Share Rating (EPS) > 90
- ❑ New 52-Week High

At the time, Taro Pharmaceutical (TARO:Nasdaq) had RS and EPS rankings of greater than 99. We are certain that a trader could make a decent living by trading just this strategy.

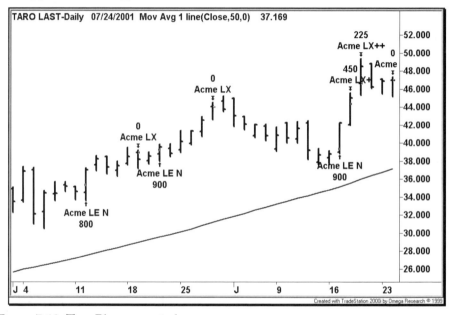

**Figure 7.10.** Taro Pharmaceutical

The number of retracement bars varies for each trade shown in Figure 7.10. The first trade pulled back two bars; the second trade two bars, including one inside day; and the third trade two bars with one inside day. A parameter to the Acme N System is *RetraceBars*–it is the minimum number of retracement bars required to trigger an N entry. If the trader chooses not to wait for a retracement and just wants to enter on a narrow range bar, then the RetraceBars parameter can be set to zero. When not using retracement bars, examine the range of the few bars preceding the NR bar. If the stock has appreciated dramatically in this period, then the trade is a pass. The advantage of using no retracement is that the N system picks up consolidations that would normally be filtered out.

### 7.4.5 Multimedia Games

The chart in Figure 7.11 shows a losing trade. Your job is to count the number of problems with this trade entry before proceeding with this example. We find at least four problems with this trade entry:

- ❏ The stock has gapped up.
- ❏ The stock has already risen 10% over two days.
- ❏ The stock is in the midst of a retracement.
- ❏ The stock's trend is not clearly defined.

This example illustrates why no automated trading system is foolproof. Yes, all of the problems could have been filtered out with the software, but automation is a tradeoff between eliminating good trading candidates and keeping bad ones. The use of retracement is a perfect example of how both good and bad trades can be eliminated. Setting the number of retracement bars to zero includes narrow range bars in consolidation patterns (good) but does not exclude stocks with strong moves in the past few days (bad). In contrast, setting the number of retracement bars to two excludes narrow range bars in consolidation patterns (bad) but also excludes stocks such as the one shown in this example (good).

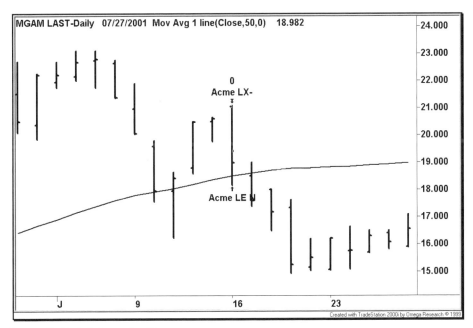

**Figure 7.11.** Multimedia Games

# 8 Market Models

*Money itself isn't lost or made,*
*it's simply transferred*
*from one perception to another.*

Gordon Gekko
*Wall Street* the Motion Picture

The market can be handicapped, just as a horseplayer bets on thoroughbreds. One might be surprised at just how complicated the betting at the track is – the average bettor is probably not aware of the potent speed sires or Diazo's Center of Distribution [8]. These data provide the edge to differentiate the professional horseplayer from the amateur. As with any game, the player competes for a statistical edge, and this search leads the player to a deeper exploration of diverse subjects such as mathematics, physics, and even philosophy. Trading evolves as a Glass Bead Game[1] as the trader attempts to build the ultimate market model.

In this chapter, we construct two market models, one using data that are relatively hard to automate. First, we apply a set of the Acme trading systems to some market and sector indices. Because indices do not have a float, we omit the Acme F system. The Acme M, N, R, and V systems are combined to form the market model; each of the systems is applied without trade filters to eliminate many of the stock-specific requirements. This first market model is our *Systems Model*.

Second, we develop a special version of the Acme M system using the market sentiment and breadth indices shown in Table 8.1. For each market index, we specify a rule based on an overbought or oversold reading; the rule interprets the reading based on the index's correlation with the market. For example, the VIX makes a new 20-day high. Because the VIX is negatively correlated with the market, the letter "V" is displayed above the current bar. As with the Acme M system, a signal is generated when a minimum number of pattern criteria in the same direction are met. This market model is our *Sentiment Model*.

---

[1] Hesse, Herman (1943) *Magister Ludi*. Bantam Books, New York, New York

**Table 8.1.** Breadth and Sentiment Indices

| Index | Chart Symbol |
|---|---|
| Volatility Index (VIX) | V |
| Put/Call Ratio | P |
| New Highs | H |
| New Lows | L |
| Arms Index (TRIN) | T |
| Bullish Consensus | B |
| Short Sales Ratio | S |

## 8.1 Systems Model

A systems model can be defined by combining the following Acme systems. In this model, we are taking a bottoms-up approach. We simply combine all of the systems into one strategy and apply that strategy to market and sector indices such as the COMPX and BTK, as well as ETFs such as the QQQ and SPY.

- ❑ Acme M System
- ❑ Acme N System
- ❑ Acme R System
- ❑ Acme V System

Figure 8.1 shows a chart of the Nasdaq-100 Series Trust (**QQQ:Amex**) with the Acme Systems Model. Each trading system has been applied unfiltered to the chart. As with any other stock, the QQQ exhibits the same characteristics with the Acme systems applied to the chart—multiple entries, profit targets, and stop losses. For market and sector indices, the rectangle is a rare occurrence, so the Acme R signal does not trigger often; however, when it does appear, prepare for some trading action over the following days.

Table 8.2 summarizes the performance of the unfiltered Systems Model for the QQQ. The profit factor is consistent with the overall Acme profit factor, so we then decided to compare the performance of the model for the sector indices versus their corresponding ETFs. Since we wanted to optimize for performance here, we applied the system filters. The results are shown in Tables 8.3 and 8.4, sorted by profit factor.

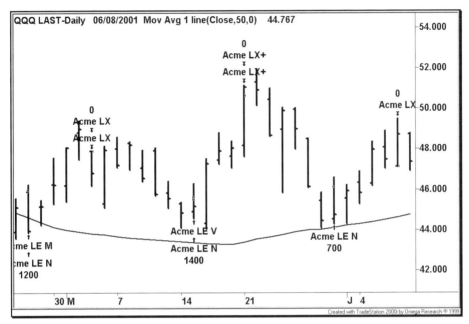

**Figure 8.1.** Systems Model for QQQ

**Table 8.2.** QQQ Performance Report (06/10/1999 – 02/15/2002)

| | | | |
|---|---|---|---|
| Total Net Profit | $24,318.00 | Open position P/L | $0.00 |
| Gross Profit | $54,059.00 | Gross Loss | ($29,741.00) |
| | | | |
| Total # of trades | 58 | Percent profitable | 53.45% |
| Number winning trades | 31 | Number losing trades | 27 |
| | | | |
| Largest winning trade | $5,424.00 | Largest losing trade | ($2,455.00) |
| Average winning trade | $1,743.84 | Average losing trade | ($1,101.52) |
| Ratio avg win/avg loss | 1.58 | Avg trade (win & loss) | $419.28 |
| | | | |
| Max consec. Winners | 6 | Max consec. losers | 5 |
| Avg # bars in winners | 3 | Avg # bars in losers | 2 |
| | | | |
| Max intraday drawdown | ($8,293.00) | | |
| Profit Factor | 1.82 | Max # contracts held | 4,200 |
| Account size required | $8,293.00 | Return on account | 293.24% |

**Table 8.3.** Market Indices

| Sector Index | # Trades | % Profitable | Win/Loss Ratio | Profit Factor |
|---|---|---|---|---|
| COMPX | 43 | 65% | 1.54 | 2.88 |
| DJI | 35 | 57% | 1.54 | 2.05 |
| MID | 55 | 53% | 1.83 | 2.04 |
| SPX | 50 | 48% | 2.03 | 1.87 |

**Table 8.4.** Market ETFs

| Sector Index | # Trades | % Profitable | Win/Loss Ratio | Profit Factor |
|---|---|---|---|---|
| QQQ | 34 | 59% | 2.07 | 2.95 |
| SPY | 47 | 43% | 1.99 | 1.47 |
| MDY | 50 | 52% | 1.25 | 1.36 |
| DIA | 39 | 44% | 1.29 | 1.00 |

**Table 8.5.** Sector Indices

| Sector Index | # Trades | % Profitable | Win/Loss Ratio | Profit Factor |
|---|---|---|---|---|
| RMS | 57 | 67% | 2.40 | 4.80 |
| DOT | 58 | 67% | 2.05 | 4.20 |
| XTC | 50 | 58% | 2.63 | 3.64 |
| NWX | 55 | 64% | 2.04 | 3.57 |
| YLS | 45 | 64% | 1.87 | 3.40 |
| FOP | 4 | 50% | 2.46 | 2.46 |
| XBD | 50 | 46% | 2.57 | 2.19 |
| XAU | 50 | 48% | 2.13 | 1.96 |
| DRG | 47 | 51% | 1.76 | 1.84 |
| BKX | 45 | 49% | 1.89 | 1.80 |
| RLX | 55 | 45% | 1.96 | 1.64 |
| OSX | 53 | 45% | 1.91 | 1.58 |
| FPP | 60 | 43% | 1.98 | 1.51 |
| BTK | 51 | 49% | 1.56 | 1.50 |
| UTY | 52 | 46% | 1.75 | 1.50 |
| SOX | 33 | 39% | 2.24 | 1.46 |
| CMR | 43 | 44% | 1.47 | 1.17 |
| CYC | 55 | 33% | 1.33 | 0.65 |

The performance results in Tables 8.3 and 8.4 illustrate the difference between performance derived from indices and their corresponding proxies. Except for the QQQ, the performance for the ETFs is mediocre at best. The problem with the other ETFs is that the spreads are higher, and more importantly they are not as volatile as the QQQ. The bottom line is that a trader will not be able to trade an ETF effectively unless it exhibits a combination of tight spreads, high trading volume, and high volatility. The QQQ fits these criteria, so we will take it.

**Table 8.6.** Sector ETFs

| Sector Index | # Trades | % Profitable | Win/Loss Ratio | Profit Factor |
|:---:|:---:|:---:|:---:|:---:|
| BHH | 52 | 62% | 1.70 | 2.73 |
| WMH | 35 | 57% | 1.83 | 2.44 |
| BBH | 46 | 59% | 1.65 | 2.35 |
| IAH | 48 | 52% | 1.72 | 1.87 |
| BDH | 50 | 48% | 2.00 | 1.85 |
| HHH | 52 | 54% | 1.54 | 1.80 |
| RKH | 48 | 44% | 1.84 | 1.43 |
| UTH | 51 | 47% | 1.57 | 1.40 |
| SMH | 33 | 58% | 0.97 | 1.31 |
| OIH | 20 | 45% | 1.42 | 1.16 |
| RTH | 21 | 38% | 1.77 | 1.09 |
| TTH | 37 | 38% | 1.74 | 1.06 |
| PPH | 29 | 31% | 2.05 | 0.92 |

Tables 8.5 and 8.6 compare the performance of the sector indices with sector ETFs, sorted by profit factor. Again, we see how the performance of the ETFs is worse than the raw indices, except in those cases where the ETF is relatively liquid and relatively volatile. Currently, the only two ETFs that we consider "trade worthy" for holding periods of five days or less are the Biotechnology HOLDRS (BBH:Amex) and the Semiconductor HOLDRS (SMH:Amex).

Notice the bottom four entries in Table 8.5; these are the four most cyclical sectors.

- Morgan Stanley Cyclical index (CYC)
- Morgan Stanley Consumer index (CMR)
- PHLX Semiconductor Sector index (SOX)
- PHLX Utility Sector index (UTY)

The interesting trend is that semiconductor stocks are becoming increasingly cyclical in their behavior, making short-term trading that much more difficult.

## 8.2 Sentiment Model

In 1986, Zweig developed a "Super Model", combining several monetary and momentum indicators to predict market direction [39]. Here, we review seven different market indicators and then incorporate them into the Pattern Trading System (Chapter 3). By encoding the behavior of each market indicator, we can construct the Sentiment Model to synthesize the bullish and bearish behavior of each indicator and generate signals to predict market direction, emulating the Acme M system.

### 8.2.1 Volatility Index (VIX)

The *Volatility Index* (VIX) measures the implied volatility of index options. The VIX is inversely related to market direction; consequently, a high VIX reading is associated with sharp corrections, while a low relative VIX reading marks the end of an uptrend.

Together on a chart, a broad-based market index and the VIX will appear as mirror images of each other (see Figures 8.2 and 8.3). Historically, high VIX readings can reach fifty and above, while low readings bottom in the twenties. The behavior of the VIX is asymmetrical because as the VIX spikes up during market corrections, it declines gradually during market advances.

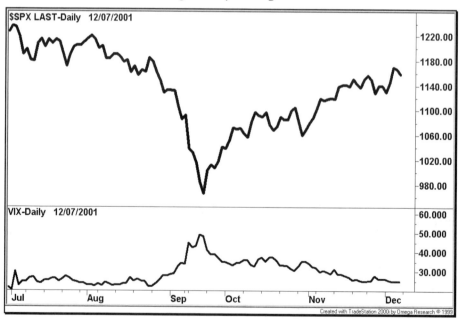

**Figure 8.2.** Volatility Index (VIX)

Since we avoid absolute values of the VIX, we look for new highs or lows in the form of spikes over a reference period. Technically, a *spike* is a combination of a channel breakout with a large range bar. If the VIX spikes up, then a Buy signal will be generated. If the VIX spikes down, then a Sell signal will be generated.

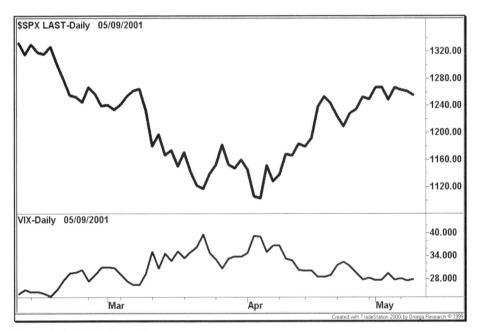

**Figure 8.3.** VIX Mirror Image

With this technique, we can identify extreme readings in the VIX and see spikes on the chart in either direction. Although this technique is good for identification, the trading signals have not been clearly defined. First, as with any trading system, we do not want to enter a trade without *confirmation*. Second, we do not want to restrict signals to spikes alone. As soon as the VIX makes a new high or low over a given range of bars, we want to prepare for a confirmation.

What do we mean by confirmation? In the case of the VIX, as the market goes down and the VIX spikes up, we want to see the VIX first tick down before going long the market. This down tick in the VIX is usually accompanied by an uptick in the market, since the two are inversely related. Clearly, we want to use this relationship as a general confirmation technique that can be applied to any indicator. The only question is whether an indicator is positively correlated with the market (indicator rises as the market rises) or negatively correlated with the market (indicator falls as the market rises, e.g., the VIX).

There are two types of confirmation: *high confirmation* and *low confirmation*. If the previous price is the highest price of a given range, but the current price is less than the previous price, then a high confirmation occurs. If the previous price is the lowest price of a given range, but the current price is higher than the previous price, then a low confirmation occurs. The interpretation of a high or low confirmation depends on whether or not the indicator is positively or negatively correlated with the market. Table 8.7 shows the signal to take based on the indicator's confirmation and its market correlation:

**Table 8.7.** Indicator Confirmation

| Confirmation | Market Correlation | Signal |
|---|---|---|
| High | Negative | Buy |
| High | Positive | Sell Short |
| Low | Negative | Sell Short |
| Low | Positive | Buy |

From this confirmation logic, we created a function called *AcmeHighLowIndex* to test for both high and low confirmations. The Acme Market System calls the *AcmeHighLowIndex* function separately for each indicator in the model. Each time, the function returns one of the following values to the Market System:

❑   0 = No Confirmation

❑   1 = High Confirmation

❑   2 = Low Confirmation

The Market System then populates its long and short pattern strings based on the confirmation values. The EasyLanguage code for the *AcmeHighLowIndex* function is shown below in Example 8.1:

**Example 8.1.** Function *AcmeHighLowIndex*

```
{**************************************************************
AcmeHighLowIndex: Calculate the High Low Index
**************************************************************}

Inputs:
    Price(Numeric),
    Length(Numeric);

AcmeHighLowIndex = 0;

If Price[1] >= Highest(Price, Length - 1)[2] and
Price < Price[1] Then
    AcmeHighLowIndex = 1
Else If Price[1] <= Lowest(Price, Length - 1)[2] and
Price > Price[1] Then
    AcmeHighLowIndex = 2;
```

### 8.2.2 Put/Call Ratio

The Put/Call ratio is an index calculated by the Chicago Board Options Exchange (CBOE). The ratio compares the total put volume with the total call volume for stock options or index options. Investors buy more calls than puts, so the ratio never reaches one unless the market is declining sharply. The put/call ratio is negatively correlated with the market because people tend to buy puts at bottoms, and historically this behavior has proven to be wrong, as shown by the circled area in Figure 8.4.

Many traders look at the value of the put/call ratio on a historical level. For example, a ratio greater than 0.8 is considered to be bullish, and a ratio less than 0.4 is considered bearish; however, we do not care about the absolute readings because we are using the confirmation technique.

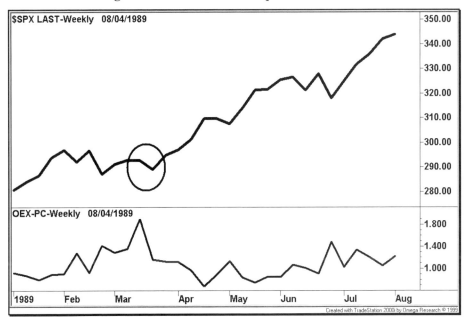

**Figure 8.4.** Put/Call Ratio Peak

Figure 8.5 shows a trough in the put/call ratio. Although spikes up are common, spikes down are rare because such a low reading means that everyone is bullish. This situation is akin to everyone running to one side of the Titanic. Essentially, the whole country was long in March 2000, and nobody was left to buy. The charts illustrate how the put/call ratio is not entirely symmetrical. The fear of losing money is much more powerful than the satisfaction in making money, and the emotional trader usually makes the wrong decision at the wrong time.

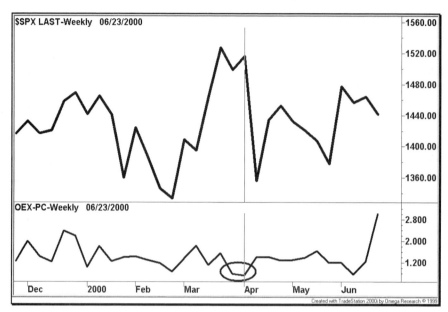

**Figure 8.5.** Put/Call Ratio Trough

### 8.2.3 New Highs

Each day, the number of stocks making 52-week highs on the New York Stock Exchange is tracked as the "NYSE New Highs" number. The New Highs indicator is positively correlated with the market. As the market goes up, so does the number of new highs; however, the behavior of the New Highs data is slightly different than the behavior of its corresponding market index. When the market attains a new peak, the number of new highs spikes at the peak. As the market pulls back, the number of new highs drops close to zero. At the next peak, the new highs will spike once again.

The key to interpreting new high data is to compare the new highs at two market peaks. If the market is higher at the second peak, but the number of new highs is lower at its second peak, then a divergence has been created, as shown in Figure 8.6. The divergence in this example occurred just before a 20% selloff in the S&P 500 in July 1998.

Fosback created an indicator in 1979 called the High Low Logic Index in order to recognize these divergences [14]. The index calculates the minimum of two ratios: the ratio of new highs to the total number of issues, and the ratio of new lows to total issues. When the index is high, the market attains both a high number of new highs and new lows, a bearish indication because market breadth is narrowing. When the index is low, then either the number of new highs or new lows is low, a bullish indication in both cases.

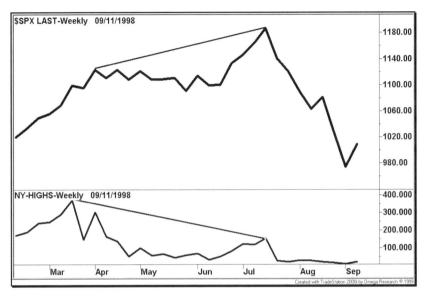

**Figure 8.6.** New Highs

### 8.2.4 New Lows

The number of stocks making 52-week lows on the NYSE is tracked as the "NYSE New Lows" number. The New Lows indicator is negatively correlated with the market, meaning that spikes in the number of new lows is a bullish indication, as shown by the circled areas in Figure 8.7.

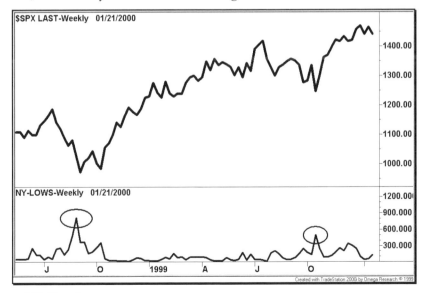

**Figure 8.7.** New Lows

## 8.2.5 Arms Index (TRIN)

Richard Arms created the Arms Index[2] in 1967 to compare a ratio of advancers to decliners (Advance/Decline Ratio) with the ratio of advancing volume to declining volume (Upside/Downside Ratio). The TRIN's behavior is similar to the VIX; it is negatively correlated with the market, i.e., a high reading means the market is oversold and a low reading means the market is overbought.

As shown in Figure 8.8, the TRIN plotted in the lower panel resembles the profile of an EKG. Spikes punctuate the chart; some technicians will smooth out the TRIN with a three-day or four-day moving average. The problem with smoothing any kind of price is that the average introduces lag, and because our trading signal would depend on a confirmation of the moving average, most of the move would already have occurred.

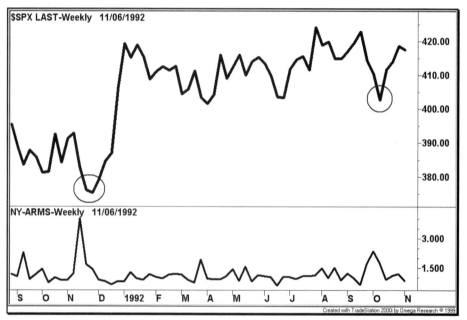

**Figure 8.8.** Arms Index, or TRIN

The TRIN is the least predictable of the indicators in the Sentiment Model. All of the other indicators show some degree of persistency from day-to-day or week-to-week. In contrast, the TRIN is a one-bar phenomenon. Its value lies more in its oversold readings (i.e., spikes) than in its overbought readings. The TRIN is another indicator that illustrates the asymmetry between corrections and rallies.

---

[2] The Arms Index is also known as the TRIN, an acronym for TRading INdex.

### 8.2.6 Bullish Consensus

The Bullish Consensus is a market sentiment indicator that was created in 1964 by Market Vane to track the buy and sell recommendations of market advisors and equity analysts. Based on their recommendations, Market Vane calculates the bullish percentage, e.g., 59% of the people are bullish, and so the remaining 41% are bearish.

Along with the New Highs indicator, the Bullish Consensus is the only other model indicator that is positively correlated with the market. The chart in Figure 8.9 shows how closely the two track together, not coincidentally. When the market is up, people are bullish, and when the market is down, people are bearish. Clearly, when people are overly bullish, the market is ripe for a fall and vice versa.

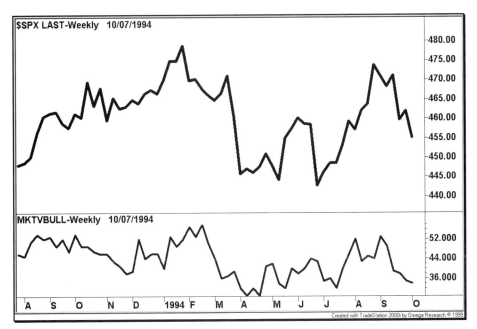

**Figure 8.9.** Bullish Consensus

### 8.2.7 Short Sales Ratio

There are a variety of short sales ratios, such as the Odd Lot Short Sales to Odd Lot Total Sales. Here, we refer to the Public to Specialist Short Sales Ratio on the NYSE. The theory behind this ratio is that the public tends to sell short at the worst times (Figure 8.10), and the statistics prove it. The bottom line is that the specialist down on the floor has a much better sense of the market.

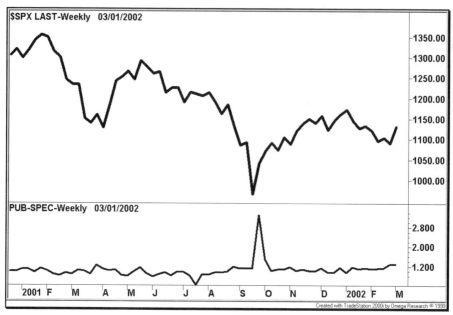

**Figure 8.10.** Public to Specialist Short Sales Ratio

The Short Sales Ratio is negatively correlated with the market. Further, it has symmetrical spikes down. The chart in Figure 8.11 shows the huge divergence that formed shortly before the market cracked in March 2000. The ratio spiked down again in June 2000, setting up another correction.

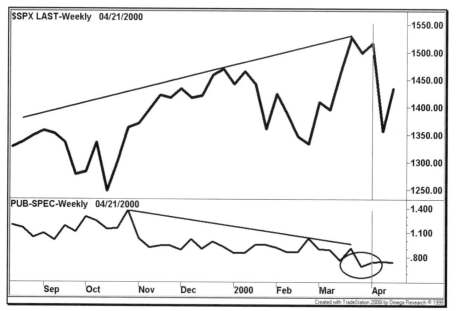

**Figure 8.11.** Short Sales Ratio

## 8.3 Market Trading System

With the sentiment indicators defined, we can now adapt the Acme M System to our Sentiment Model as a general market system. The Acme Market System simply counts the number of bullish or bearish patterns on any given bar. If the number of patterns is greater than the minimum number of patterns specified by the system, then a signal is generated; no other conditions apply.

The Acme Market System uses the *AcmeHighLowIndex* function for pattern confirmation. For any indicators with negative correlations, a high confirmation (return value of 1) means the pattern is added to the *LongString* variable. A low confirmation (return value of 2) means the pattern is added to the *ShortString* variable. For indicators with positive correlations, the logic is reversed. For a high confirmation, the pattern is added to the *ShortString*, and for a low confirmation, the pattern is added to the *LongString*.

> The Acme Market System uses weekly data for its trading signals because some of the data are not available electronically on a daily basis. Although data such as the Bullish Consensus are published on a daily basis, the data feeds do not transmit this data, making the collection of sentiment data difficult to automate[3]. This system can certainly be adapted to daily data, as most of the indicators are available electronically.

Before we define the rules of the system, we review the market correlations of each indicator in the Sentiment Model, as shown in Table 8.8. As with the Acme pattern model, the Sentiment model can be extended with other data, e.g., margin debt. The trader determines the market correlation of a new index, assigns a letter to it, and encodes it in the Acme Market System. When adding new indicators, find ones that represent different interpretations of the market to keep the Sentiment Model in balance.

**Table 8.8.** Market Correlations

| Index | Market Correlation |
|---|---|
| Volatility Index (VIX) | Negative |
| Put/Call Ratio | Negative |
| New Highs | Positive |
| New Lows | Negative |
| Arms Index (TRIN) | Negative |
| Bullish Consensus | Positive |
| Short Sales Ratio | Negative |

---

[3] We use a historical database published by Pinnacle Data Corporation. As an alternative, the trader can use data provided by Barron's in its Market Lab section.

### 8.3.1 Long Signal

| Calculations |
|---|

1. Total the number of Bullish Patterns.
2. Calculate the ATR for the last 20 bars ($ATR_{20}$).

| Entry Rules |
|---|

1. Number of Bullish Patterns >= 2
2. **Buy** the next bar at or above the High + (EntryFactor * $ATR_{20}$)

| Exit Rules: Profit Target |
|---|

1. **Sell** half of the position at or above the High + (ProfitFactor * $ATR_{20}$)
2. **Sell** half of the position at or above the High of ProfitBars ago + (2 * ProfitFactor * $ATR_{20}$)

| Exit Rules: Stop Loss |
|---|

1. **Sell** all shares at or below the Lowest Low for StopBars − (ExitFactor * $ATR_{20}$)

### 8.3.2 Short Signal

| Calculations |
|---|

1. Total the number of Bearish Patterns.
2. Calculate the ATR for the last 20 bars ($ATR_{20}$).

| Entry Rules |
|---|

1. Number of Bearish Patterns >= 2
2. **Sell Short** the next bar at or below the Low − (EntryFactor * $ATR_{20}$)

| Exit Rules: Profit Target |
|---|

1. **Cover** half of the position at or below the Low − (ProfitFactor * $ATR_{20}$)
2. **Cover** half of the position at or below the Low of ProfitBars ago − (2 * ProfitFactor * $ATR_{20}$)

---

| Exit Rules: Stop Loss |
| --- |

1. **Cover** all shares at or above the Highest High for StopBars + (ExitFactor * $ATR_{20}$)

The code for the Acme Market System is shown in Example 8.2.

**Example 8.2.** Acme Market System

```
{*****************************************************************
Acme Market System: Look for combinations of multiple market patterns

1. VIX (V)
2. Put/Call Ratio (P)
3. New Highs (H)
4. New Lows (L)
5. Arms Index, or TRIN (T)
6. Bullish Consensus (B)
7. Short Sales Ratio (S)

Data1: Market Index
Data2: VIX
Data3: Put/Call Ratio
Data4: New Highs
Data5: New Lows
Data6: TRIN
Data7: Market Vane Bullish Consensus
Data8: Public/Specialist Short Sales Ratio
*****************************************************************}

Inputs:
    {Market Parameters}
    MinimumPatterns(2),
    Length(20),
    {Position Parameters}
    Equity(100000),
    RiskModel(3),
    RiskPercent(2.0),
    RiskATR(1.0),
    EntryFactor(0.2),
    DrawTargets(True);

Variables:
    N(0),
    ATR(0.0),
    PatternString(""),
    LongString(""),
    ShortString(""),
    ReturnValue(0),
    PriceDelta(0),
    HighLow(0),
```

```
    Smooth(4),
    BuyStop(0.0),
    ShortStop(0.0);

ATR = Average(Range, Length);
BuyStop = High + (EntryFactor * ATR);
ShortStop = Low - (EntryFactor * ATR);

If DataCompression < 2 Then
    Commentary("This indicator must be applied to a daily bar " +
    "interval or longer.")
Else Begin
    PatternString = "";
    LongString = "";
    ShortString = "";
    ATR = Volatility(Length);
    PriceDelta = ATR / 4;

    If Close of Data2 > 0 Then Begin
        PatternString = "V";
        HighLow = AcmeHighLowIndex(Close of Data2, Length);
        If HighLow = 1 Then
            LongString = LongString + PatternString
        Else If HighLow = 2 Then
            ShortString = ShortString + PatternString;
    End;

    If Close of Data3 > 0 Then Begin
        PatternString = "P";
        HighLow = AcmeHighLowIndex(Close of Data3, Length);
        If HighLow = 1 Then
            LongString = LongString + PatternString
        Else If HighLow = 2 Then
            ShortString = ShortString + PatternString;
    End;

    If Close of Data4 > 0 Then Begin
        PatternString = "H";
        HighLow = AcmeHighLowIndex(Close of Data4, Length);
        If HighLow = 2 Then
            LongString = LongString + PatternString
        Else If HighLow = 1 Then
            ShortString = ShortString + PatternString;
    End;

    If Close of Data5 > 0 Then Begin
        PatternString = "L";
        HighLow = AcmeHighLowIndex(Close of Data5, Length);
        If HighLow = 1 Then
            LongString = LongString + PatternString
        Else If HighLow = 2 Then
            ShortString = ShortString + PatternString;
    End;
```

```
    If Close of Data6 > 0 Then Begin
        PatternString = "T";
        HighLow = AcmeHighLowIndex(Average(Close of Data6, Smooth),
        Length);
        If HighLow = 1 Then
            LongString = LongString + PatternString
        Else If HighLow = 2 Then
            ShortString = ShortString + PatternString;
    End;

    If Close of Data7 > 0 Then Begin
        PatternString = "B";
        HighLow = AcmeHighLowIndex(Close of Data7, Length);
        If HighLow = 2 Then
            LongString = LongString + PatternString
        Else If HighLow = 1 Then
            ShortString = ShortString + PatternString;
    End;

    If Close of Data8 > 0 Then Begin
        PatternString = "S";
        HighLow = AcmeHighLowIndex(Close of Data8, Length);
        If HighLow = 1 Then
            LongString = LongString + PatternString
        Else If HighLow = 2 Then
            ShortString = ShortString + PatternString;
    End;

    {Calculate shares based on risk model}
    N = AcmeGetShares(Equity, RiskModel, RiskPercent, RiskATR);

    {Multiple Pattern Buy Signal}

    If StrLen(LongString) >= MinimumPatterns Then Begin
        {Draw Entry Targets on the Chart}
        If DrawTargets Then
            Condition1 = AcmeEntryTargets("M", BuyStop, 0, 0, 0);
        Buy("Acme LE Market") N Shares Next Bar on BuyStop Stop;
    End;

    {Multiple Pattern Sell Signal}

    If StrLen(ShortString) >= MinimumPatterns Then Begin
        {Draw Entry Targets on the Chart}
        If DrawTargets Then
            Condition1 = AcmeEntryTargets("M", 0, 0, ShortStop, 0);
        Sell("Acme SE Market") N Shares Next Bar on ShortStop Stop;
    End;
End;
```

## 8.4 Examples

Figure 8.12 displays the chart of the S&P 500 index from September 2001 to March 2002. The third bar in the chart shows a bullish "VS" bar (VIX and Short Sales Ratio), but a long entry was not triggered. The fifth bar shows a bullish "VHLB" bar with the following confirmations:

- ❑ High Confirmation for the VIX
- ❑ Low Confirmation for New Highs
- ❑ High Confirmation for New Lows
- ❑ High Confirmation for the Bullish Consensus

A long entry was triggered the first week of October, and the market rallied 10% over the next two months. Shortly after the rally stalled in January of 2002, a bearish "VHLBS" bar occurred with the following confirmations:

- ❑ Low Confirmation for the VIX
- ❑ High Confirmation for New Highs
- ❑ Low Confirmation for New Lows
- ❑ Low Confirmation for the Bullish Consensus
- ❑ Low Confirmation for the Short Sales Ratio

A short entry was triggered the following week with a subsequent 7% decline.

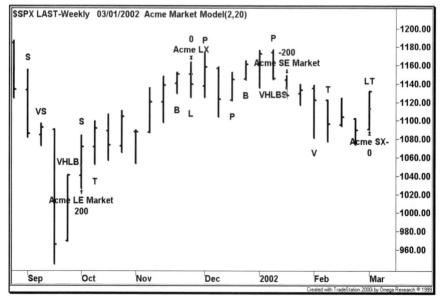

**Figure 8.12.** S&P 500 Index (09/01 – 02/02)

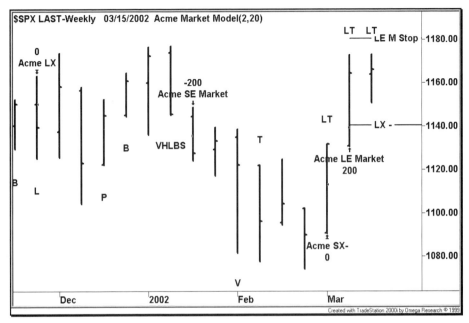

**Figure 8.13.** S&P 500 Index (12/01 – 03/02)

Figure 8.13 is an extension of the chart in Figure 8.12. A bullish "LT" bar occurs in early March 2002, and a long entry is triggered the following week with these confirmations:

❏  High Confirmation for New Lows

❏  High Confirmation for the TRIN

The chart in Figure 8.13 is unfolding as of the time of this writing[4]. The profit target is not shown, but the stop loss denoted by `LX-` has been established at an index price of ~1140. Further, just after the long position was opened, another LT bar occurred the following week (last bar on the chart), with an `LE M Stop` just above 1180.

Table 8.9 shows the results for the S&P 500 from 1985 to 2002. Over this period, there were 37 weekly signals based on a pattern minimum of two and a study length of 20 weeks. Over a period of 800 weeks, that equates to about one signal every five months. Eventually, this system will be adjusted to a daily time frame when all of the data are available electronically. Certainly, the system can be run for the subset of indicators that are available on a daily basis.

---

[4]  A week after this chapter was written, yet another LT bar occurred the week of March 18th, 2002. The LE M Stop order remained in place, and the S&P 500 was approaching a triple top with overhead resistance at 1180. A market breakout above 1180 could portend a big rally in the weeks ahead; otherwise, the February lows will be retested.

**Table 8.9.** Performance (20) - Acme Market Strategy $SPX-Weekly (11/29/1985-3/1/2002)

| | | | |
|---|---|---|---|
| Total Net Profit | $94,895.00 | Open position P/L | $0.00 |
| Gross Profit | $158,545.00 | Gross Loss | ($63,650.00) |
| Total # of trades | 37 | Percent profitable | 54.05% |
| Number winning trades | 20 | Number losing trades | 17 |
| Largest winning trade | $19,926.00 | Largest losing trade | ($11,568.00) |
| Average winning trade | $7,927.25 | Average losing trade | ($3,744.12) |
| Ratio avg win/avg loss | 2.12 | Avg trade (win & loss) | $2,564.73 |
| Max consec. Winners | 4 | Max consec. losers | 3 |
| Avg # bars in winners | 5 | Avg # bars in losers | 2 |
| Max intraday drawdown | ($20,388.00) | | |
| Profit Factor | 2.49 | Max # contracts held | 200 |
| Account size required | $20,388.00 | Return on account | 465.45% |

**Table 8.10.** Performance (30) - Acme Market Strategy $SPX-Weekly (11/29/1985-3/1/2002)

| | | | |
|---|---|---|---|
| Total Net Profit | $112,270.00 | Open position P/L | $0.00 |
| Gross Profit | $138,510.00 | Gross Loss | ($26,240.00) |
| Total # of trades | 22 | Percent profitable | 68.18% |
| Number winning trades | 15 | Number losing trades | 7 |
| Largest winning trade | $19,935.00 | Largest losing trade | ($7,328.00) |
| Average winning trade | $9,234.00 | Average losing trade | ($3,748.57) |
| Ratio avg win/avg loss | 2.46 | Avg trade (win & loss) | $5,103.18 |
| Max consec. Winners | 5 | Max consec. losers | 2 |
| Avg # bars in winners | 6 | Avg # bars in losers | 2 |
| Max intraday drawdown | ($9,772.00) | | |
| Profit Factor | 5.28 | Max # contracts held | 200 |
| Account size required | $9,772.00 | Return on account | 1148.89% |

Table 8.10 shows the results of running the Market System on a 30-week cycle. The profit factor on the 30-week cycle is 5.28, an improvement over the profit

factor of 2.49 on the 20-week cycle. By lengthening the study cycle, the number of trades has been reduced from 37 to 22.

Think of the market cycle in terms of each of our sentiment indicators. The trader makes the choice of how often each indicator will be making new highs and lows based on the cycle length. As the cycle is shortened, the number of trading signals increases with a decrease in profit factor. Similarly, as the cycle is lengthened, the number of signals decreases with an increase in profit factor.

If a trader cannot use the Sentiment Model on a daily basis[5], the model is still useful for identifying significant market turning points. Figure 8.14 shows a subtle example of a bullish "HLS" bar in June 1998. Typically, a bullish bar will occur at the end of a downtrend, but here it occurs after eight weeks of a trading range. From the price bars alone, there are no apparent signs of an impending rally; however, the bar is confirming the following:

❑  Low Confirmation for New Highs

❑  High Confirmation for New Lows

❑  High Confirmation for Short Sales Ratio (this is the key)

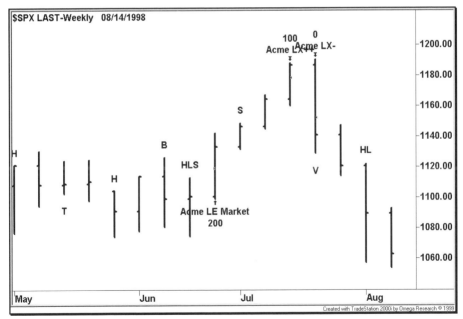

**Figure 8.14.** S&P 500 Index June 1998

The following week, a long entry triggered, and the market rallied 6.5% over the next month. The key to the trade was the Short Sales Ratio – it is an example of

---

[5] Imagine the trader of the 21st century making one trade every five months.

data revealing hidden market information that could otherwise not be gleaned from a typical bar chart.

## 8.5 Data Sources

For more information on the indicators in the Sentiment Model, refer to the sources in Table 8.11.

**Table 8.11.** Data Sources

| Data | Source |
|------|--------|
| Volatility Index (VIX) | Chicago Board Options Exchange |
| Put/Call Ratio | Chicago Board Options Exchange |
| New Highs | New York Stock Exchange |
| New Lows | New York Stock Exchange |
| Arms Index (TRIN) | New York Stock Exchange |
| Bullish Consensus | Market Vane |
| Short Sales Ratio | NYSE Members Report |

# 9 Tools of the Trade

*Generally he who first occupies the field*
*of battle to await the enemy will be rested;*
*He who comes later and hastens*
*into battle will be weary.*

Sun-tzu, *The Art of Warfare*

Preparation for the next trading day begins at the closing bell, and by the time the opening bell rings, the trader's work should be done for the rest of the day, except for the simple matter of executing the trades when alerts are received. During the trading day, the priorities are order entry and money management instead of trade selection – an exercise of managing risk rather than creating it.

Some traders like to come in with a blank slate. If one chooses to trade this way, then discipline is a greater factor. As long as risk is managed, discretionary trading can be equally rewarding. As an analogy, system trading is like listening to classical music, interrupted occasionally by the counterpoint of subtle mouse clicks. In contrast, discretionary trading is like blasting rock music, punctuated by the sensory overload of tick data.

Even with discretionary trading, preparation is the key to success. Knowing when to pull the trigger and to wait patiently for the right trade will eliminate some of the angst. The only requirement is that the trade must have a *catalyst*. Just because a Level II screen is showing upward momentum does not mean the trade has a catalyst, but combine that momentum with a catalyst and there is a basis for the trade.

Consider the example of a stock in a strong downtrend that a trader knows is heavily shorted. In the middle of the day, the company announces a big stock buyback. The trader sees the news release and buys the stock instantaneously. The trader does not hesitate because the catalyst is apparent. The foundation of success here is the trader's knowledge of the stock's fundamental and technical condition, an awareness of a catalyst that can change it, and a definition of risk (e.g., exit the position if the low of the previous five-minute bar is broken).

## 9.1 Tyco Case Study

Consider the case of Tyco (TYC:NYSE) in Figure 9.1. Over a period of three weeks in early 2002, the stock dropped in price from the mid-fifties to the low thirties because of accounting concerns. Furthermore, the company announced that it would spin off some of its operating companies rather than continue its acquisition strategy (note the gap up and reversal on January 22nd).

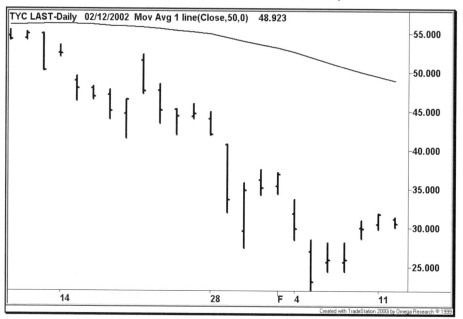

**Figure 9.1.** Tyco Daily Chart

On January 30th, the stock gapped down over three points. Given the possibility of a positive catalyst, the stock was placed on the watch list. After the stock gapped down, it drifted downwards and languished the rest of the morning.

At 12:08 pm, Tyco issued a press release that the CEO and CFO would be purchasing 500,000 shares apiece with their own money. The timing of the release could not have been more perfect. While some traders were eating lunch[1], others were having it eaten because the price spiked from 28 to 30 in a matter of minutes (Figure 9.2) and then climbed the rest of the afternoon to close near 35. When a stock has declined as much as Tyco, only a positive catalyst is required to reverse the stock's direction in a matter of hours. We recommend that the trader set up a *watch list* of stocks in the news to be alerted to potential reversal catalysts.

---

[1] In the movie *Wall Street* (1987), directed by Oliver Stone, starring Michael Douglas, the character Gordon Gekko uttered one of the more memorable lines "Lunch is for wimps."

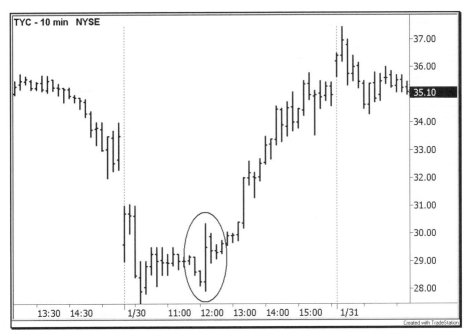

**Figure 9.2.** Tyco Intraday Chart

Some traders prefer not to watch or monitor the news at all, but the trader gains an edge in situations like Tyco – these situations do not occur often, but the key is that the news must be a reversal catalyst. In contrast, if a company reports bad news while its stock remains in a downtrend, fighting the tape is futile.

## 9.2 Preparation

To prepare for the next trading day, we take the following steps at the end of the current trading day. All of the work for the next trading day is done the previous night. For all intents and purposes, the trader walks in the following morning, gets trading alerts, and executes orders. The time between 9:30 am and 4:00 pm should be the most boring hours of a trader's life.

1. After the close, download today's closing prices.
2. Run the scanning software to generate orders and new alerts.
3. Review the open positions.
4. Analyze the charts with new alerts.
5. Assign priorities to charts for trading the next day.
6. Enter the symbols and/or alerts into the trading software.

Eventually, the trader's routine should become fairly rigid. Occasionally, panic will strike when the trader is trying to liquidate a large position in an illiquid stock (hint), or when the Federal Reserve Board decides to unleash a surprise interest rate cut on the market in the middle of the day [2]. The old saying "hours of boredom interrupted by moments of panic" applies to the trader, which is equally appreciated by sports fishermen and the guy holding the down marker at a professional football game.

### 9.2.1 Software

The key to establishing a trading routine is to automate as much of the process as possible, and that means investing in software and hardware. The minimum requirements are: one computer, two data feeds (for redundancy), two monitors (one for trading and one for analysis), and one technical analysis product.

We use the TradeStation 2000*i* software for nightly scans. The new version of the product, TradeStation 6, does not include end-of-day scans on a portfolio of stocks, so after the nightly scan, we take the candidates for the next day from version 2000i and track them real-time in the version 6 product (*N.B.* the Acme software runs on both versions). A software alternative to TradeStation is the MetaStock Professional product.

Other products such as FirstAlert® are designed to scan the whole market, not just a portfolio of stocks. The advantage of real-time scanning programs is that their formula languages are optimized for speed, creating dynamic lists of stocks on a tick-by-tick basis. The disadvantage is that a real-time scanner can generate sensory overload, and the trader may be tempted to jump from one stock to another.

Other traders prefer and need the discipline of a program like TradeStation because everything can be automated: the number of shares to trade, the exact entry and exit points displayed on the charts, and even order execution itself. Further, one can code an idea quickly and view the results of back testing.

The most important issue is the "cleanliness" of the data, which is affected by bad ticks. When analyzing performance, review each trade to ensure that the results are not flawed, looking for unusually good or bad outlier trades. Just a single erroneous trade can skew the results. Finally, realize that no one product offers the ultimate trading machine. Each programs has its strengths and weaknesses, and no program is bug-free. Trading software is very difficult to write

---

[2] On January 3rd, 2001, the Federal Reserve cut interest rates in the middle of the day, sending the QQQ from an open of 52 to a close of 62, a 19% move in a single day. For system testing purposes, we are happy to have these data because we need to assess statistics such as maximum loss size and maximum drawdown during the worst possible moments.

properly, so the vendor must be able to respond to problems in real-time with a competent technical support department.

## 9.3 A Trading Day

Think of this chapter as a "real time" chapter. Today is Monday, February 25, 2002, and we are preparing for Tuesday's trading. The beauty of this experiment is that we have no idea what is going to happen with our stock selections, so at the end of this trading week, we are going to appear as either Adam Vinatieri or Scott Norwood[3].

**Table 9.1.** Nightly Download

|     | Symbol | Description | Exchange | Category |
| --- | --- | --- | --- | --- |
| 494 | OPWV | Openwave Systems | Nasdaq | Stock |
| 495 | ORBK | Orbotech LTD | Nasdaq | Stock |
| 496 | ORCL | Oracle Corp | Nasdaq | Stock |
| 497 | OSIP | OSI Pharmaceuticals Inc | Nasdaq | Stock |
| 498 | OSIS | OSI Sys Inc | Nasdaq | Stock |
| 499 | OVER | Overture Services Inc | Nasdaq | Stock |
| 500 | PAYX | Paychex Inc | Nasdaq | Stock |
| 501 | PB-CONT | Pork Bellies Continuous | CME | Index |
| 502 | PCAR | Paccar Inc | Nasdaq | Stock |
| 503 | PCLN | Priceline.com | Nasdaq | Stock |
| 504 | PCRATIO | CBOE Put-Call Ratio | CALC | Index |
| 505 | PCSA | AirGate PCS Inc | Nasdaq | Stock |

The first step is to download the closing prices, as shown in Table 9.1. After the download, Table 9.2 shows all of the open positions (17) in the database. On any given night, the number of open positions will vary from ten to thirty for a database of approximately 500 stocks. Note that eleven of the positions were opened on today, February 25th, and that nine of the signals were long entries. Within the context of the market, this behavior is logical because the Nasdaq Composite Index had just completed a five-day downtrend, reversing to close above the open on February 22nd, as shown in Figure 9.3.

---

[3] The former kicked a 48-yard field goal with seven seconds remaining in the game to win Super Bowl XXXVI for the New England Patriots; the latter missed a 47-yard field goal with four seconds remaining in the game to lose Super Bowl XXV.

**Table 9.2.** Open Positions

| Symbol | Signal | Position | Entry Price | Last | Profit | Entry Time |
|--------|--------|----------|-------------|------|--------|------------|
| AMHC | Acme SE R | Short 1100 | 20.5 | 20.05 | 495.00 | 2/25/2002 4:00 PM |
| BCC | Acme LE V | Long 1050 | 34.375 | 35.37 | 1044.75 | 2/20/2002 4:00 PM |
| BJ | Acme LE M | Long 1400 | 41.375 | 41.34 | -49.00 | 2/25/2002 4:00 PM |
| BREL | Acme LE R | Long 1000 | 18.75 | 18.79 | 40.00 | 2/21/2002 4:00 PM |
| C | Acme LE M | Long 1300 | 43 | 43.79 | 1027.00 | 2/25/2002 4:00 PM |
| COGN | Acme LE M | Long 1900 | 25.25 | 25.39 | 266.00 | 2/25/2002 4:00 PM |
| CTX | Acme LE M | Long 1000 | 54.25 | 55.43 | 1180.00 | 2/25/2002 4:00 PM |
| DST | Acme LE M | Long 1500 | 41.75 | 41.74 | -15.00 | 2/21/2002 4:00 PM |
| ESIO | Acme LE M | Long 1300 | 31.625 | 31.28 | -448.50 | 2/25/2002 4:00 PM |
| ESRX | Acme LE V | Long 1000 | 52.5 | 53.7 | 1200.00 | 2/20/2002 4:00 PM |
| GS | Acme LE M | Long 700 | 79.875 | 81.96 | 1459.50 | 2/25/2002 4:00 PM |
| IMPH | Acme SE FB | Short 900 | 35.125 | 34.9 | 202.50 | 2/21/2002 4:00 PM |
| IONA | Acme LE M | Long 1400 | 16.25 | 16.15 | -140.00 | 2/25/2002 4:00 PM |
| ITG | Acme LE V | Long 1600 | 43.375 | 43.22 | -248.00 | 2/20/2002 4:00 PM |
| MERQ | Acme LE M | Long 900 | 33.75 | 34.63 | 792.00 | 2/25/2002 4:00 PM |
| ORBK | Acme SE N | Short 1400 | 23.75 | 23.98 | -322.00 | 2/25/2002 4:00 PM |
| PCAR | Acme LE FB | Long 900 | 69.5 | 70.88 | 1242.00 | 2/25/2002 4:00 PM |

This example illustrates several important points when analyzing trades for the next day. First, always examine the condition of the market and sectors to get a sense of the signals that will be triggered the following day. Second, run each of the Acme systems unfiltered for the broad market and sector indices, e.g., the HOLDRS[4]. Finally, highlight any stocks that are running against the general market trend; these stocks are bucking the market for a reason.

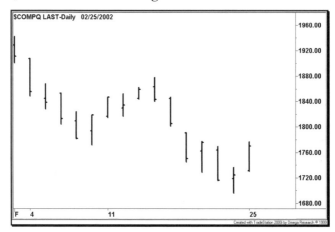

**Figure 9.3.** Nasdaq Composite Index Reversal

---

[4] HOLDRS are exchange-traded stocks that represent sectors such as biotechnology, broadband, oil services, and semiconductors. The Web address is http://www.holdrs.com.

Table 9.3 shows all of the active orders generated for February 26th, 2002. The window shows both entry and exit orders, consisting of stop orders, limit orders, and market orders. Three of the stocks (BCC, ESRX, and ITG) have market orders; these stocks have reached the end of the holding period, i.e., the profit target and stop loss orders never triggered. The top half of the window shows long entries, and the last entry in the window (DST) shows a limit order for a single-bar profit target.

**Table 9.3.** Active Orders

| Symbol | Signal | Order | Last | Time Placed |
|---|---|---|---|---|
| EASI | Acme LE FB | Buy 1000 at 39.125 Stop | 37.79 | 2/26/2002 2:06 AM |
| ABC | Acme LE FB | Buy 1200 at 65.375 Stop | 64.66 | 2/26/2002 2:06 AM |
| CECO | Acme LE FB | Buy 1200 at 37.750 Stop | 37.05 | 2/26/2002 2:06 AM |
| BOBJ | Acme LE M | Buy 1100 at 36.500 Stop | 36.1 | 2/26/2002 2:06 AM |
| ORBK | Acme LE R | Buy 1500 at 24.750 Stop | 23.98 | 2/26/2002 2:06 AM |
| CACI | Acme LE R | Buy 800 at 36.000 Stop | 34.81 | 2/26/2002 2:06 AM |
| MMS | Acme LE R | Buy 1400 at 34.000 Stop | 33.52 | 2/26/2002 2:06 AM |
| ORBK | Acme LE R | Buy 1400 at 24.750 Stop | 23.98 | 2/26/2002 2:06 AM |
| IONA | Acme LE R | Buy 1400 at 17.000 Stop | 16.15 | 2/26/2002 2:06 AM |
| DST | Acme LE R | Buy 1500 at 42.375 Stop | 41.74 | 2/26/2002 2:06 AM |
| CMNT | Acme LE R | Buy 1300 at 12.625 Stop | 11.45 | 2/26/2002 2:06 AM |
| NOC | Acme LE V | Buy 600 at 108.750 Stop | 108.44 | 2/26/2002 2:06 AM |
| ACAM | Acme LE V | Buy 1000 at 49.500 Stop | 49.15 | 2/26/2002 2:06 AM |
| CBRL | Acme LE V | Buy 2300 at 31.500 Stop | 31.15 | 2/26/2002 2:06 AM |
| BCC | Acme LX | Sell 1050 at Market | 35.37 | 2/26/2002 2:06 AM |
| ESRX | Acme LX | Sell 1000 at Market | 53.7 | 2/26/2002 2:06 AM |
| ITG | Acme LX | Sell 1600 at Market | 43.22 | 2/26/2002 2:06 AM |
| DST | Acme LX+ | Sell 750 at 43.375 Limit | 41.74 | 2/26/2002 2:06 AM |

For each open position, we review the profit targets and stop losses drawn on the chart. The Trade Manager calls the *AcmeExitTargets* function to mark each price level with a horizontal trend line. This function allows the caller to specify a stop loss price, a first profit target price, and a second profit target price. Trade entries are drawn with the *AcmeEntryTargets* function. The trader can identify a stop price or limit price on the chart with the same horizontal line.

Figure 9.4 shows an example of a stop loss for an Acme V entry, denoted by LX- at a price of 34.65. The horizontal line is drawn under the low of the bar, adjusted downward for the *ExitFactor* multiplied by the ATR. The chart also shows an Acme N short entry, denoted by SE N Stop. This is an example of a "stop and reverse" trade. The short entry serves a dual purpose by selling out the long entry and simultaneously taking the short position. When executing the trade, the short entry order is entered as double the size of the long position.

Figure 9.5 shows a multi-bar profit target denoted by **LX++**, the single-bar profit target marked by **LX+**, and a stop loss marked by **LX-** for the Acme N long entry.

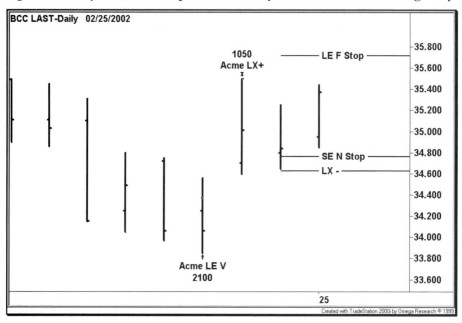

**Figure 9.4.** Boise Cascade Position Open Orders

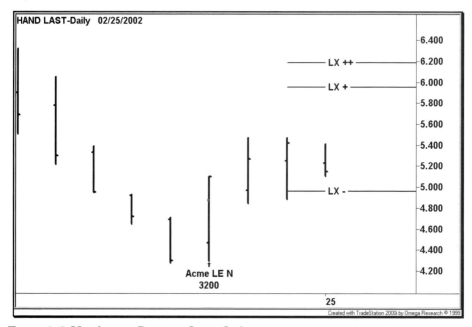

**Figure 9.5.** Handspring Position Open Orders

After the scanner has generated new signals for the next day, the trader reviews the charts to select the best candidates using qualitative and quantitative criteria, i.e., experience matched with measures such as volatility, ATR, and liquidity. The end-of-day scan for February 26th generated fourteen new long orders and fourteen new short orders, as shown in Tables 9.4 and 9.5, respectively.

**Table 9.4.** New Long Orders

| Symbol | Signal | Order | Last | Time Placed |
|---|---|---|---|---|
| EASI | Acme LE FB | Buy 1000 at 39.125 Stop | 37.79 | 2/26/2002 2:06 AM |
| ABC | Acme LE FB | Buy 1200 at 65.375 Stop | 64.66 | 2/26/2002 2:06 AM |
| CECO | Acme LE FB | Buy 1200 at 37.750 Stop | 37.05 | 2/26/2002 2:06 AM |
| BOBJ | Acme LE M | Buy 1100 at 36.500 Stop | 36.1 | 2/26/2002 2:06 AM |
| ORBK | Acme LE R | Buy 1500 at 24.750 Stop | 23.98 | 2/26/2002 2:06 AM |
| CACI | Acme LE R | Buy 800 at 36.000 Stop | 34.81 | 2/26/2002 2:06 AM |
| MMS | Acme LE R | Buy 1400 at 34.000 Stop | 33.52 | 2/26/2002 2:06 AM |
| ORBK | Acme LE R | Buy 1400 at 24.750 Stop | 23.98 | 2/26/2002 2:06 AM |
| IONA | Acme LE R | Buy 1400 at 17.000 Stop | 16.15 | 2/26/2002 2:06 AM |
| DST | Acme LE R | Buy 1500 at 42.375 Stop | 41.74 | 2/26/2002 2:06 AM |
| CMNT | Acme LE R | Buy 1300 at 12.625 Stop | 11.45 | 2/26/2002 2:06 AM |
| NOC | Acme LE V | Buy 600 at 108.750 Stop | 108.44 | 2/26/2002 2:06 AM |
| ACAM | Acme LE V | Buy 1000 at 49.500 Stop | 49.15 | 2/26/2002 2:06 AM |
| CBRL | Acme LE V | Buy 2300 at 31.500 Stop | 31.15 | 2/26/2002 2:06 AM |

**Table 9.5.** New Short Orders

| Symbol | Signal | Order | Last | Time Placed |
|---|---|---|---|---|
| CACI | Acme SE R | Sell 800 at 33.125 Stop | 34.81 | 2/26/2002 2:06 AM |
| IONA | Acme SE R | Sell 1400 at 14.750 Stop | 16.15 | 2/26/2002 2:06 AM |
| CMNT | Acme SE R | Sell 1300 at 10.250 Stop | 11.45 | 2/26/2002 2:06 AM |
| MMS | Acme SE R | Sell 1400 at 32.125 Stop | 33.52 | 2/26/2002 2:06 AM |
| DST | Acme SE R | Sell 1500 at 40.375 Stop | 41.74 | 2/26/2002 2:06 AM |
| ORBK | Acme SE R | Sell 1500 at 23.125 Stop | 23.98 | 2/26/2002 2:06 AM |
| CYTC | Acme SE N | Sell 1600 at 22.500 Stop | 22.96 | 2/26/2002 2:06 AM |
| MCSI | Acme SE N | Sell 1700 at 19.750 Stop | 20.19 | 2/26/2002 2:06 AM |
| EPG | Acme SE N | Sell 800 at 44.875 Stop | 45.72 | 2/26/2002 2:06 AM |
| OVER | Acme SE N | Sell 700 at 26.375 Stop | 27.30 | 2/26/2002 2:06 AM |
| ADLAC | Acme SE N | Sell 1400 at 21.000 Stop | 21.64 | 2/26/2002 2:06 AM |
| BVF | Acme SE M | Sell 1000 at 47.625 Stop | 48.06 | 2/26/2002 2:06 AM |
| CDN | Acme SE FB | Sell 2600 at 20.250 Stop | 20.99 | 2/26/2002 2:06 AM |
| DST | Acme SE FB | Sell 1500 at 40.625 Stop | 41.74 | 2/26/2002 2:06 AM |

The number of new long orders and new short orders is encouraging because we want to see a balance between the two. Clearly, the market has periods where one can throw money at the wall, but these periods are extremely rare. Most of the time, we want to hedge our portfolio with both long and short positions. In general, a trader can find several sectors with good volatility while other sectors languish. The shift in emphasis from investment to trading (e.g., money flow shifting into hedge funds) has encouraged the practice of hot money chasing two or three specific sectors.

The next step is to review the charts with new orders. We will not analyze every chart here but select only those with large ranges and high volatilities. Eventually, the trader will instinctively weed out those stocks that do not have high risk/reward ratios. We selected the following stocks for review (with their corresponding ATRs):

- Engineered Support Systems (**EASI:Nasdaq**)  1.83
- Business Objects (**BOBJ:Nasdaq**)              1.71
- Overture Services (**OVER:Nasdaq**)            2.87
- CACI International (**CACI:Nasdaq**)            2.24

The reader is encouraged to go through every chart to see how each of the trades panned out. Although automation eliminates much of the work, the new trader should review as many charts as possible. If the scanner generates too many potential entries, then limit this number by tightening the filters or by restricting the system-specific parameters. First, increase the volatility parameters such as Historical Volatility and Average True Range. Second, adjust any parameters that are range-restrictive such as the Range Percentage.

### 9.3.1 Chart Review

Starting with the EASI chart in Figure 9.6, we see a slightly ascending triple top, and the last three bars show highs near the upper float channel. The float box extends back to January 22nd, two days before a strong up move. As a result, the chart is at a point where the float has turned over and has consolidated near the highs for the past two weeks. As shown on the chart, the buy stop is 0.625 above the upper float channel of 38.5. In conclusion, this is a promising chart, so we will enter a trade on any signal.

The next chart is BOBJ, as shown in Figure 9.7. TradeStation has generated a long M entry to buy 1100 shares at 36.5 stop. Although the stock is in a downtrend, the narrow bar limits risk, and the market has reversed course today. Still, the stock closed slightly lower on the day – a weak stock in a strong market. As a result, this chart is a coin flip. If a signal occurs, then we will enter the trade on an "available equity" basis. The trader should establish a priori how many new positions can be taken on any given day and then arrange the charts in order of perceived signal strength.

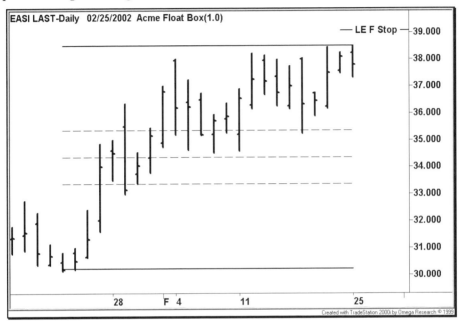

**Figure 9.6.** Engineered Support Systems Entry Order

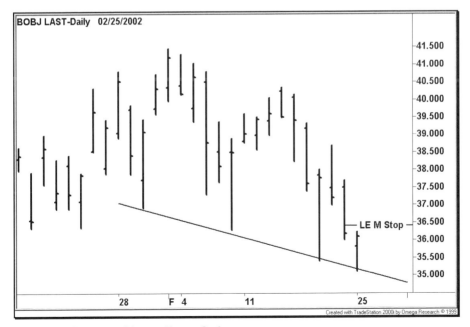

**Figure 9.7.** Business Objects Entry Order

OVER in Figure 9.8, there is an order to sell short 700 shares at 26.375. This is a good chart for several reasons. First, the stock is poised to break out of a symmetrical triangle formed over the past several weeks. Second, today's range is only 1.04, a fraction of the ATR of 2.87, a good risk/reward ratio. Finally, the stock gapped down strongly on February 8th, so fear is built into the stock. On a fundamental note, Overture sold off again after the last pivot high because of a competitive product in the Internet advertising marketplace.

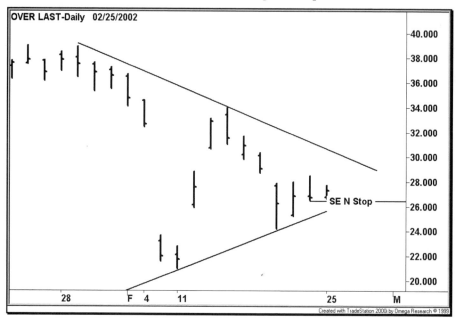

**Figure 9.8.** Overture Services Entry Order

The chart in Figure 9.9 is CACI. The stock is in a four-day rectangle, it has formed a triple bottom, and it is bounded by a large descending triangle. Based on these conditions, the stock chart is bearish because the rectangle is unbiased, the triple bottom is bearish, and the descending triangle is bearish. Since we have an Acme R entry, we can simply wait for a breakout in either direction.

Certainly, a trader can have an opinion about a trade, but the opinion means nothing. A market opinion never matters except for the shameless money managers "talking their book". Either they are stuck in a position that needs a boost, or they want to sell at a higher price – to you. Be skeptical of market gurus who raise their equity weightings in public. If the guru works for a major investment bank, then all of his or her clients have been clued in the day before, and releasing this news to the public is a chance to unload short-term trading positions. For further information about these market gurus, read Niederhoffer's hilarious taxonomy of market forecasters [21].

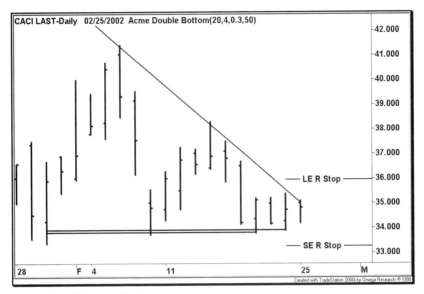

**Figure 9.9.** CACI Entry Order

## *Update*

Today is Friday, March 1st. We will now review each of the long and short trade entries from February 26th. First, the chart of EASI is shown in Figure 9.10. As expected, price broke the upper float channel, and the trade was exited within two days. When a stock moves this quickly in two days, profits should be taken on half of the position. Later that day, the remaining half was stopped out.

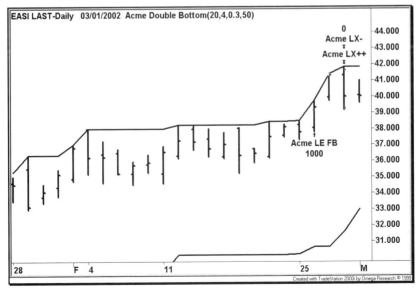

**Figure 9.10.** Engineered Support Systems Update

Remember the chart of Business Objects? We thought that this was the weakest chart, but this signal turned out to be the best trade (Figure 9.11), a testament to our chart reading skills.

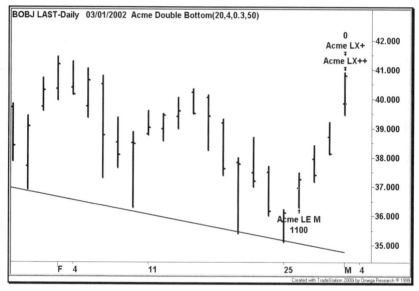

**Figure 9.11.** Business Objects Position

The Acme N short entry never triggered for OVER, as shown in Figure 9.12; however, it did break out of its symmetrical triangle.

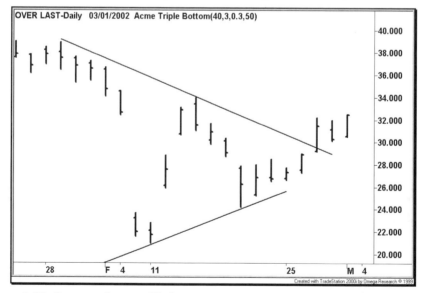

**Figure 9.12.** Overture Services Update

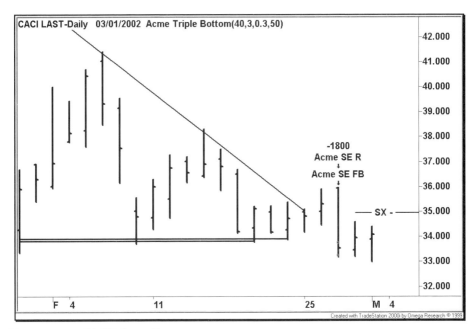

**Figure 9.13.** CACI Open Position

The CACI rectangle in Figure 9.13 triggered to the short side with both an R and FB signal. After two days, the chart showed conviction in neither direction. Although not shown here, the following day, the trade was stopped out before a three-point move to the upside during a market rally.

Overall, the systems performed better than our chart analysis, as is usually the case. The two long trades (EASI and BOBJ) were clear winners, supported by the rally in the Nasdaq. The short trade (CACI) stayed flat during the market reversal but was eventually a loser. Finally, the remaining stock (OVER) did not trigger a trade.

Next, we show the trader some inspirational charts in Figures 9.14 and 9.15. In early 2002, Rent-a-Center (RCII:Nasdaq) had an exceptional three-month Relative Strength reading of 97. During this period, all of the Acme entries were long trades. In June 2001, the Relative Strength of Corporate Executive Board (EXBD:Nasdaq) was 95. Five long signals were generated in a little over a month. Four out of five trades were winners, and two of the long positions were created with multiple trade entries.

The reason for presenting these charts is to bolster the claim that a trader's overall profit factor can be improved by selecting high RS stocks [4]. By using these measures such as RS and EPS, the trading systems presented in this book can be used as a platform to build better systems. Make the systems your own, and you will have the confidence to trade them.

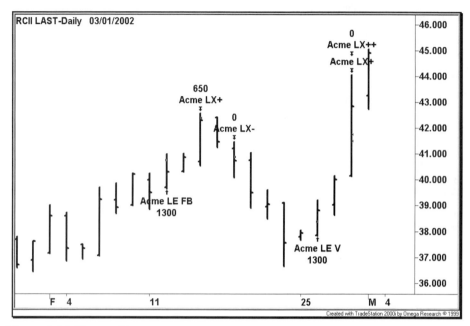

**Figure 9.14.** Rent-a-Center

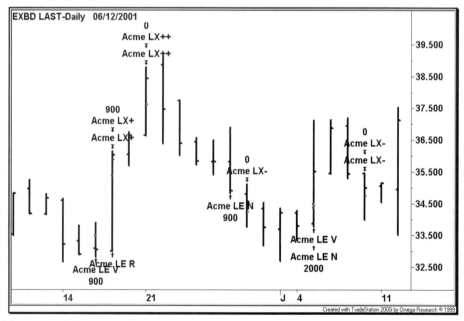

**Figure 9.15.** Corporate Executive Board

# 10 Day Trading

*At first be like a modest maiden,*
*and the enemy will open his door;*
*Afterward be as swift as a scurrying rabbit,*
*and the enemy will be too late to resist you.*

Sun-tzu, *The Art of Warfare*

Welcome to the highly evolved battlefield of electronic day trading, an arena littered with the remains of computers masquerading as slot machines with empty coin hoppers. A confluence of technology and online trading created a network of traders with access to real-time quotes, news, and instantaneous executions. As a tide of liquidity flooded into the market, the technology stocks soared, and just as quickly the tide went out–along with the fortunes of many traders.

At last count, Amazon.com had over one hundred books on day trading, but unfortunately nobody is left to read them. The world probably does not need another Level II tutorial, but in the interest of completeness, every tool has its place. This chapter offers some traditional technical analysis techniques for day trading and presents some actual trading examples where tools such as Level II quotes have proven to be extremely useful.

Before taking the first trade, follow these steps. Most traders will fail, and this is not a "you too can succeed in day trading" chapter.

1. Get the proper training from a professional mentor. Learn from a trader, not a teacher.
2. Choose a professional trading firm that invests in the latest technology and that has excellent customer service.
3. Read the tape and understand the intraday trading cycle. Understand the implications of trading the open and the close.
4. Trading is a business. Calculate your trading costs and set daily, weekly, and monthly goals based on a conservative return.

5. Invest in technical analysis software. Automate the trading process as much as possible.

## 10.1 Finding a Day Trading Firm

Selecting the right trading firm is the second most important decision a trader will make – the firm must demonstrate that it is interested in your success, not in burning through your capital by encouraging excessive trading. During the evaluation period, you are assessing each firm's package of technology, training, customer service, and costs. Make a checklist of the following items:

- Investment in software and hardware technology
- Training and mentoring
- Broad ECN access
- Commission rates and seat costs
- Technical analysis software
- Customer service
- Technical support
- NASD member and SIPC account insurance

When investigating a firm, find out what their traders are doing: day trading, position trading, system trading, or a combination. A *day trader* executes trades that last from as little as a few seconds to as long as a few hours; the day trader carries no overnight positions, i.e., is "all cash" at the end of the day, carrying no exposure to overnight risk. The *swing trader*, or *position trader*, executes trades that usually last several days. The swing trader uses short-term technical analysis indicators to enter and exit positions. Finally, the *system trader* uses computer programs to generate automatic buy and sell signals with predefined entry and exit prices, spanning all time frames.

The second decision a trader must make is whether or not to trade on-site or remotely. The advantage of trading on a floor is that other traders can be a source of ideas (just make sure they make money). The trading floors have distinct atmospheres; either the floor is noisy with traders exchanging ideas, or it is quiet with concentration. Question whether or not you will be able to tolerate a trader looking over your shoulder and pestering you for ideas. For some, the banter is good; for others, it is irritating.

When visiting a floor, go ten minutes before the market opens. At 9:30 am on a busy day, the software vendors send out a burst of market data, and some brokers are ill equipped to distribute the data fast enough. We have seen real-time quotes that have been delayed by as much as ten seconds, an eternity in the life of a day trader.

Access to the best technology is essential for the day trader. When evaluating a trading firm, evaluate the software features developed specifically for the day trader. Most of the direct access brokers have Level II quotes, point-and-click execution, and rudimentary charting, but offer little else. Advanced software has programmable features such as:

- Universal symbol filtering to eliminate unnecessary data
- Hot keys for fast execution (the mouse is too slow)
- Technical alerts such as three-day highs or volume spikes
- Real-time position, profit, and buying power information
- Market maker movement information (level changes)
- Custom tickers with filtering by symbol and volume
- Quote lists with custom fields
- Access to all ECNs with advanced order entry (e.g., reserve orders)
- Technical analysis software such as TradeStation or FirstAlert
- Bloomberg terminal
- Data feed services such as OpenBook™

Assess the number and quality of the technical support staff. If they spend their time rebooting the server during the trading day, then their technical support is inadequate. If you trade from home and they can tell you the frame relay delay in milliseconds over a DSL line, then they probably understand the technology. Finally, corner one of the traders to ask about delays or outages.

Service extends to other areas such as the back office, and a trader will want to ask questions such as:

- How does the firm treat its clients?
- What is the trading atmosphere like?
- Who clears the broker's trades?
- How soon are trade confirmations received?

Finally, ask about the experience of the traders on the floor. The truly successful day trader has been trading profitably for a minimum of several years in all kinds of markets. Many firms are populated with part-time position traders who have other jobs. There are many traders that come and go within several months.

Although there is no substitute for learning how to trade other than from a seasoned professional, look for someone who is willing to teach you specific techniques. In the following sections, we review the basic Level II trading technique and then present some advanced trading techniques with a set of case studies.

## 10.2 Trading the Nasdaq

The trading of a Nasdaq stock is shaped by the following attributes:

- Number of market makers (depth)
- Average Daily Volume (ADV)
- Float
- Average True Range (ATR)
- Spread
- Volatility Percentage (VP)

Table 10.1 shows the relationship between the market maker coverage and the spread. As the number of market makers, ADV, and float decreases, the value of the spread naturally increases. The trader wants the combination of a tight spread and volatility, using measures such as the VP and ADV/Float ratio. For example, trading 1000 shares of VRSN will average about $40 per round trip in slippage ($1000 \times 2 \times .02$), reducing the trading cost substantially.

**Table 10.1.** Nasdaq Trading Characteristics

| Symbol | Market Makers | ADV (millions) | Float (millions) | ATR | Spread | VP | ADV/Float |
|--------|--------|--------|--------|------|------|-------|------|
| CSCO | 106 | 79.39 | 7180.0 | 0.80 | .01 | 5.71 | 1.11 |
| MSFT | 88 | 27.42 | 4510.0 | 1.89 | .01 | 3.63 | 0.61 |
| VRSN | 77 | 18.79 | 195.9 | 1.98 | .02 | 11.00 | 9.59 |
| NVDA | 68 | 9.72 | 108.4 | 2.82 | .06 | 8.06 | 8.97 |
| MERQ | 63 | 2.90 | 77.6 | 2.29 | .06 | 6.36 | 3.74 |
| HOTT | 42 | 0.39 | 30.2 | 0.92 | .10 | 4.00 | 1.29 |
| PNRA | 31 | 0.28 | 12.3 | 2.44 | .30 | 3.75 | 2.28 |

### 10.2.1 Nasdaq Market Participants

Each Nasdaq stock is represented by a group of market makers and electronic communications networks that compete to buy and sell shares on a computerized exchange. Investment banks such as Goldman Sachs, Merrill Lynch, and Morgan Stanley are *market makers*. Each market maker is an NASD member firm and must register to quote a security; each market maker displays both bid and offer price quotations for a certain number of shares.

When a market maker "makes a market", it is providing a dual function – it fills customer orders for that stock (agency trades), and it buys and sells for its own account (principal trades). Each market maker is assigned a four-letter code, a *Market Participant ID* (MPID). For example, the acronym GSCO represents Goldman Sachs, and MSCO is Morgan Stanley.

The strongest market maker at any given time is known as the *Ax*. The Ax is typically the company's lead underwriter and investment banker, but this role changes from day to day. Other traders attempt to follow the Ax's lead by highlighting certain market makers, but lack of access to order flow puts the trader at a disadvantage. Be skeptical of anyone who claims to know how to follow the Ax; however, look for a *public display of affection* (PDA) on the Level II window, a sudden jump onto the best bid or offer.

The theory behind market maker analysis is that if a key market maker goes high bid, then a buying situation is created, and if the market maker goes low offer, then a selling situation is created. This is another myth perpetrated by the churners and burners. The smart market maker is accumulating shares through an ECN. The perfect time to dump these shares is to pop up on the bid with a PDA and then be ready and waiting to sell to all comers on the offer through an ECN. The difficulty of day trading with Level II quotes is that the risk/reward ratio is skewed, a pursuit similar to picking up dimes in front of bulldozers.

The trader may feel that becoming wise to a market maker's movement is a ticket to profits. Suppose in our previous example that the trader decides to fade the PDA. This time, the market maker really wants the shares, so the trader goes short. Guess what happens – the market maker buys all the shares because he is filling an order, going high bid one distressing level after another. Again, this is an issue of order flow and the requirements of the market maker filling an order [17]. A trader who sees a market maker as a conspirator should probably be writing the screenplay for a sequel to *JFK*.

*Electronic communications networks*, or ECNs, are trading exchanges that are directly accessible to the public through various online brokers (hence the term direct access broker). The well-known day trading firms give access to all of the ECNs. Note that each ECN is also assigned an MPID. For example, the MPID of Island is ISLD, and the MPID of Instinet is INCA. ECN symbols are listed along with the market maker symbols at the Nasdaq Trader Web site.

The influx of ECNs changed the basic momentum game into a complicated puzzle of analyzing individual market maker movements. Market makers developed techniques for enticing day traders into buying stock that they wished to sell and vice versa. Consequently, software developers added features to alert traders to market maker movements, but the result was a Pyrrhic victory in the absence of any order flow. When first introduced, Level II quotations gave the trader an advantage; now, they are just a minimum requirement for day trading.

## 10.2.2 Level II Quotations

Together, the best bid price (highest) and the best offer price (lowest) comprise a *Level I* quote. The current bid and ask price are displayed in combination as the *inside market*. The other bids at lower prices and other offers at higher prices are outside the market. For example, if a stock is quoting 17.38 × 17.39, then 17.38 is the highest bid price and 17.39 is the lowest offer price – other bids start at 17.37 and lower, with other offers at 17.40 or higher. The difference between the best offer price and best bid price is known as the *spread*. The spread on the sample quote here is 17.39 minus 17.38 equals 0.01, or one cent.

A *Level II* display shows all of the bid and ask prices for a stock, i.e., all of the bid prices are in descending order (from highest to lowest) on the left-hand side, and the ask prices are shown in ascending order (lowest to highest) on the right-hand side. Each bid or offer price is associated with either a market maker or an ECN in the first column. The number of shares that the market maker is bidding or offering is shown in the third column in units of 100. Note how each price tier is delineated by color.

In the Level II window in Figure 10.1, Goldman Sachs (GSCO) is bidding 1000 shares of Cisco at 17.38. The Island ECN (ISLD) is bidding 2500 shares at 17.38, and Instinet (INCA) is offering 2300 shares of Cisco at 17.39.

| CSCO | 17.38 | Chg | -1.23 | Lst Trd | 1000 |
|------|-------|-----|-------|---------|------|
| Close | 18.61↓ | Bid | 17.38 | Ask | 17.39 |
| Open | 17.92 | High | 18.00 | Low | 17.07 |
| GSCO | 17.38 | 10 | MSCO | 17.39 | 10 |
| ISLD | 17.38 | 25 | INCA | 17.39 | 23 |
| SCHB | 17.38 | 10 | COWN | 17.40 | 10 |
| SBSH | 17.37 | 10 | MLCO | 17.40 | 10 |
| REDI | 17.37 | 10 | SBSH | 17.40 | 10 |
| MLCO | 17.37 | 10 | REDI | 17.41 | 10 |
| COWN | 17.36 | 10 | NFSC | 17.41 | 10 |
| MSCO | 17.36 | 10 | GSCO | 17.41 | 10 |

**Figure 10.1.** Level II Window

The Level II window is modeled on the Nasdaq Workstation that each market maker uses to display quotes, adjust quotes, and enter orders. Software vendors implemented a facsimile of this display based on the Nasdaq data feed so that online traders could see the same information.

### 10.2.3 Level II Tutorial

Before understanding the details of Level II, one must appreciate the history of its usage. Originally, the Level II quote screen was the basis of a momentum technique known as "SOESing", where a trader could profit simply by buying out all of the market makers at the best offer price and then selling back to them at a higher price, based on the illusion of upside momentum. However, market makers learned the game quickly, and trading with Level II degenerated into a game of head fakes, firepower, and spoofing[1].

| CSCO | 17.38↓ | Chg | -1.23 | Lst Trd | 1000 |
|------|--------|------|-------|---------|------|
| Close | 18.61 | Bid | 17.38 | Ask | 17.39 |
| Open | 17.92 | High | 18.00 | Low | 17.07 |
| GSCO | 17.38 | 10 | MSCO | 17.39 | 10 |
| ISLD | 17.38 | 25 | INCA | 17.39 | 23 |
| SCHB | 17.38 | 10 | COWN | 17.40 | 10 |
| SBSH | 17.37 | 10 | MLCO | 17.40 | 10 |
| REDI | 17.37 | 10 | SBSH | 17.40 | 10 |
| MLCO | 17.37 | 10 | REDI | 17.41 | 10 |
| COWN | 17.36 | 10 | NFSC | 17.41 | 10 |
| MSCO | 17.36 | 10 | GSCO | 17.41 | 10 |

**Figure 10.2.** Level II Snapshot 1

Figure 10.2 shows the first Level II snapshot in the tutorial. The current quote for Cisco (Nasdaq:CSCO) is 17.38 bid × 17.39 offer—three market participants for a total of 4500 shares on the bid, and two market participants for a total of 3300 shares at the offer. The last trade was 1000 shares @ 17.38, and the stock is on a down bid (denoted by the ↓ arrow).

Suppose that after several minutes, the market maker window in Figure 10.2 changes to the display in Figure 10.3:

---

[1] Spoofing is the illegal practice of flashing a large number of shares on Level II (e.g., 50000 shares) in an attempt to scare the market in a certain direction.

| CSCO | 17.39↑ | Chg | -1.22 | Lst Trd | 2300 |
|------|--------|-----|-------|---------|------|
| Close | 18.61 | Bid | 17.38 | Ask | 17.39 |
| Open | 17.92 | High | 18.00 | Low | 17.07 |

| GSCO | 17.38 | 10 | MSCO | 17.39 | 10 |
|------|-------|----|------|-------|----|
| ISLD | 17.38 | 25 | ISLD | 17.40 | 18 |
| SCHB | 17.38 | 10 | COWN | 17.40 | 10 |
| SBSH | 17.38 | 10 | MLCO | 17.40 | 10 |
| REDI | 17.38 | 10 | SBSH | 17.40 | 10 |
| MLCO | 17.37 | 10 | REDI | 17.41 | 10 |
| COWN | 17.36 | 10 | NFSC | 17.41 | 10 |
| MSCO | 17.36 | 10 | GSCO | 17.41 | 10 |

**Figure 10.3.** Level II Snapshot 2

Although the Level I quote has remained the same (17.38 x 17.39), 2300 shares of Cisco have been bought at 17.39, and two other market makers have joined the best bid. A buying situation is created when the best bid tier expands, and the best offer tier contracts. Likewise, a selling situation is created when the best offer tier expands, and the best bid tier contracts. In this situation, momentum traders will rush in to buy CSCO at 17.39 since only one market maker remains, hoping that Morgan Stanley (MSCO) will finish selling shares at 17.39 and raise the offer to a price of 17.40 or higher.

So, the momentum trader has bought shares at 17.39 and is now waiting for a higher offer. Before continuing with our example, we examine the practice of Level II trading before decimalization (B.D.) and after decimalization (A.D.). In 1995 B.D., a trader could SOES in for 1000 shares at 17 ¼, and as soon as the offer was raised, try to sell it immediately for 17 3/8 in order to pocket a quick $125 (not including commissions). In 2002 A.D., a stock such as Cisco has a penny spread, which invalidates the original SOES strategy. As a result, some traders have adapted by trading more size and staying in the trade longer, in contrast to the virtually risk-free trade of the past.

Several minutes later, CSCO is trading up to 17.45. Now, the trader can act as a market maker and use any of the ECNs to sell 1000 shares of CSCO at the offer price of 17.45. For example, the trader may use ISLD to display its offer as shown in Figure 10.4. If the momentum continues, then the trader will sell the shares and make six cents in several minutes. For 1000 shares, the profit will be $60 minus commissions.

| CSCO | 17.45↑ | Chg | -1.16 | Lst Trd | 1000 |
|------|--------|-----|-------|---------|------|
| Close | 18.61 | Bid | 17.44 | Ask | 17.45 |
| Open | 17.92 | High | 18.00 | Low | 17.07 |

| GSCO | 17.44 | 10 | MSCO | 17.45 | 10 |
|------|-------|-----|------|-------|-----|
| ISLD | 17.44 | 72 | ISLD | 17.45 | 44 |
| SCHB | 17.44 | 33 | COWN | 17.45 | 10 |
| SBSH | 17.44 | 10 | MLCO | 17.45 | 10 |
| REDI | 17.44 | 10 | SBSH | 17.45 | 10 |
| MLCO | 17.43 | 10 | REDI | 17.46 | 10 |
| COWN | 17.42 | 10 | NFSC | 17.46 | 10 |
| MSCO | 17.42 | 10 | GSCO | 17.46 | 10 |

**Figure 10.4.** Level II Snapshot 3

Suppose that the momentum stalls before the trader is able to sell the shares. Further, the Level II window shows that market makers are lowering their bids and/or offers. If momentum is reversing, then the trader should be able to sell at the best bid price, in this case at 17.44.

### 10.2.4 Case Study: ImClone Systems

The case of ImClone Systems (IMCL:Nasdaq) is an example of combining news and tracking market maker movement to predict price direction. The company was expecting the FDA to approve its cancer drug Erbitux before the end of calendar year 2001. The stock had been sliding from the seventies into the fifties near the end of December. On the morning of December 27th, a Merrill Lynch analyst issued the following comments regarding the drug's approval:

> It's "not uncommon" for companies to be asked for more information about their drugs and the analyst said Erbitux still appears to be headed for approval in the coming year. "We believe that over the next six months ImClone will have its file activated and we expect the product to be approved in 2002."

Given that Merrill Lynch is a top market maker by volume in ImClone, the logical step was to monitor the market maker MLCO on the Level II window. Most direct access software lets the trader highlight market makers or ECNs in the Level II window. The trader can learn much by observing the actions of a highlighted key market maker.

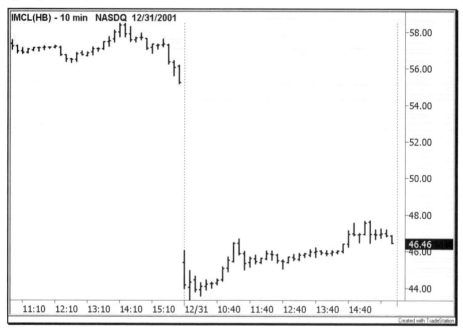

**Figure 10.5.** ImClone Intraday

At approximately 3:30 pm on the Friday afternoon of December 28th, Merrill Lynch went low offer on IMCL. For the next thirty minutes until the closing bell, MLCO remained on the best offer. As ECNs rushed to step in front of MLCO to sell shares, the market maker aggressively lowered its offer price to sell stock. The price plummeted several points over the last three bars, as shown in Figure 10.5.

> Then, with the whir of a fax machine in ImClone's offices on Dec. 28, the FDA's letter arrived, rejecting the ballyhooed Erbitux trial and casting doubt over the drug's future.          *Wall Street Journal, February 7, 2002*

At 7:14 pm that evening, ImClone announced that the FDA had decided not to accept the filing for the Erbitux application. On Monday morning, January 31st, IMCL opened at 45.39, down 9.86 points from Friday's closing price (refer to Figure 10.6). An investor may have been inclined to listen to the analyst's positive comments for guidance and buy the stock, but the astute trader lets price do the talking and typically does the opposite of the investor.

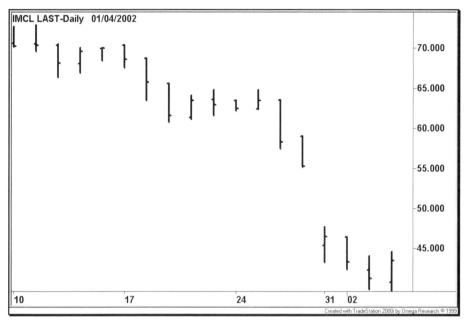

**Figure 10.6.** ImClone Daily

As shown in the ImClone example, Level II trading is not about plopping in front of the screen and hitting hot keys. Use the technology and combine it with market knowledge to exploit unique trading opportunities. Further, use other data sources to refine your understanding of any given stock and understand its pattern of trading.

The Nasdaq Market Data Web site offers detailed data reports such as the Market Maker Price Movement Report and the Time and Sales Report; these are daily replays of Level II price movements and trade history, respectively. Order a few of these reports and track a stock's price movement throughout the entire trading day.

### 10.2.5 Case Study: Comverse Technology

The following example illustrates the power of tape reading—no multi-colored screens or multiple time frame charting. We think a trader just starting out should sit down in front of the television, tune into CNBC, and then hit the mute button. For the next few days, the trader should just read the tape, watching the ticker scroll across the bottom of the screen.

As the symbols pass by, certain patterns begin to emerge. Focus on the trades in ten thousand share blocks and higher, e.g., 10K, 20K, 50K, etc. Then note whether the trades are printed in green (up ticks) or red (down ticks). The usual large-cap suspects will appear on the tape. Newsworthy stocks will appear as well, but we want to focus on those stocks with no apparent news, so review the morning news to eliminate the known ones. This skill becomes second nature with experience.

On July 9th and July 10th, 2001, several casual glances at the ticker revealed some unusual activity in Comverse Technology. Large blocks of CMVT were crossing the tape, and no news had been released about the company. All of the trades were at least 10000 shares in size, and all of the trades were occurring on down ticks.

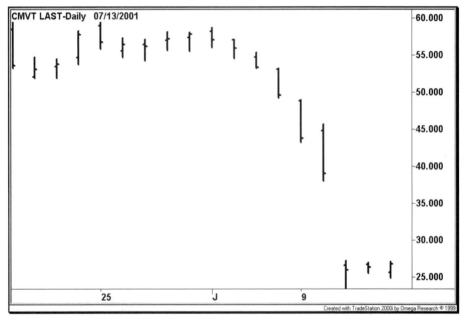

**Figure 10.7.** Comverse Technology

On July 10th, Comverse announced that they were cutting earnings estimates for the next two years. The stock gapped down over twelve points that morning (Figure 10.7). In retrospect, one wonders whether or not anyone knew about these cuts ahead of the announcement (tongue planted firmly in cheek). One month later, investment houses upgraded the stock (tongue deeply embedded).

In the following sections, we show the trader how to analyze stocks based on their block volume, and explore how to detect unusual trading volume in small-cap stocks. As with our trading systems, we want to analyze the market from as many perspectives as possible.

## 10.2.6 Case Study: OSCA Inc.

In early 2002, OSCA had an average daily volume of 85,000 shares. Then, on February 19th, the average daily volume was exceeded at 9:55 am, in the absence of news. After spiking up to 22, the stock pulled back to 20 and then slowly gained ground for the rest of the day on heavy volume. At 2:30 pm, the price spiked back to 22, where it closed on the day (Figure 10.8).

The various news organizations had picked up stories of acquisition rumors throughout the afternoon, but an average volume filter detected this unusual movement early in the morning. The formula is easy: calculate the average daily volume of the stock for the past twenty days; we want to focus on illiquid stocks with average daily volumes of between fifty to two hundred thousand shares. Then, compare the volume of the current trading day to the highest volume of the past sixty days to see if volume is tracking higher.

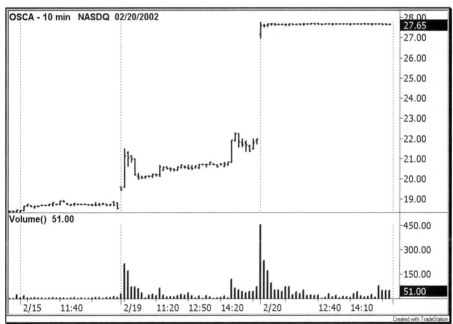

**Figure 10.8.** OSCA, Inc.

Example 10.1 is an example of a FirstAlert filter for detecting unusual volume in a low-capitalization stock:

**Example 10.1.** Unusual Volume Filter

```
#1 Volume > (VolHigh60 d% 1)
#2 Volume > 30000
#3 VolAvg20 > 50000
#4 VolAvg20 < 200000
```

## 10.3 Day Trading Techniques

Day trading is simply the application of technical analysis to a smaller time frame. To illustrate this point, consider the *Money Flow Index*, or MFI. The MFI formula uses the high, low, close, and volume of a bar to calculate a value known as *Money Flow*, or MF. If the MF of the current bar is greater than the MF of the previous bar, then money is flowing into the stock; a declining MF implies that money is flowing out of the stock. Without getting into the details of the calculation, clearly the MFI can be calculated on any kind of bar – daily or intraday. Figure 10.9 shows a divergence on a daily chart of Ciena.

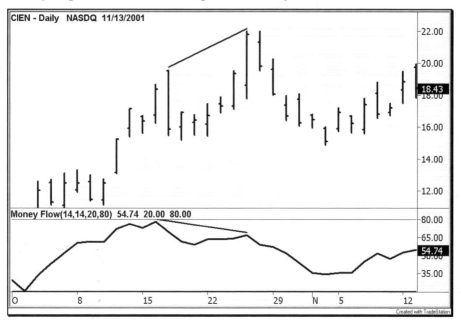

**Figure 10.9.** Daily Money Flow

On the intraday chart shown in Figure 10.10, Ciena gapped up on the morning of November 13th, creating a divergence between its price and the MFI. The declining MFI from the previous day was a signal to sell short Ciena on the open. Here, the strategy for the trader is to locate stocks gapping in either direction before the opening bell and filter them with the MFI from the previous day to identify divergence patterns.

The chief objective is to combine the tools provided by the direct access software (e.g., gap scanning) with traditional technical analysis to identify high probability price patterns. Direct access software makers are just beginning to add other filters and built-in scans to complement their charting features.

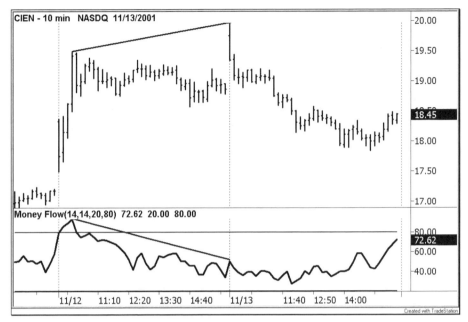

**Figure 10.10.** Intraday Money Flow

## 10.3.1 Gap Trading

As discussed in Chapter 2, gaps are critical to strategies such as pair trading. Successful day trading requires mastery of the gap, and while gaps can result in fast profits, they are the source of major trading mistakes. The first mistake is the bargain complex discussed in Chapter 6. Just as investors are attracted to falling prices, traders are attracted to stocks that gap down. A key to trading down gaps is to distinguish between stocks that are gapping because of news affecting the whole market or because of news about the company itself.

The other key to trading gaps is to wait for confirmation. The temptation is always there to scoop up a stock before the market opens because the price appears cheap. If the stock has bad news and is cheap at 8:30 am, then it will probably be cheaper at 9:30. Wait until the last possible minute to assess the direction of the stock before the market opens.

Remember that the gap price reflects all of the known information about the stock. The point is not to dwell on the fact that the price was 58 yesterday and now 55. The trader wants to wait for others to commit themselves and then take a trade in whichever direction price leads him or her. Let the stock establish its range, and then wait for any breakout. This technique is known as an *opening range breakout* [6].

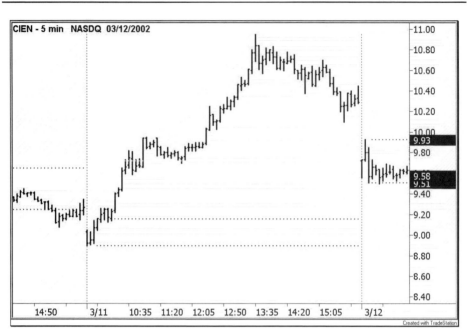

**Figure 10.11.** Ciena Opening Range Breakout

On March 11th, Ciena gapped down and established an opening range between 8.90 and 9.16, as shown in Figure 10.11. At 9:55 am, the stock broke through the upper band of the opening range, rallying for most of the day. The advantage of using an opening range breakout (ORB) is that the risk is bounded by the distance between the upper and lower band (9.16 − 8.90) = 0.26 points. The reward is defined by the trader's choice of exit technique, e.g., a moving average crossover or ATR-based profit target.

As spreads have narrowed, gaps have become increasingly important to the market maker. When spreads were wider, the market maker made most of his profits from the spread by buying at the bid and selling at the offer. As spreads in large-cap stocks have virtually dried up, the profit potential has shifted from spread trading to position trading.

A market maker trading a gap is similar to the specialist on the NYSE handling an order imbalance. A market maker buying shares from an institutional seller is taking the other side of the trade and has an interest in buying these shares as cheaply as possible. Thus, the collective objective is to create a gap as wide as possible before the open and then wait for a counter-move to sell the shares. Barring any disastrous news, a counter-move will occur most of the time in the first few minutes of trading, no matter how abbreviated.

Another effective gap strategy is gap continuation trading. This strategy is explored in Section 10.3.2.

## 10.3.2 Continuation Trading

We define *continuation* trading as the connection between the last hour of one trading day and the first hour of the following trading day. Stocks that move in either direction the last hour of a session tend to continue in the same direction the following morning. A stock will lie dormant all day, trend into the closing bell, and then follow through the next day, barring a major gap. Continuation patterns fall into three general categories:

❑  Gap Continuation

❑  News Continuation

❑  Breakout Continuation

### *Gaps*

*Gap continuation* is the strategy of finding gaps in strongly trending stocks that are created by general market conditions, not by company-specific news. For example, if futures are weak and a stock in a strong up trend gaps down, then we want to buy that stock before the open. Similarly, if the futures are strong and a weak stock gaps up, then we want to go short (refer to Table 10.2).

**Table 10.2.** Gap Continuation Strategy

| Futures | Stock Gap | Stock Trend | Trade |
|---------|-----------|-------------|-------|
| Down | Down | Up | Buy |
| Up | Up | Down | Sell Short |

Gap continuation is a relative strength strategy. Just as a lioness hunts for the weakest prey under good conditions, the trader is looking for the weakest stock when futures are strong. Examine the price percentage gainers and losers from the previous day in addition to stocks with strong percentage increases or decreases over the past few days, filtering out those stocks with light volume. If the futures are up strongly, then check each of the price percentage losers to see if any of them are gapping up. Likewise, if the futures are down strongly, check the percentage gainers for down gaps.

On March 20th, 2002, the Nasdaq futures opened down over twenty points. While the Nasdaq was in a downtrend, Panera (**PNRA:Nasdaq**) was in an uptrend, as shown in Figure 10.12. That morning, Panera gapped down to 62.76, down 63 cents from the previous day's close of 63.39. By the end of the day, the Nasdaq Composite Index closed down over fifty points, while Panera closed almost two points above the open at 64.70.

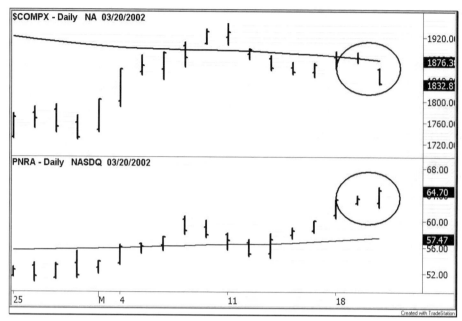

**Figure 10.12.** Panera Bread Gap Continuation

## News

When a company reports earnings after the bell, the perception of its earnings is altered by the tone of the market during the day. If a company reports good earnings but the market was down on the day, then people will tend to find a troubling element in the earnings report that sends the stock down after the bell. The odds are in favor of the stock trading even lower the following morning, but its opening price is subject to the opinion of analysts who will issue upgrades or downgrades. Analysts being only human, their comments echo the sentiment of the market, and everyone piles on[2].

**Table 10.3.** News Continuation Strategy

| Market Tone | Earnings | Morning Gap | Earnings | Morning Gap |
|-------------|----------|-------------|----------|-------------|
| Bullish | Positive | Strong Up | Negative | Down |
| Bearish | Positive | Up | Negative | Strong Down |
| Neutral | Positive | Up | Negative | Down |

---

[2] The Market Vane Bullish Consensus confirms this fact—a person's perception of the market rises and falls with market action.

Table 10.3 shows the impact of market tone upon a company's earnings report. The issue is how the trader uses this information to establish a position. When a company reports its earnings, unless the stock is halted for news pending, the price develops in two stages. First, the stock reacts to the earnings number. The company beats, meets, or misses its number[3], and within minutes the stock finds its new price level. Then, the waiting game begins for the company conference call, a game of corporate spin. Unless the company mentions forward guidance in its earnings report, people will be eagerly awaiting that guidance during the call. When the guidance is released, the stock finds its second price level (refer to Section 10.4.5 on trading after the bell).

Because the actions of analysts can be unpredictable, the news continuation strategy should be traded only when the market tone and earnings tone match. If the market tone is bullish and earnings guidance is positive, then the stock should be bought after-hours. In contrast, if the market tone is bearish and earnings guidance is negative, then the stock should be shorted after-hours. Bear in mind that the stock price has absorbed most of the news already, so the difference in price between the after-hours close and next morning's open will not be nearly as large as the gap between the regular market close and the open.

The trader is simply trying to wring out an extra point or two because the emotional market participants will be eager to bail out or bolster their position early on the following morning, and there will be added pressure on the stock in the direction of the after-hours move. Even in instances where the market tone is neutral, a bullish earnings report will generally get a slight bump up from the after-hours close the next day.

The same principle applies to other news released after hours, such as a new contract announcement or an SEC investigation. On November 28th, 2001, at 4:15 pm, the United States government announced a $428 million contract for a smallpox vaccine to Acambis (**ACAM:Nasdaq**). The stock closed near 38 and traded up to the low 40's after-hours. Watching the stock rise over three points within minutes, we decided not to take the trade.

The following day, Acambis opened above 48–it had traded as high as 50 before the open. At the time, if we had known the float of the stock were less than 8 million shares, then the trade would have been more appealing. Clearly, the magnitude of the gap is directly related to the significance of the news and the capitalization of the stock. The enterprising trader should be able to develop general trading guidelines by studying the interaction between news and stock float. Figure 10.13 shows the intraday chart of Acambis preceding the contract announcement. Notice the subtle signs of accumulation beginning on the afternoon of November 27th and the expanding session width of the 5-minute chart.

---

[3] Certain companies always seem to beat their earnings estimate by one penny per share. We are currently in the era of managed earnings and creative accounting, but this too shall pass.

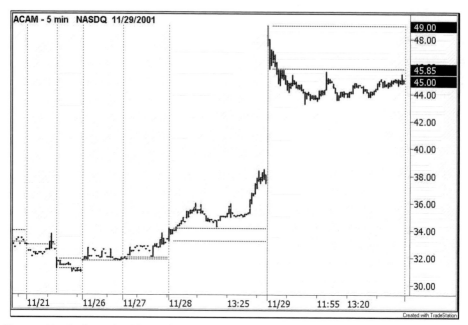

**Figure 10.13.** Acambis News Continuation

### Breakouts

The *breakout continuation* is a two-day pattern. On Day One, the stock must consolidate the entire day until later in the afternoon. Then, one or two hours before the closing bell, the stock trends strongly in either direction. This is an example of a pent-up move that will probably continue on Day Two, unlike a stock that trends all day on Day One and continues into Day Two. The strategy is a simple application of the alternation principle that a trending day follows a non-trending day, but the key is to recognize the beginning of the trend phase late in the afternoon of a predominantly flat day.

The breakout continuation is a pattern for real-time scanning programs such as FirstAlert. The breakout follows the pattern principle of a rectangle, where the rectangle height of the breakout period is compared to a smaller range height for a longer time frame preceding the rectangle. In this case, we divide the trading day into half-hour intervals, so the trading day has a total of thirteen intervals. Since we scan for a breakout during the last two hours of the trading day, we want to calculate the ratio of the range height of the last four thirty-minute intervals divided by the range height of the previous nine thirty-minute intervals, e.g., a ratio of 2:1 or 3:1. Further, the height of the reference range must be narrow, as little as 10%-20% of the stock's ATR. Figure 10.14 shows a breakout continuation for Rambus (**RMBS:Nasdaq**).

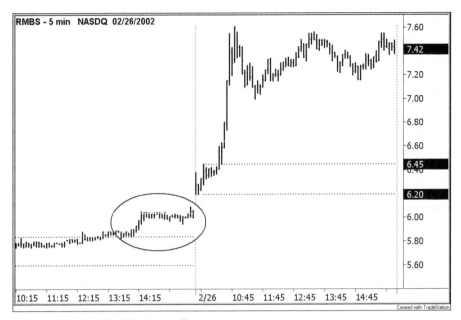

**Figure 10.14.** Rambus Breakout Continuation

### 10.3.3 Block Trading

Previously, we presented some examples of how block trade analysis can detect unusual activity in a stock. Before we explore the mechanics of this technique further, let's compare the average block trade with the average trade size for the Nasdaq stock market. As shown in Table 10.4, the average block size is over twenty thousand shares, but remember that a trade qualifies as a block only in the context of a stock's average daily volume (ADV).

For example, if the ADV of one stock is 100,000 shares, then a trade of 5000 shares could be considered a block trade. For a stock with an ADV of one million shares, then trades of 25K and 50K would be considered block trades. For stocks such as Cisco Systems with an ADV of millions of shares, blocks become more difficult to interpret.

**Table 10.4.** Nasdaq Block Size

| Year | Average Trade Size | Average Block Size |
|------|--------------------|--------------------|
| 1999 | 800                | 20,000             |
| 2000 | 700                | 22,000             |
| 2001 | 800                | 24,000             |

One accepted truism of day trading is that large blocks signal a trend reversal. This concept has appeal because a large block to be sold will temporarily force down the price. A trader who is alerted to a large block on the tape may be able to ride the momentum back up; however, this type of trade has two problems. First, by the time the "print" occurs in Time & Sales, the stock may have already reversed because Nasdaq members have up to ninety seconds after execution to report transactions; thus, the print can be delayed. Second, the trader has no idea whether or not another large block is coming down the pipe.

Without any insight as to order flow, fading a block trade may not be worth the risk. Only the participant with access to order flow can buy or sell ahead. A trader of NYSE stocks subscribing to the OpenBook service (released January 24th, 2002) can view the specialist's limit order book from 7:30 am to 4:30 pm. Here, the trader can develop a sense of the technical levels that may be breached and anticipate any movement towards those areas.

The key to block trading is to measure the frequency of certain block sizes across the spectrum of market capitalization. If a large block needs to be bought or sold for a small-cap stock, then the probability is greater that the block is a one-off, and the trader may be able to participate in a reversal. We recommend that the trader set up a group of separate tickers, segregated by ADV to display only those trades that meet the minimum block size. Table 10.5 shows sample block sizes sorted by ADV.

**Table 10.5.** Volume-Based Block Size

| ADV Range | | Block Size |
|---|---|---|
| 50,000 – | 200,000 | 2,000 |
| 200,000 – | 500,000 | 5,000 |
| 500,000 – | 1,000,000 | 7,000 |
| 1,000,000 – | 2,000,000 | 10,000 |
| 2,000,000 – | 10,000,000 | 25,000 |

We caution the trader not to place too much emphasis on a single block trade. People seem to get excited about seeing a large print above the offer if they are long or a large print below the bid if they are short. The isolated print serves only as a psychological boost to the nervous trader, who should probably not be in that position if he or she is dwelling on every tick and consulting the oracle of the Yahoo board. More importantly, examine a string of block trades to see how many were executed on downticks and how many on up ticks. The trader is simply trying to assess trend and possibly impending news. When a low-cap stock suddenly shows up on the ticker, then that is a sign to get involved.

### 10.3.4 Spread Trading

When spreads were wider in the fractional days, spread trading was an activity best reserved for the market maker. Still, a trader could "play market maker" in a liquid stock by simultaneously placing a buy order at the best bid price and a sell order at the best offer price using an ECN such as the Island. For example, if a stock were trading at 40 ¼ x 41, then a trader could bid the stock at 40 5/16 and offer it at 40 15/16 – there may have been a seller and buyer who were willing to take advantage of the better prices given by the spread trader.

Unfortunately, for stocks with wide spreads, the trader with no knowledge of order flow is a sitting duck. If a trader's bid is hit, then it probably happened for one reason – the stock is going down, and the trader still has an offer to sell his or her shares. Now, other market participants see that the bid was hit, and start going low offer. In an attempt to sell the shares, the trader goes low offer as well, cutting the spread and sowing the seeds of the stock's demise. The trader will be lucky to get out of the trade without a loss.

Currently, the spreads are as narrow as possible, so unless the practice can be automated, spread trading is intense and is not the best use of the trader's time. A large-cap stock such as Cisco trades with a penny spread. To make money on the spread, the commission costs must be factored into both sides of the spread trade. For example, if the commission is $10, then the total cost of the trade is $20, one trade for the bid and one trade for the offer. At least 2100 shares must be spread (2100 × $0.01 = $21 - $20 = $1) to make any profit at all. Even with a stock such as Cisco, a price jump could move the stock twenty or thirty cents, and all of a sudden, the trader has risked several hundred dollars to make a buck, converting a spread trade into a position trade.

Spread trading has been subsumed almost entirely within the domain of the computer. For the large-cap stocks, many of the ECNs are lined up on either side of the Level II window with thousands of shares displayed on the screen. Traders that used to watch the volatility on the Level II screen are now forced to watch as automated programs swap hundreds of thousands of shares before any appreciable price movement. The free-flowing volatility of the past has evolved into a pattern of tight consolidations alternating with sudden price shocks.

So far, we have covered the following day trading techniques:

❑   Gap Trading

❑   Continuation Trading

❑   Block Trading

❑   Spread Trading

Next, we examine the intraday market cycle.

## 10.4 The Trading Day

The stock market is expanding on either end of the day, a natural extension into round-the-clock trading. Assuming a 24-hour trading day, we divide the day into five natural segments as shown in Table 10.6.

**Table 10.6.** Trading Day Segments

| Segment | Time Period |
|---|---|
| Before the Bell | 08:00 pm – 09:30 am EST |
| The Open | 09:30 am – 11:00 am |
| Lunch Hour[4] | 11:00 am – 02:00 pm |
| The Close | 02:00 pm – 04:00 pm |
| After the Bell | 04:00 pm – 08:00 pm |

The time period in the first row is not a typographical error. The new trading day starts just after the close of after-hours trading at 08:00 pm, putting us on the 24-hour cycle. One may question our designation of the Open and Close segments with their expanded time frames, but they serve to delineate the time periods when trades are entered. New trading positions between 11:00 am and 02:00 pm are rare.

### 10.4.1 Before the Bell

The period before the bell is divided into two phases:

- ❑ Research phase (08:00 pm – 08:00 am)
- ❑ Trading phase (08:00 am – 09:30 am)

The research phase–the process of downloading price data, scanning charts, and selecting stocks is discussed in Chapter 9. The trader should have all of this work done before trading begins at 08:00 am, although some traders prefer not to trade either before or after the bell, in which case the trader can hit the snooze button. Use the time before the opening bell to set up charts, enter alerts, and scan for gaps. The trader may also have other research services and publications to review beforehand. Finally, any remaining time can be spent laughing at the guys on Squawk Box[5].

---

[4] Lunch is three hours, one for each martini.
[5] Squawk Box is the morning program on CNBC business television.

*Fair Value*

It is a daily morning ritual for some traders – the business section, coffee, and the futures check. One of the first things to do is flip on the television and get the latest S&P futures quote displayed in the lower-right hand corner of the screen. This quote, also known as the *S&P bug*, shows the positive or negative change from yesterday's S&P 500 futures contract close.

The purpose of watching the S&P futures in the morning is to assess the general direction of stocks because futures are a leading indicator of stock prices. Unless the futures are very strong (e.g., greater than +5.00 or less than –5.00), then the market open will be difficult to predict. As a trader eventually learns, a positive futures change does not imply a strong opening, and a negative futures change does not imply a weak opening. This price discrepancy is explained by the trading concept known as *fair value*.

Fair value[6] is an estimate of what an S&P 500 futures contract is worth; it is a formula that factors in borrowing costs and dividends. Fair value is computed at the end of each trading day to compare with the actual futures price. Before the market opens, the S&P futures serve as a market proxy, digesting any news to trade above or below fair value. For example, a bullish economic release at 8:30 am will send the futures soaring beyond their fair value. The key point is to know where futures are trading relative to fair value. Some business channels such as CNBC display this value before the opening bell.

Market commentators always give their perception of a strong open or weak open for the market. For now, hit the mute button to make your own determination. First, calculate the net change for the S&P futures from yesterday's close. This value is displayed with a "+" or "-" point value on the television screen. For example, if the S&P futures are +2.50, then the futures are trading two and a half points higher in the morning trading session. Then, get the fair value displayed on the screen; this value is also displayed as a "+" or "-" point value. For example, if fair value is "-6.00", then futures closed six points above fair value yesterday. If the fair value is "+6.00", then the futures closed six points below fair value yesterday.

Now, compare the current S&P futures quote against fair value to determine how the market is going to open this morning. Simply subtract the fair value number (F) from the S&P futures quote (S). A positive number indicates a bias to the upside; a negative number indicates a downside bias; and zero means that the market will open flat. Some sample combinations of fair value and futures are shown in Table 10.7.

---

[6] The Nasdaq Stock Market computes an estimate of the open called the *Pre-Market Indicator*, or PMI. The PMI is calculated for the Nasdaq 100 from 08:15 to 09:30 am.

**Table 10.7.** Fair Value

| S&P Futures (S) | Fair Value (F) | (S) – (F) | Market Opening |
|:---:|:---:|:---:|:---:|
| +5.00 | +1.00 | +4.00 | Up |
| +2.00 | +6.00 | -4.00 | Down |
| -2.00 | -4.00 | +2.00 | Up |
| -6.00 | +7.00 | -13.00 | Down |
| -2.50 | -2.50 | 0.00 | Neutral |
| +4.50 | -3.50 | +8.00 | Up |

Most of the time, the fair value is a small number, and the S&P futures quote by itself is an indication of how the market will open. Do not make this assumption, however – always check the fair value delta (S) – (F). Still, the S&P futures close at 09:15 am, and stocks continue to trade during the fifteen minutes before the market opens, so even this figure can be misleading.

Once we have made an assessment of the general market, we turn to the subject of individual stock picking. If the market bias is up, then we focus on our long selections. If the market bias is down, then we focus on the shorts. With our stock selections in place from last night's analysis, we want to review each of these stocks for any news before the opening bell.

### Case Study: Ciena

Companies are revising their earnings guidance on an increasingly regular basis, with an attendant rise in the number of conference calls being held before and after market hours. Depending on the severity of the news, the stock may or may not be halted. Companies with bad news are more likely to be halted than companies with good news, so companies with good news create more opportunity for traders.

The problem with trading halts is that news does not go through the normal dissemination process, so when a stock reopens for trading, it will gap and find its equilibrium almost immediately, similar to a specialist delaying the opening of a stock until the imbalance can be resolved (unless the stock is halted, there may be some liquidity on the ECNs for an NYSE stock).

One company, Ciena (CIEN:Nasdaq), has held several morning conference calls, creating opportunity for the early bird trader. On November 12th, 2001, Ciena held a conference call before the bell to update its guidance. The positive news sent Ciena from a price of 17.18 to well over 18 at the open, as shown in

Figure 10.15. Trading was never halted in the stock, so a trader listening to the conference call could have gotten in immediately.

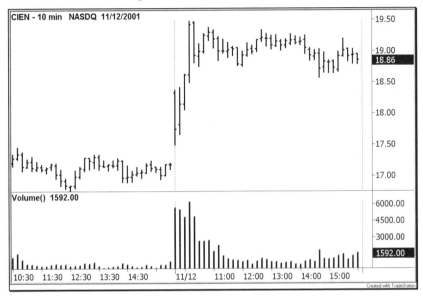

**Figure 10.15.** Ciena: November 12, 2001

Ciena's conference call that was held on February 5th, 2002, was a warning. The stock was halted for almost one hour. Note the opening counter-move from the gap down in Figure 10.16.

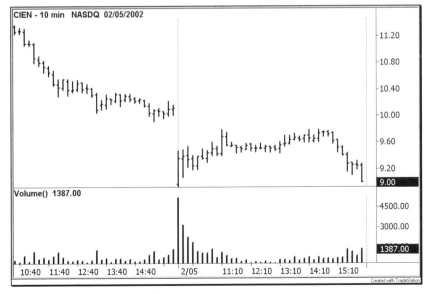

**Figure 10.16.** Ciena: February 5, 2002

Another source of critical data before the bell are the government's economic reports released at 08:30 am, such as the following:

❑ Non-Farm Payrolls
❑ Gross Domestic Product (GDP)
❑ Factory Orders
❑ Consumer Price Index (CPI)
❑ Producer Price Index (PPI)

On the dates of these key government reports, either avoid trading before 08:30 am or wait until after the report is released. Further, do not trade off these data except for a fade – the reaction to these numbers is usually unpredictable and characterized by zigzags. The whole point of professional trading is to eliminate as much uncertainty as possible, not to place one's capital on black or red.

## 10.4.2 The Open

The worst time for an investor to buy stock is at the open (once the investing public catches on, this will change because conventional wisdom translates into lighter wallets). Conversely, the open is usually the best time for the trader to sell a long position and initiate a short position[7]. In his *Stock Trader's Almanac*, Hirsch plots the performance of the market by percentage each half-hour of the day [16]. For the period between January 1987 and December 2000, the market rose 52.8% of the time on the open.

The market rarely sprints from the open because even in the case of exceptionally good or bad news, the market needs time to digest the offsetting orders just after the opening bell. Thus, the market will spend from fifteen minutes to one hour settling into a range before committing to a certain direction[8]. At this point, either the long signals or short signals for the swing trades are going to start firing, giving an indication as to the direction of the market. As the open develops, the trader builds up his or her portfolio of positions and lets price do the rest. When the market is split, both long and short signals will trigger. This is the optimal scenario.

The cutoff for new signals is 11:00 am. Even 11:00 am is a little late to take signals because the major trend decision of the market will almost always be made within the first hour of the trading day.

---

[7] In its treatment of holding period, the Acme Trade Manager subtracts one day from the holding period and then exits a long position the following day on the open. Statistically, this technique provides a real edge.

[8] Other influential economic reports are released between 09:30 and 10:00 am EST, such as the ISM index (manufacturing) and the Michigan Consumer Sentiment Survey.

### 10.4.3 Lunch Hour

For obvious reasons, the trader should focus on the open and close, while avoiding lunch hour. Market makers like to eat day traders for lunch. Still, companies have been known to slip in news announcements with traders on siesta, creating a scramble (refer to the Tyco example in Chapter 9).

By definition, the lunch hour is a time for consolidation, so many rectangles and triangles set up during this period. Scan for stocks and sectors that trended strongly in the morning and that are poised to continue in the afternoon (e.g., percentage gainers or losers). Use the rectangle[9] to predict market direction for the afternoon.

During lunch, the worst action a trader can take is to buy a stock that is up on the day in anticipation that it will resume its upward move in the afternoon (see the Rambus example in Chapter 5). Wait for a confirmation before taking any long trades because the 01:30 and 02:00 pm half-hour periods are the worst performing market intervals [16].

### 10.4.4 The Close

In general, the intraday trend is persistent, i.e., the morning trend will usually resume in the afternoon. Intraday V patterns are rare except for certain days of the week (Chapter 6). Beginning at 02:00 pm, the trader should be looking for reversal patterns to assess whether or not the morning trend will resume. If a rectangle forms, then the breakout of the rectangle will dictate whether or not the position should be covered or maintained.

To exit long positions or initiate new short positions, look for "M" tops. To exit short positions and enter long positions, look for "W" bottoms. Combine these patterns with Bollinger Bands to maximize trading profits near highs and lows of the day [1]. The circled areas in Figures 10.17 and 10.18 show examples of M top and W bottom patterns, respectively.

The reversal pattern is a great tool because it serves two functions. First, it protects the trader from giving back the bulk of any profits attained during the day. Second, it frees the trader's capital for other strategies that trigger towards the end of the day. Furthermore, the reversal pattern is the only other decision point for determining whether or not to stay in a position until the rest of the day (in addition to the profit target and stop loss).

Do not be anxious to cover short positions for rallies that occur early in the close period. Rallies around 02:00 pm tend to fizzle, while rallies starting closer

---

[9] The rectangle is a geometric pattern covered in Chapter 5. Use other patterns such as the "M" top and "W" bottom to detect reversals as well [1].

to 03:00 pm are more successful (47.9% versus 53.7%). Exaggerated moves occur in the last fifteen minutes of the trading day.

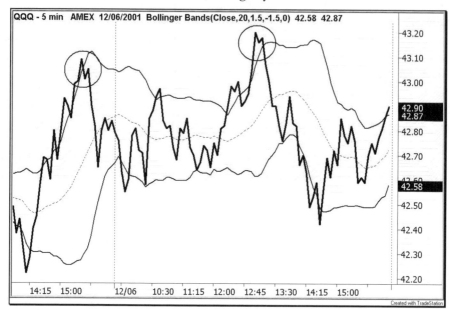

**Figure 10.17.** M Tops with Bollinger Bands

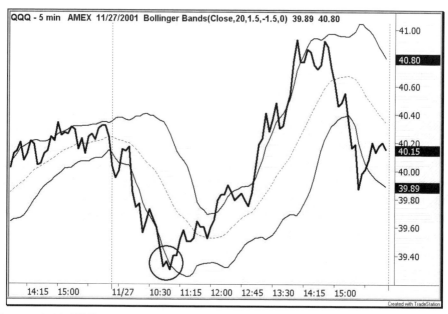

**Figure 10.18.** W Bottom with Bollinger Bands

## 10.4.5 After the Bell

Welcome to the money pit. Trading stocks after the bell is the Tombstone of trading[10]. It is a game of firepower, so traders with small accounts are advised to holster their mouse. As with any trading rule, however, there are exceptions. Here, we discuss two strategies where the odds are tilted in the trader's favor. Both are news-driven strategies and should be used in exceptional cases.

### Earnings

Previously, we discussed the impact of market tone upon a company's earnings report and explained the News Continuation strategy. Most earnings reports are released shortly after 4:00 pm, with a conference call beginning around 5:00 pm. The most important advice we can give about earnings is to keep your finger on the trigger and an ear to the conference call. Do not trade the stock blindly with a Level II window unless you know exactly what is happening during the conference call, unless trading is your substitute for craps.

A trader with direct access usually can jump on a stock as soon as forward guidance is announced. By the time others have touched the keypad on their mobile phones, one can quickly establish a small position in a stock, albeit with some degree of slippage; however, as with any other trading position, there are no guarantees. This strategy is designed for the trader with direct access, quick fingers, and hot keys.

### News

Every major newspaper has an online evening edition that includes stories to be released in the print edition the following day. Typically, these stories appear in the online edition after 6 pm, so a trader aware of an important story about a public company may be able to capitalize on this news after the bell.

The effect is especially dramatic when a small-cap company is profiled in a technology or science section of newspapers such as the Wall Street Journal, the New York Times, and Investor's Business Daily. On October 8th, 2001, the evening edition of the New York Times profiled a small biotechnology company named Cepheid (CPHD:Nasdaq) in the midst of the anthrax crisis. The stock had closed at 4.40, but quickly climbed above five in the evening as news of the Times story spread. The following morning, the stock gapped up to 6.70, over 50% from the close (Figure 10.19).

---

[10] Tombstone, Arizona is the home of the Gunfight at the OK Corral. The city is also the home of Boothill Cemetery, plotted in 1878. One of its more famous epitaphs is: "Here lies Lester Moore, Four Slugs from a 44, No Les No More."

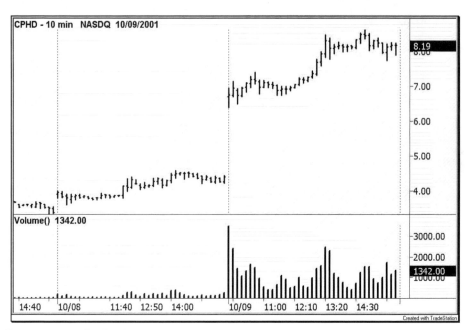

**Figure 10.19.** Cepheid

# 11 Source Code

*The bitter and the sweet*
*Come from the outside,*
*The hard from within,*
*from one's own efforts.*

Albert Einstein, *Out of My Later Years*

The history of trading is a pyramid of knowledge that has been constructed over the past century. From Livermore to Gann to Edwards and Magee, only time will tell which of the modern-day technicians will be mentioned in the same breath. The important point to remember is that trading is a collective effort in the sense that one draws inspiration from many sources. This book is a synthesis of many who have contributed to the body of work in technical analysis.

The evolution of trading software has been a catalyst for developing new prototypes of technical analysis in a short period of time, especially with the development of programming languages designed specifically for trading.

All of the source code here is written in EasyLanguage, a language for technical analysis and trade management. The code was originally written for the TradeStation 2000*i* platform, but can be imported into TradeStation 6. Note the difference in signal names in Table 11.1 between the TradeStation 2000*i* platform and the TradeStation 6 platform:

**Table 11.1.** TradeStation Signal Names

| Signal | TradeStation 2000i | TradeStation 6 |
|---|---|---|
| Long Entry | Buy | Buy |
| Short Entry | Sell | Sell Short |
| Long Exit | ExitLong | Sell |
| Short Exit | ExitShort | Buy To Cover |

## 11.1 Inventory

All of the EasyLanguage code is grouped by function and roughly by chapter. Start with the Money Management code because it is the foundation for the rest of the code. Then, choose the system(s) to build. After the files have been created, verify the entire Acme code base, selecting the appropriate signal names in Table 11.1 based on the platform.

If using the TradeStation 2000*i* and TradeStation 6 platforms, create the source code using the PowerEditor, verify the source, and then export all of the code with the Acme prefix to an ELS archive file. Finally, import the archive into TradeStation 6 for automatic conversion.

> The EasyLanguage code in this chapter is based on TradeStation 2000*i*. If using TradeStation 6, the signal names *Sell*, *ExitLong*, and *ExitShort* must be replaced with the signals *SellShort*, *Sell*, and *BuyToCover*, respectively.

### 11.1.1 Web Site

A professional CD-ROM product containing the source code in this book can be purchased in EasyLanguage archive file format from the Acme Trader Web site at http://www.acmetrader.com. The product can simply be installed into TradeStation, and the trader can then open pre-defined workspaces provided on the CD-ROM.

### 11.1.2 Money Management

**Table 11.2.** Money Management Modules

| Name | Type | Description |
|------|------|-------------|
| Acme HV | Indicator | Display the historic volatility of an instrument |
| Acme Trade Manager | Signal | Set stops and profit targets |
| AcmeEntryTargets | Function | Plot the entry points for stop and limit orders |
| AcmeExitTargets | Function | Plot the stop loss points and profit targets |
| AcmeGetShares | Function | Calculate the shares based on the risk model |
| AcmeLogTrades | Function | Log trades to a file for spreadsheet import |
| AcmeVolatility | Function | Calculate the historic volatility |

### 11.1.3 Geometric Trading

**Table 11.3.** Geometric Trading Modules

| Name | Type | Description |
| --- | --- | --- |
| Acme Double Bottom | Indicator | Draw a line forming a double bottom |
| Acme Double Top | Indicator | Draw a line forming a double top |
| Acme R Strategy | Strategy | R Signal with the Acme Trade Manager |
| Acme R System | Signal | Look for rectangle breakouts |
| Acme Rectangle | Indicator | Draw a rectangle |
| Acme Triangle | Indicator | Draw a triangle |
| Acme Triple Bottom | Indicator | Draw a line forming a triple bottom |
| Acme Triple Top | Indicator | Draw a line forming a triple top |
| AcmeDoubleBottom | Function | Find a double bottom formation |
| AcmeDoubleTop | Function | Find a double top formation |
| AcmeRectangular | Function | Is the current region a rectangle? |
| AcmeTripleBottom | Function | Find a triple bottom formation |
| AcmeTripleTop | Function | Find a triple top formation |

### 11.1.4 Market Models

**Table 11.4.** Market Model Modules

| Name | Type | Description |
| --- | --- | --- |
| Acme All Strategies | Strategy | Combination of F, M, N, R, and V strategies |
| Acme Market Model | Indicator | Label market sentiment patterns |
| Acme Market Strategy | Strategy | Market Signal with the Acme Trade Manager |
| Acme Market System | Signal | Look for multiple market sentiment patterns |
| AcmeHighLowIndex | Function | Check for an index confirmation |

## 11.1.5 Pair Trading

**Table 11.5.** Pair Trading Modules

| Name | Type | Description |
|---|---|---|
| Acme P Strategy | Strategy | P Signal (does not use Acme Trade Manager) |
| Acme P System | Signal | Pair trading system |
| Acme Spread | Indicator | Display the spread between two instruments |

## 11.1.6 Range Trading

**Table 11.6.** Range Trading Modules

| Name | Type | Description |
|---|---|---|
| Acme ID2 | PaintBar | Mark an inside day within an inside day |
| Acme IDNR | PaintBar | Mark inside day/narrow range combinations |
| Acme N Strategy | Strategy | N Signal with the Acme Trade Manager |
| Acme N System | Signal | Range ratio and narrow range pattern system |
| Acme NR | PaintBar | Mark the narrowest range in n bars |
| Acme NR% | PaintBar | Mark a narrow range bar based on % of ATR |
| Acme NR2 | PaintBar | Mark two consecutive narrow range bars |
| Acme Range Ratio | Indicator | Display the ratio of two bar ranges |
| AcmeInsideDay2 | Function | Search for two consecutive inside days |
| AcmeInsideDayNR | Function | Find an inside day/narrow range bar |
| AcmeNarrowRange | Function | Is the specified bar a narrow range bar? |
| AcmeRangePercent | Function | Calculate the range percentage over n bars |
| AcmeRangeRatio | Function | Calculate the range ratio |

## 11.1.7 Pattern Trading

**Table 11.7.** Pattern Trading Modules

| Name | Type | Description |
|---|---|---|
| Acme M Strategy | Strategy | M Signal with the Acme Trade Manager |
| Acme M System | Signal | Look for multiple pattern combinations |
| Acme Market Patterns | Indicator | Label bar patterns |
| AcmeCobra | Function | Find a Cobra pattern |
| AcmeHarami | Function | Search for the extended Harami pattern |
| AcmeHook | Function | Search for a Hook pattern |
| AcmeOnAverage | Function | Is the current bar sitting on the moving average? |
| AcmePullback | Function | Search for a Gann pullback pattern |
| AcmeRetraceDown | Function | Identify an n-bar pullback |
| AcmeRetraceUp | Function | Identify an n-bar upward retracement |
| AcmeTail | Function | Identify a Tail pattern |
| AcmeTest | Function | Identify a Test pattern |

## 11.1.8 Volatility Trading

**Table 11.8.** Volatility Trading Modules

| Name | Type | Description |
|---|---|---|
| Acme V High Zone | PaintBar | Mark when the V High Zone is hit |
| Acme V Low Zone | PaintBar | Mark when the V Low Zone is hit |
| Acme V Strategy | Strategy | V Signal with the Acme Trade Manager |
| Acme V System | Signal | Find V bottoms based on linear regression |
| AcmeVHigh | Function | Find an inverted V high |
| AcmeVLow | Function | Find a V low |

## 11.1.9 Float Trading

**Table 11.9.** Float Trading Modules

| Name | Type | Description |
|------|------|-------------|
| Acme F Strategy | Strategy | F Signal with the Acme Trade Manager |
| Acme F System | Signal | Float Breakouts and Pullbacks |
| Acme Float Box | Indicator | Plot parallel lines indicating float turnover |
| Acme Float Channel | Indicator | Plot the high and low float channels |
| Acme Float Percent | Indicator | Plot the float turnovers on base breakouts |
| AcmeFloatChannelHigh | Function | Return the value of the upper float channel |
| AcmeFloatChannelLow | Function | Return the value of the lower float channel |
| AcmeGetFloat | Function | Return the float of a given stock |
| AcmeGetFloatBars | Function | Calculate the bar number for a float turnover |

## 11.2 Compilation

### 11.2.1 Creating an Archive

Once the code has been created and verified in TradeStation, the user should create an EasyLanguage archive file to store all of the Acme code. Further, if the trader uses the combination of TradeStation 2000*i* and TradeStation 6, then the archive should be created in 2000*i* and then imported into TradeStation 6 because the old signal names will be automatically converted.

### *TradeStation 2000i*

To create an archive in TradeStation 2000*i* application, follow these steps:

1. In the EasyLanguage PowerEditor, select:
   `File->Import and Export…`
2. Click on:
   `Export EasyLanguage Storage File (ELS)`
3. Click:
   `Next >`
4. Under the `Analysis Type:` dropdown menu, select:
   `All Techniques`

5. Scroll down until you see the Acme prefix. Highlight:
   `Acme All Strategies`

6. Click the > button repeatedly until all of the Acme techniques have been transferred to the `Techniques to Export:` pane on the right.

7. Click:
   `Next >`

8. Enter the location and name where the archive file will be created, e.g.,
   `c:\temp\Acme.els`

9. Click:
   `Finish`

10. A `Reminder` dialog box will appear saying:
    `Functions used by functions you selected will be automatically`
    `transferred as well.`

11. Click:
    `OK`

12. The transfer process will begin. Possibly, a `Confirm file replace` dialog box will appear asking if you would like to replace an existing analysis technique. Click:
    `No to all`

13. A `Reminder` dialog box will appear saying:
    `Signals and Functions used by the selected Strategies and Signals`
    `will be automatically transferred as well.`

14. Click:
    `OK`

15. A `Reminder` dialog box will appear saying:
    `Functions used by Studies you selected will be automatically trans-`
    `ferred as well.`

16. Click:
    `OK`

17. An `Export Success` dialog box will appear saying:
    `You have successfully exported your analysis techniques`

18. Click:
    `OK`

19. The archive file named `Acme.els` has been created in the directory:
    `c:\temp\`

The archive file can now be distributed and imported into both TradeStation 2000*i* and TradeStation 6.

*TradeStation 6*

To create an archive in TradeStation 6, take the following steps:

1. In the TradeStation 6 application, select:
   `File->Import/Export EasyLanguage…`
2. Click on:
   `Export EasyLanguage Documents File (ELD)`
3. Click:
   `Next >`
4. Under the `Analysis Type:` dropdown menu, select:
   `All Techniques`
5. Scroll down until you see the Acme prefix. Highlight:
   `Acme All Strategies`
6. Click the > button repeatedly until all of the Acme techniques have been transferred to the `Techniques to Export:` pane on the right.
7. Click:
   `Next >`
8. Enter the location and name where the archive file will be created, e.g.,
   `c:\temp\Acme.eld`
9. Click:
   `Finish`
10. A `Reminder` dialog box will appear saying:
    `Strategies and Functions used by the selected Strategies will be automatically transferred as well.`
11. Click:
    `OK`
12. The transfer process will begin. An `Export Success` dialog box will appear saying:
    `You have successfully exported your analysis techniques`
13. Click:
    `OK`
14. The archive file named `Acme.eld` has been created in the directory:
    `c:\temp\`

The archive file can now be distributed and imported into TradeStation 6.

## 11.2.2 Importing the Code into TradeStation 6

Once the archive has been created, it can be imported into TradeStation 6 with the following steps:

1. In the TradeStation 6 application, select:
   `File->Import/Export EasyLanguage…`
2. Click on:
   `Import EasyLanguage file (ELD, ELS, or ELA)`
3. Click:
   `Next >`
4. Type the location and name where the archive file is located, e.g.,
   `c:\temp\Acme.els`
5. Click:
   `Next >`
6. The analysis types will be displayed and checked. If not checked, click:
   `Select All`
7. Click:
   `Next >`
8. The available analysis techniques will be displayed and checked. If not checked, click:
   `Select All`
9. Click:
   `Finish`
10. A `Reminder` dialog box will appear saying:
    `Strategies and Functions used by the selected Strategies will be automatically transferred as well.`
11. Click:
    `OK`
12. The transfer process will begin. Possibly, a `Confirm file replace` dialog box will appear asking if you would like to replace an existing analysis technique. Depending on whether or not the file to import is newer than the existing one, select `Yes` if newer, `No` if not.
13. TradeStation will begin verifying all of the code.
14. An `Import Success` dialog box will appear saying:
    `You have successfully imported your analysis techniques`
15. Click:
    `OK`

## 11.3 Using the Software

The Acme systems and indicators are applied using the standard TradeStation Windows menus:

- ❑  Insert→Indicator…
- ❑  Insert→PaintBar…
- ❑  Insert→Strategy…

### 11.3.1 Acme All Strategies

A Strategy named *Acme All Strategies* has been created that combines the Acme Systems F, M, N, R, and V. This strategy can be inserted into a TradeStation chart like any other strategy (the Acme P system has been excluded because it is a special intraday strategy).

### 11.3.2 Acme Spread Indicator

The *Acme Spread* Indicator requires four Data charts for the two stock symbols in its Chart window. The first two charts are intraday (Data1 and Data2), and the second two charts are daily (Data3 and Data4) as follows:

1. Stock A : Intraday
2. Stock B : Intraday
3. Stock A : Daily (hidden optional)
4. Stock B : Daily (hidden optional)

The spread indicator uses the daily data for calculating historical volatility and correlation values. The daily data is required in the chart window but does not need to be displayed. We recommend 3- or 5-minute charts for pair trading.

### 11.3.3 AcmeGetFloat Function

The Acme F System requires the use of a function *AcmeGetFloat*. Since the float is fundamental information and cannot be obtained through the TradeStation interface, the *AcmeGetFloat* function contains the float values for over 1500 commonly traded stocks. If a symbol is not listed in this function, then the float analysis techniques simply do nothing because the float value is zero. To add a stock to the list in the *AcmeGetFloat* function, perform the following steps:

1. Open the EasyLanguage function *AcmeGetFloat*.

2. Scroll down the document to insert the new symbol alphabetically. The function uses a binary sort to locate a symbol quickly, so it must be in alphabetical order; otherwise, it will not be found.

3. Copy and paste one of the surrounding lines in the function. Update the line with the new symbol and float value (refer to Chapter 4 for getting the float value).

4. After the symbol has been added, Verify the function (F3).

5. The float analysis techniques should now appear in the symbol's chart window.

## 11.4 Source Code

All of the Acme code is listed in alphabetical order. Every signal, indicator, and function has been written in EasyLanguage. To build each of the strategies, use the TradeStation StrategyBuilder™ to create a new strategy using the following steps:

❑ Create the new strategy with the proper name.

❑ Add each signal to the strategy.

❑ Each strategy should contain the signals shown in each table.

For TradeStation 6, insert each system from the table into the chart window to form the overall strategy.

### Acme All Strategies

*Strategy*

**Table 11.10.** Acme All Strategies

| Signal Name | Long Entry | Long Exit | Short Entry | Short Exit |
|---|---|---|---|---|
| Acme F System | ✔ | | ✔ | |
| Acme M System | ✔ | | ✔ | |
| Acme N System | ✔ | | ✔ | |
| Acme R System | ✔ | | ✔ | |
| Acme V System | ✔ | | | |
| Acme Trade Manager | | ✔ | | ✔ |

## Acme Double Bottom

*Indicator*

```
{******************************************************************
Acme Double Bottom: Draw a double bottom line
******************************************************************}

Inputs:
    LookbackBars(20),
    Strength(4),
    RangeFactor(0.3),
    MALength(50);

Variables:
    DBBar(-1),
    DBLine(-1),
    AlertString("");

DBBar = AcmeDoubleBottom(LookbackBars, Strength, RangeFactor);
If DBBar <> -1 Then Begin
    DBLine = TL_New(Date[0], Time[0], Low, Date[DBBar], Time[DBBar],
    Low);
    AlertString = "Acme Double Bottom";
    If DMIPlus(LookbackBars) > DMIMinus(LookbackBars) Then
        Condition1 = AbsValue(Low - Average(Close, MALength)) <=
        RangeFactor * Volatility(LookbackBars)
    Else If DMIPlus(LookbackBars) < DMIMinus(LookbackBars) Then
        Condition1 = AbsValue(High - Average(Close, MALength)) <=
        RangeFactor * Volatility(LookbackBars);
    If Condition1 Then
        AlertString = AlertString + " Near " + NumToStr(MALength, 0) +
        " Bar Moving Average";
    If AlertEnabled or Condition1 Then
        Alert(AlertString);
End;
```

## Acme Double Top

*Indicator*

```
{*********************************************************************
Acme Double Top: Draw a double top line
*********************************************************************}

Inputs:
    LookbackBars(20),
    Strength(4),
    RangeFactor(0.3),
    MALength(50);

Variables:
    DTBar(-1),
    DTLine(-1),
    AlertString("");

DTBar = AcmeDoubleTop(LookbackBars, Strength, RangeFactor);
If DTBar <> -1 Then Begin
    DTLine = TL_New(Date[0], Time[0], High, Date[DTBar], Time[DTBar],
    High);
    AlertString = "Acme Double Top";
    If DMIPlus(LookbackBars) > DMIMinus(LookbackBars) Then
        Condition1 = AbsValue(Low - Average(Close, MALength)) <=
        RangeFactor * Volatility(LookbackBars)
    Else If DMIPlus(LookbackBars) < DMIMinus(LookbackBars) Then
        Condition1 = AbsValue(High - Average(Close, MALength)) <=
        RangeFactor * Volatility(LookbackBars);
    If Condition1 Then
        AlertString = AlertString + " Near " + NumToStr(MALength, 0) +
        " Bar Moving Average";
    If AlertEnabled or Condition1 Then
        Alert(AlertString);
End;
```

## Acme F Strategy

*Strategy*

**Table 11.11.** Acme F Strategy

| Signal Name | Long Entry | Long Exit | Short Entry | Short Exit |
|---|---|---|---|---|
| Acme F System | ✔ | | ✔ | |
| Acme Trade Manager | | ✔ | | ✔ |

## Acme F System

*Signal*

```
{*******************************************************************
Acme F System: Look for float breakouts and pullbacks
*******************************************************************}

Inputs:
    {F Parameters}
    FloatFactor(1.0),
    BaseBars(7),
    BaseFactor(0.25),
    TableBars(3),
    TableFactor(0.35),
    {Filter Parameters}
    FiltersOn(True),
    FilterLength(30),
    MinimumPrice(15),
    {Position Parameters}
    Equity(100000),
    RiskModel(3),
    RiskPercent(2.0),
    RiskATR(1.0),
    EntryFactor(0.3),
    DrawTargets(True);

Variables:
    N(0),
    ATR(0.0),
    ATRLength(20),
    MA(0.0),
    MALength(50),
    TradeFilter(True),
    BuyStop(0.0),
    ShortStop(0.0),
    {F Variables}
    TheFloat(0.0),
    FloatHigh1(0.0),
    FloatHigh2(0.0),
    HighBaseCount(1),
    FloatLow1(0.0),
    FloatLow2(0.0),
    LowBaseCount(1),
    BaseDelta(0.0),
    TableDelta(0.0);

If TheFloat = 0.0 Then
Begin
    {Compute the number of base bars based on float turnover}

    TheFloat = FloatFactor * AcmeGetFloat(GetSymbolName);
```

```
End Else If TheFloat > 0.0 Then
Begin
   {Initialize variables}

   ATR = Average(Range, ATRLength);
   MA = Average(Close, MALength);
   FloatHigh1 = AcmeFloatChannelHigh(TheFloat);
   FloatLow1 = AcmeFloatChannelLow(TheFloat);

   {Run trade filters}

   If FiltersOn Then
      TradeFilter = Close >= MinimumPrice;

   If TradeFilter Then Begin

      {Calculate shares based on risk model}
      N = AcmeGetShares(Equity, RiskModel, RiskPercent, RiskATR);

      {Entry Signals}

      BuyStop = High + (EntryFactor * ATR);
      ShortStop = Low - (EntryFactor * ATR);
      BaseDelta = BaseFactor * ATR;
      TableDelta = TableFactor * ATR;

      If HighBaseCount >= BaseBars and
      High > (FloatHigh1 - ATR) and
      Highest(High, TableBars) - Lowest(High, TableBars) <= TableDelta and
      Close > MA Then Begin
         {Draw Entry Targets on the Chart}
         If DrawTargets Then
            Condition1 = AcmeEntryTargets("F", BuyStop, 0, 0, 0);
         Buy("Acme LE FB") N Shares Next Bar at BuyStop Stop;
      End;

      If LowBaseCount >= BaseBars and
      Low < (FloatLow1 + ATR) and
      Highest(Low, TableBars) - Lowest(Low, TableBars) <= TableDelta and
      Close < MA Then Begin
         {Draw Entry Targets on the Chart}
         If DrawTargets Then
            Condition1 = AcmeEntryTargets("F", 0, 0, ShortStop, 0);
         Sell("Acme SE FB") N Shares Next Bar at ShortStop Stop;
      End;

      If Low <= (FloatLow1 + ATR) and
      DMIPlus(FilterLength) > DMIMinus(FilterLength) and
      Close > MA Then Begin
         {Draw Entry Targets on the Chart}
         If DrawTargets Then
            Condition1 = AcmeEntryTargets("F", BuyStop, 0, 0, 0);
         Buy("Acme LE FP") N Shares Next Bar on BuyStop Stop;
```

```
        End;

        If High >= (FloatHigh1 - ATR) and
        DMIMinus(FilterLength) > DMIPlus(FilterLength) and
        Close < MA Then Begin
            {Draw Entry Targets on the Chart}
            If DrawTargets Then
                Condition1 = AcmeEntryTargets("F", 0, 0, ShortStop, 0);
            Sell("Acme SE FP") N Shares Next Bar on ShortStop Stop;
        End;
    End;

    {Calculate running base count and changing float channel values}

    If AbsValue(FloatHigh1 - FloatHigh2) <= BaseDelta Then
        HighBaseCount = HighBaseCount + 1
    Else
        HighBaseCount = 1;
    FloatHigh2 = FloatHigh1;

    If AbsValue(FloatLow1 - FloatLow2) <= BaseDelta Then
        LowBaseCount = LowBaseCount + 1
    Else
        LowBaseCount = 1;
    FloatLow2 = FloatLow1;
End;
```

## Acme Float Box

*Indicator*

```
{*******************************************************************
Acme Float Box: Plot the upper and lower float indicator lines

This is an implementation of the Cumulative-Volume
Float Indicator described on Page 74 of the book
"The Precision Profit Float Indicator" by Steve Woods.

Three dashed lines have been added to indicate
Fibonacci retracement levels at the 38%, 50%, and
62% mark.
*******************************************************************}

Inputs:
    FloatFactor(1.0);

Variables:
    TheFloat(0.0),
    FloatBars(0),
    FloatHigh(0.0),
    FloatLow(0.0),
```

```
    Float38(0.0),
    Float50(0.0),
    Float62(0.0),
    PlotColor(Black),
    UpperLine(-1),
    LowerLine(-1),
    Line38(-1),
    Line50(-1),
    Line62(-1);

If LastBarOnChart Then Begin
    FloatBars = 0;
    TheFloat = FloatFactor * AcmeGetFloat(GetSymbolName);
    If TheFloat > 0 Then Begin
        FloatBars = AcmeGetFloatBars(TheFloat);
        If FloatBars > 0 Then Begin
            FloatHigh = AcmeFloatChannelHigh(TheFloat);
            FloatLow = AcmeFloatChannelLow(TheFloat);
            If GetBackGroundColor = 1 Then
                PlotColor = White;
            UpperLine = TL_New(Date[0], Time[0], FloatHigh,
            Date[FloatBars], Time[FloatBars], FloatHigh);
            If UpperLine >= 0 Then Begin
                TL_SetColor(UpperLine, PlotColor);
                TL_SetSize(UpperLine, 1);
            End;
            LowerLine = TL_New(Date[0], Time[0], FloatLow,
            Date[FloatBars], Time[FloatBars], FloatLow);
            If LowerLine >= 0 Then Begin
                TL_SetColor(LowerLine, PlotColor);
                TL_SetSize(LowerLine, 1);
            End;
            Float38 = FloatHigh - 0.38 * (FloatHigh - FloatLow);
            Line38 = TL_New(Date[0], Time[0], Float38,
            Date[FloatBars], Time[FloatBars], Float38);
            If Line38 >= 0 Then Begin
                TL_SetStyle(Line38, Tool_Dashed);
                TL_SetColor(Line38, PlotColor);
                TL_SetSize(Line38, 0);
            End;
            Float50 = FloatHigh - 0.50 * (FloatHigh - FloatLow);
            Line50 = TL_New(Date[0], Time[0], Float50,
            Date[FloatBars], Time[FloatBars], Float50);
            If Line50 >= 0 Then Begin
                TL_SetStyle(Line50, Tool_Dashed);
                TL_SetColor(Line50, PlotColor);
                TL_SetSize(Line50, 0);
            End;
            Float62 = FloatHigh - 0.62 * (FloatHigh - FloatLow);
            Line62 = TL_New(Date[0], Time[0], Float62,
            Date[FloatBars], Time[FloatBars], Float62);
            If Line62 >= 0 Then Begin
                TL_SetStyle(Line62, Tool_Dashed);
```

```
            TL_SetColor(Line62, PlotColor);
            TL_SetSize(Line62, 0);
         End;
      End;
   End;
End;
```

## Acme Float Channel

*Indicator*

```
{******************************************************************
Acme Float Channel: Plot the float channels based on turnover

This is an implementation of the Cumulative-Volume Channel
Indicator described on Page 78 of the book
"The Precision Profit Float Indicator" by Steve Woods
******************************************************************}

Inputs:
    FloatFactor(1.0),
    BaseBars(7),
    RangeFactor(0.3);

Variables:
    TheFloat(0.0),
    {High Parameters}
    FloatHigh1(0.0),
    FloatHigh2(0.0),
    HighBaseCount(1),
    {Low Parameters}
    FloatLow1(0.0),
    FloatLow2(0.0),
    LowBaseCount(1),
    {Alert Parameters}
    AlertString(""),
    RangeDelta(0.0),
    PercentLimit(0.25),
    LookbackBars(20),
    ADXLimit(20),
    Strength(3),
    Length2(0);

If TheFloat = 0.0 Then Begin
    {Compute the number of base bars based on float turnover}

    TheFloat = FloatFactor * AcmeGetFloat(GetSymbolName);

End Else If TheFloat > 0.0 Then Begin
    {Compute the channel lines}

    FloatHigh1 = AcmeFloatChannelHigh(TheFloat);
```

```
Plot1(FloatHigh1, "High");

FloatLow1 = AcmeFloatChannelLow(TheFloat);
Plot2(FloatLow1, "Low");

{Generate alerts}

RangeDelta = RangeFactor * Volatility(LookbackBars);

If (High >= Plot1 or (High + RangeDelta >= Plot1 and
AcmeRangePercent(Close, 1) >= (1 - PercentLimit))) and
HighBaseCount >= BaseBars Then Begin
    AlertString = "Upper Float Channel Breakout: Long";
    Alert(AlertString);
End;

If (Low <= Plot2 or (Low - RangeDelta <= Plot2 and
AcmeRangePercent(Close, 1) <= PercentLimit)) and
LowBaseCount >= BaseBars Then Begin
    AlertString = "Lower Float Channel Breakout: Short";
    Alert(AlertString);
End;

If High + RangeDelta >= Plot1 and
ADX(LookbackBars) >= ADXLimit and
DMIMinus(LookbackBars) > DMIPlus(LookbackBars) Then Begin
    AlertString = "Touch Upper Float Channel in Downtrend: Short";
    AlertString = AlertString +
    " (ADX: " + NumToStr(ADX(LookbackBars), 0) + ")";
    Alert(AlertString);
End;

If Low - RangeDelta <= Plot2 and
ADX(LookbackBars) >= ADXLimit and
DMIPlus(LookbackBars) > DMIMinus(LookbackBars) Then Begin
    AlertString = "Touch Lower Float Channel in Uptrend: Long";
    AlertString = AlertString +
    " (ADX: " + NumToStr(ADX(LookbackBars), 0) + ")";
    Alert(AlertString);
End;

Length2 = AcmeDoubleTop(LookbackBars, Strength, RangeFactor);
If High + RangeDelta >= Plot1 and
Length2 > 0 Then Begin
    AlertString = "Double Top: Short";
    AlertString = AlertString +
    " (Length: " + NumToStr(Length2, 0) + ")";
    Alert(AlertString);
End;

Length2 = AcmeDoubleBottom(LookbackBars, Strength, RangeFactor);
If Low - RangeDelta <= Plot2 and
Length2 > 0 Then Begin
```

```
        AlertString = "Double Bottom: Long";
        AlertString = AlertString +
        " (Length: " + NumToStr(Length2, 0) + ")";
        Alert(AlertString);
    End;

    {Calculate running base count and changing float channel values}

    If FloatHigh1 - FloatHigh2 = 0 Then
        HighBaseCount = HighBaseCount + 1
    Else
        HighBaseCount = 1;
    FloatHigh2 = FloatHigh1;

    If FloatLow1 - FloatLow2 = 0 Then
        LowBaseCount = LowBaseCount + 1
    Else
        LowBaseCount = 1;
    FloatLow2 = FloatLow1;
End;
```

## Acme Float Percent

*Indicator*

```
{*********************************************************************
Acme Float Percent: Display the float turnovers on base breakouts

This is an implementation of the Cumulative-Volume Percentage
Indicator described on Page 76 of the book
"The Precision Profit Float Indicator" by Steve Woods
*********************************************************************}

Inputs:
    FloatFactor(1.0),
    BaseBars(7),
    PercentAlert(90.0),
    RangeFactor(0.3);

Variables:
    TheFloat(0.0),
    {High Parameters}
    FloatHigh1(0.0),
    FloatHigh2(0.0),
    FoundHighBase(False),
    HighBaseCount(1),
    HighBaseVolume(0),
    HighPercent(0.0),
    Percent95(95.0),
    {Low Parameters}
    FloatLow1(0.0),
    FloatLow2(0.0),
```

```
    FoundLowBase(False),
    LowBaseCount(1),
    LowBaseVolume(0),
    LowPercent(0.0),
    {Alert Parameters}
    AlertString(""),
    RangeDelta(0.0);

If TheFloat = 0.0 Then Begin
    TheFloat = FloatFactor * AcmeGetFloat(GetSymbolName);
End Else If TheFloat > 0 Then Begin
    {Calculations}
    FloatHigh1 = AcmeFloatChannelHigh(TheFloat);
    FloatLow1 = AcmeFloatChannelLow(TheFloat);
    RangeDelta = RangeFactor * Volatility(BaseBars);
    {High Logic}
    If HighBaseCount >= BaseBars and High > FloatHigh2 Then Begin
        FoundHighBase = True;
        HighBaseVolume = 0;
    End;
    If FoundHighBase Then Begin
        If HighBaseVolume <= TheFloat Then Begin
            HighBaseVolume = HighBaseVolume + Volume;
            HighPercent = 100.0 * HighBaseVolume / TheFloat;
            If HighPercent >= PercentAlert Then
                Plot1(HighPercent, "High %", DarkBlue)
            Else
                Plot1(HighPercent, "High %", Blue);
            If Plot1 >= PercentAlert Then Begin
                If High >= (FloatHigh1 - RangeDelta) Then Begin
                    If HighPercent >= Percent95 Then Begin
                        AlertString = "High Break Turnover (" +
                        NumToStr(HighPercent, 0) + "%) at High: Short ";
                        Alert(AlertString);
                    End;
                End;
                If Low <= (FloatLow1 + RangeDelta) Then Begin
                    If HighPercent >= Percent95 Then Begin
                        AlertString = "High Break Turnover (" +
                        NumToStr(HighPercent, 0) + "%) at Low: Long ";
                        Alert(AlertString);
                    End;
                End;
            End;
        End Else Begin
            FoundHighBase = False;
            HighBaseVolume = 0;
        End;
    End;
    If FloatHigh1 - FloatHigh2 = 0 Then
        HighBaseCount = HighBaseCount + 1
    Else
        HighBaseCount = 1;
```

```
    FloatHigh2 = FloatHigh1;
    {Low Logic}
    If LowBaseCount >= BaseBars and Low < FloatLow2 Then Begin
        FoundLowBase = True;
        LowBaseVolume = 0;
    End;
    If FoundLowBase Then Begin
        If LowBaseVolume <= TheFloat Then Begin
            LowBaseVolume = LowBaseVolume + Volume;
            LowPercent = 100.0 * LowBaseVolume / TheFloat;
            If LowPercent >= PercentAlert Then
                Plot2(LowPercent, "Low %", DarkRed)
            Else
                Plot2(LowPercent, "Low %", Red);
            If Plot2 >= PercentAlert Then Begin
                If Low <= (FloatLow1 + RangeDelta) Then Begin
                    If LowPercent >= Percent95 Then Begin
                        AlertString = "Low Break Turnover (" +
                        NumToStr(LowPercent, 0) + "%) at Low: Long ";
                        Alert(AlertString);
                    End;
                End;
                If High >= (FloatHigh1 - RangeDelta) Then Begin
                    If LowPercent >= Percent95 Then Begin
                        AlertString = "Low Break Turnover (" +
                        NumToStr(LowPercent, 0) + "%) at High: Short ";
                        Alert(AlertString);
                    End;
                End;
            End;
        End Else Begin
            FoundLowBase = False;
            LowBaseVolume = 0;
        End;
    End;
    If FloatLow1 - FloatLow2 = 0 Then
        LowBaseCount = LowBaseCount + 1
    Else
        LowBaseCount = 1;
    FloatLow2 = FloatLow1;
End;
```

## Acme HV

*Indicator*

```
{*******************************************************************
Acme HV: Display the Historical Volatility
*******************************************************************}

Inputs:
    Length(30),
    Cutoff(0.5);

Plot1(AcmeVolatility(Length), "HV");
Plot2(Cutoff, "Cutoff");
```

## Acme ID2

*PaintBar*

```
{***************************************************
Acme ID2: Mark an inside day within an inside day
***************************************************}

If Low > Low[1] and High < High[1] and
Low[1] > Low[2] and High[1] < High[2] Then Begin
    PlotPaintBar(High, Low, "Acme ID2");
    Alert("Acme ID2 Alert");
End
Else Begin
    NoPlot(1);
    NoPlot(2);
End;
```

## Acme IDNR

*PaintBar*

```
{***************************************************
Acme IDNR: Display Inside Day / Narrow Range Combinations
***************************************************}

Inputs:
    RangeLength(4);

If AcmeInsideDayNR(RangeLength, 0) Then Begin
    PlotPaintBar(High, Low, "Acme IDNR");
    Alert("Acme IDNR Alert");
End
Else Begin
```

```
    NoPlot(1);
    NoPlot(2);
End;
```

## Acme M Strategy

*Strategy*

**Table 11.12.** Acme M Strategy

| Signal Name | Long Entry | Long Exit | Short Entry | Short Exit |
|---|---|---|---|---|
| Acme M System | ✔ | | ✔ | |
| Acme Trade Manager | | ✔ | | ✔ |

## Acme M System

*Signal*

```
{******************************************************************
Acme M System: Look for multiple combinations of market patterns

1. Cobra (C)
2. Hook (H)
3. Inside Day 2 (I)
4. Tail (L)
5. Harami (M)
6. 1-2-3 Pullback (P)
7. Test (T)
8. V Zone (V)

Qualifiers

1. Moving Average (A)
2. Narrow Range (N)

******************************************************************}

Inputs:
    {M Parameters}
    MinimumPatterns(3),
    {Filter Parameters}
    FiltersOn(True),
    FilterLength(14),
    MinimumPrice(15),
    MinimumATR(1.0),
    {Position Parameters}
```

```
       Equity(100000),
       RiskModel(3),
       RiskPercent(2.0),
       RiskATR(1.0),
       EntryFactor(0.10),
       DrawTargets(True);

Variables:
       N(0),
       ATR(0.0),
       ATRLength(20),
       TradeFilter(True),
       BuyStop(0.0),
       ShortStop(0.0),
       {M Variables}
       PatternString(""),
       LongString(""),
       ShortString(""),
       ReturnValue(0),
       ALength(50),
       ACondition(False),
       CPercent(0.25),
       CRangeFactor(0.8),
       HLength(1),
       HPercent(0.2),
       LPercent(0.3),
       LLength(7),
       PADX(25),
       PLength(14),
       VFactor(1.5),
       NRFactor(0.7),
       NLength1(5),
       NLength2(10),
       NLength3(4),
       MRange(5),
       MRangePercent(0.4),
       HighText(0),
       LowText(0);

ATR = Average(Range, ATRLength);
BuyStop = High + (EntryFactor * ATR);
ShortStop = Low - (EntryFactor * ATR);

{Run trade filters}

If FiltersOn Then
       TradeFilter = Close > MinimumPrice and ATR >= MinimumATR;

If TradeFilter Then Begin

       PatternString = "";
       LongString = "";
       ShortString = "";
```

```
ReturnValue = AcmeCobra(CPercent, CRangeFactor);
If ReturnValue > 0 Then Begin
    PatternString = "C";
    If ReturnValue = 1 Then
        LongString = LongString + PatternString
    Else
        ShortString = ShortString + PatternString;
End;

ReturnValue = AcmeHook(HLength, HPercent);
If ReturnValue > 0 Then Begin
    PatternString = "H";
    If ReturnValue = 1 Then
        LongString = LongString + PatternString
    Else
        ShortString = ShortString + PatternString;
End;

If AcmeInsideDay2 Then Begin
    PatternString = "I";
    LongString = LongString + PatternString;
    ShortString = ShortString + PatternString;
End;

ReturnValue = AcmeTail(LPercent, LLength);
If ReturnValue > 0 Then Begin
    PatternString = "L";
    If ReturnValue = 1 Then
        LongString = LongString + PatternString
    Else
        ShortString = ShortString + PatternString;
End;

ReturnValue = AcmeHarami;
If ReturnValue > 0 Then Begin
    PatternString = "M";
    If ReturnValue = 1 Then
        LongString = LongString + PatternString
    Else
        ShortString = ShortString + PatternString;
End;

ReturnValue = AcmePullback(PADX, PLength);
If ReturnValue > 0 Then Begin
    PatternString = "P";
    If ReturnValue = 1 Then
        LongString = LongString + PatternString
    Else
        ShortString = ShortString + PatternString;
End;

ReturnValue = AcmeTest;
```

```
If ReturnValue > 0 Then Begin
   PatternString = "T";
   If ReturnValue = 1 Then
      LongString = LongString + PatternString
   Else
      ShortString = ShortString + PatternString;
End;

If High >= AcmeVHigh(VFactor, FilterLength) Then
   ShortString = ShortString + "V";

If Low <= AcmeVLow(VFactor, FilterLength) Then
   LongString = LongString + "V";

{Pattern Qualifiers}

ACondition = AcmeOnAverage(ALength);
If ACondition Then Begin
   PatternString = "A";
   LongString = LongString + PatternString;
   ShortString = ShortString + PatternString;
End;

Condition1 = AcmeNarrowRange(NLength1, 1) and
AcmeNarrowRange(NLength1, 0)[1];

Condition2 = Low > Low[1] and High < High[1] and
Low[1] > Low[2] and High[1] < High[2];

Condition3 = AcmeNarrowRange(NLength2, 0);
Condition4 = AcmeInsideDayNR(NLength3, 0);
Condition5 = Range <= NRFactor * ATR;

If (Condition1 or Condition2 or Condition3 or
Condition4 or Condition5) Then Begin
   PatternString = "N";
   If StrLen(LongString) > 0 Then
      LongString = LongString + PatternString;
   If StrLen(ShortString) > 0 Then
      ShortString = ShortString + PatternString;
End;

{Calculate shares based on risk model}
N = AcmeGetShares(Equity, RiskModel, RiskPercent, RiskATR);

{Multiple Pattern Buy Signal}

If StrLen(LongString) >= MinimumPatterns and
Low < Lowest(Low, MRange - 1)[1] and
AcmeRangePercent(High, MRange) <= MRangePercent and
High > Low[1] Then Begin
   {Draw Entry Targets on the Chart}
   If DrawTargets Then
```

```
        Condition1 = AcmeEntryTargets("M", BuyStop, 0, 0, 0);
    Buy("Acme LE M") N Shares Next Bar on BuyStop Stop;
End;

{Multiple Pattern Sell Signal}

If StrLen(ShortString) >= MinimumPatterns and
High > Highest(High, MRange - 1)[1] and
AcmeRangePercent(Low, MRange) >= (1 - MRangePercent) and
Low < High[1] Then Begin
    {Draw Entry Targets on the Chart}
    If DrawTargets Then
        Condition1 = AcmeEntryTargets("M", 0, 0, ShortStop, 0);
    Sell("Acme SE M") N Shares Next Bar on ShortStop Stop;
End;
End;
```

## Acme Market Model

*Indicator*

```
{****************************************************************
Acme Market Model: Label Market Model Patterns

1. VIX (V)
2. Put/Call Ratio (P)
3. New Highs (H)
4. New Lows (L)
5. Arms Index, or TRIN (T)
6. Bullish Consensus (B)
7. Short Sales Ratio (S)

Data1: Market Index
Data2: VIX
Data3: Put/Call Ratio
Data4: New Highs
Data5: New Lows
Data6: TRIN
Data7: Market Vane Bullish Consensus
Data8: Public / Specialist Short Sales Ratio

****************************************************************}

Inputs:
    MinimumPatterns(2),
    Length(20);

Variables:
    PatternString(""),
    LongString(""),
    ShortString(""),
    ReturnValue(0),
```

```
    PriceDelta(0),
    HighLow(0),
    ATR(0.0),
    Smooth(4),
    HighText(0),
    LowText(0);

If DataCompression < 2 Then
    Commentary("This indicator must be applied to a daily bar " +
    "interval or longer.")
Else Begin
    PatternString = "";
    LongString = "";
    ShortString = "";
    ATR = Volatility(Length);
    PriceDelta = ATR / 4;

    If Close of Data2 > 0 Then Begin
        PatternString = "V";
        HighLow = AcmeHighLowIndex(Close of Data2, Length);
        If HighLow = 1 Then
            LongString = LongString + PatternString
        Else If HighLow = 2 Then
            ShortString = ShortString + PatternString;
    End;

    If Close of Data3 > 0 Then Begin
        PatternString = "P";
        HighLow = AcmeHighLowIndex(Close of Data3, Length);
        If HighLow = 1 Then
            LongString = LongString + PatternString
        Else If HighLow = 2 Then
            ShortString = ShortString + PatternString;
    End;

    If Close of Data4 > 0 Then Begin
        PatternString = "H";
        HighLow = AcmeHighLowIndex(Close of Data4, Length);
        If HighLow = 2 Then
            LongString = LongString + PatternString
        Else If HighLow = 1 Then
            ShortString = ShortString + PatternString;
    End;

    If Close of Data5 > 0 Then Begin
        PatternString = "L";
        HighLow = AcmeHighLowIndex(Close of Data5, Length);
        If HighLow = 1 Then
            LongString = LongString + PatternString
        Else If HighLow = 2 Then
            ShortString = ShortString + PatternString;
    End;
```

```
If Close of Data6 > 0 Then Begin
    PatternString = "T";
    HighLow = AcmeHighLowIndex(Average(Close of Data6, Smooth),
    Length);
    If HighLow = 1 Then
        LongString = LongString + PatternString
    Else If HighLow = 2 Then
        ShortString = ShortString + PatternString;
End;

If Close of Data7 > 0 Then Begin
    PatternString = "B";
    HighLow = AcmeHighLowIndex(Close of Data7, Length);
    If HighLow = 2 Then
        LongString = LongString + PatternString
    Else If HighLow = 1 Then
        ShortString = ShortString + PatternString;
End;

If Close of Data8 > 0 Then Begin
    PatternString = "S";
    HighLow = AcmeHighLowIndex(Close of Data8, Length);
    If HighLow = 1 Then
        LongString = LongString + PatternString
    Else If HighLow = 2 Then
        ShortString = ShortString + PatternString;
End;

If LongString <> "" Then Begin
    Value1 = Text_New(Date, Time, High + PriceDelta, LongString);
    HighText = Text_SetStyle(Value1, 2, 2);
    If GetBackGroundColor = 1 Then
        Text_SetColor(Value1, Tool_Yellow)
    Else
        Text_SetColor(Value1, Tool_Black);
    If AlertEnabled or StrLen(LongString) >= MinimumPatterns Then
        Alert("Long " + LongString);
End;

If ShortString <> "" Then Begin
    Value1 = Text_New(Date, Time, Low - PriceDelta, ShortString);
    If GetBackGroundColor = 1 Then
        Text_SetColor(Value1, Tool_Yellow)
    Else
        Text_SetColor(Value1, Tool_Black);
    LowText = Text_SetStyle(Value1, 2, 0);
    If AlertEnabled or StrLen(ShortString) >= MinimumPatterns Then
        Alert("Short " + ShortString);
End;
End;
```

## Acme Market Patterns

*Indicator*

```
{*****************************************************************
Acme Market Patterns: Label Bar Patterns

1. Cobra (C)
2. Hook (H)
3. Inside Day 2 (I)
4. Tail (L)
5. Harami (M)
6. 1-2-3 Pullback (P)
7. Test (T)
8. V Zone (V)

Qualifiers

1. Average (A)
2. Narrow Range (N)

*****************************************************************}

Inputs:
    MinimumPrice(10),
    Length(10);

Variables:
    PatternString(""),
    LongString(""),
    ShortString(""),
    ReturnValue(0),
    PriceDelta(0),
    ADR(0.0),
    ALength(50),
    ACondition(False),
    CPercent(0.25),
    CRangeFactor(0.8),
    HLength(1),
    HPercent(0.2),
    LPercent(0.3),
    LRangeLength(10),
    PADX(25),
    PLength(14),
    VFactor(3.0),
    VHighZone(0.0),
    VLowZone(0.0),
    NLength1(5),
    NLength2(10),
    NLength3(4),
    HighText(0),
    LowText(0);
```

```
If DataCompression = 0 and BarInterval <= 5 Then
    Commentary("This indicator must be applied to a bar interval" +
    " larger than 5 ticks.")
Else
    If DataCompression = 5 Then
        Commentary("This indicator cannot be applied to" +
        " Point and Figure charts. ")
    Else If Close >= MinimumPrice Then Begin
        PatternString = "";
        LongString = "";
        ShortString = "";
        PriceDelta = Volatility(Length) / 4;
        ADR = Average(Range, Length);

        ReturnValue = AcmeCobra(CPercent, CRangeFactor);
        If ReturnValue > 0 Then Begin
            PatternString = "C";
            If ReturnValue = 1 Then
                LongString = LongString + PatternString
            Else
                ShortString = ShortString + PatternString;
        End;

        ReturnValue = AcmeHook(HLength, HPercent);
        If ReturnValue > 0 Then Begin
            PatternString = "H";
            If ReturnValue = 1 Then
                LongString = LongString + PatternString
            Else
                ShortString = ShortString + PatternString;
        End;

        If AcmeInsideDay2 Then Begin
            PatternString = "I";
            LongString = LongString + PatternString;
            ShortString = ShortString + PatternString;
        End;

        ReturnValue = AcmeTail(LPercent, LRangeLength);
        If ReturnValue > 0 Then Begin
            PatternString = "L";
            If ReturnValue = 1 Then
                LongString = LongString + PatternString
            Else
                ShortString = ShortString + PatternString;
        End;

        ReturnValue = AcmeHarami;
        If ReturnValue > 0 Then Begin
            PatternString = "M";
            If ReturnValue = 1 Then
                LongString = LongString + PatternString
            Else
```

```
        ShortString = ShortString + PatternString;
End;

ReturnValue = AcmePullback(PADX, PLength);
If ReturnValue > 0 Then Begin
    PatternString = "P";
    If ReturnValue = 1 Then
        LongString = LongString + PatternString
    Else
        ShortString = ShortString + PatternString;
End;

ReturnValue = AcmeTest;
If ReturnValue > 0 Then Begin
    PatternString = "T";
    If ReturnValue = 1 Then
        LongString = LongString + PatternString
    Else
        ShortString = ShortString + PatternString;
End;

VHighZone = AcmeVHigh(VFactor, Length);
If High >= VHighZone and VHighZone > 0 Then
    ShortString = ShortString + "V";

VLowZone = AcmeVLow(VFactor, Length);
If Low <= VLowZone and VLowZone > 0 Then
    LongString = LongString + "V";

{Qualifiers}

ACondition = AcmeOnAverage(ALength);
If ACondition Then Begin
    PatternString = "A";
    LongString = LongString + PatternString;
    ShortString = ShortString + PatternString;
End;

Condition1 = AcmeNarrowRange(NLength1, 1) and
AcmeNarrowRange(NLength1, 0)[1];

Condition2 = Low > Low[1] and High < High[1] and
Low[1] > Low[2] and High[1] < High[2];

Condition3 = AcmeNarrowRange(NLength2, 0);
Condition4 = AcmeInsideDayNR(NLength3, 0);
Condition5 = Range <= CRangeFactor * ADR;
If (Condition1 or Condition2 or Condition3 or
Condition4 or Condition5) Then Begin
    PatternString = "N";
    If StrLen(LongString) > 0 Then
        LongString = LongString + PatternString;
    If StrLen(ShortString) > 0 Then
```

```
            ShortString = ShortString + PatternString;
    End;

    If LongString <> "" Then Begin
        Value1 = Text_New(Date, Time, High + PriceDelta, LongString);
        HighText = Text_SetStyle(Value1, 2, 2);
        If GetBackGroundColor = 1 Then
            Text_SetColor(Value1, Tool_Yellow)
        Else
            Text_SetColor(Value1, Tool_Black);
        If AlertEnabled or StrLen(LongString) >= 2 Then
            Alert("Long " + LongString);
    End;

    If ShortString <> "" Then Begin
        Value1 = Text_New(Date, Time, Low - PriceDelta, ShortString);
        If GetBackGroundColor = 1 Then
            Text_SetColor(Value1, Tool_Yellow)
        Else
            Text_SetColor(Value1, Tool_Black);
        LowText = Text_SetStyle(Value1, 2, 0);
        If AlertEnabled or StrLen(ShortString) >= 2 Then
            Alert("Short " + ShortString);
    End;
End;
```

## Acme Market Strategy

*Strategy*

**Table 11.13.** Acme Market Strategy

| Signal Name | Long Entry | Long Exit | Short Entry | Short Exit |
|---|---|---|---|---|
| Acme Market System | ✔ | | ✔ | |
| Acme Trade Manager | | ✔ | | ✔ |

## Acme Market System

*Signal*

```
{****************************************************************
Acme Market System: Look for combinations of multiple market patterns

1. VIX (V)
2. Put/Call Ratio (P)
3. New Highs (H)
4. New Lows (L)
5. Arms Index, or TRIN (T)
6. Bull/Bear Consensus (B)
7. Short Sales Ratio (S)

Data1: Market Index
Data2: VIX
Data3: Put/Call Ratio
Data4: New Highs
Data5: New Lows
Data6: TRIN
Data7: Market Vane Bullish Consensus
Data8: Public / Specialist Short Sales Ratio

*****************************************************************}

Inputs:
    {Market Parameters}
    MinimumPatterns(2),
    Length(20),
    {Position Parameters}
    Equity(100000),
    RiskModel(3),
    RiskPercent(2.0),
    RiskATR(1.0),
    EntryFactor(0.2),
    DrawTargets(True);

Variables:
    N(0),
    ATR(0.0),
    PatternString(""),
    LongString(""),
    ShortString(""),
    ReturnValue(0),
    PriceDelta(0),
    HighLow(0),
    Smooth(4),
    BuyStop(0.0),
    ShortStop(0.0);

ATR = Average(Range, Length);
```

```
BuyStop = High + (EntryFactor * ATR);
ShortStop = Low - (EntryFactor * ATR);

If DataCompression < 2 Then
   Commentary("This indicator must be applied to a daily bar " +
   "interval or longer.")
Else Begin
   PatternString = "";
   LongString = "";
   ShortString = "";
   ATR = Volatility(Length);
   PriceDelta = ATR / 4;

   If Close of Data2 > 0 Then Begin
      PatternString = "V";
      HighLow = AcmeHighLowIndex(Close of Data2, Length);
      If HighLow = 1 Then
         LongString = LongString + PatternString
      Else If HighLow = 2 Then
         ShortString = ShortString + PatternString;
   End;

   If Close of Data3 > 0 Then Begin
      PatternString = "P";
      HighLow = AcmeHighLowIndex(Close of Data3, Length);
      If HighLow = 1 Then
         LongString = LongString + PatternString
      Else If HighLow = 2 Then
         ShortString = ShortString + PatternString;
   End;

   If Close of Data4 > 0 Then Begin
      PatternString = "H";
      HighLow = AcmeHighLowIndex(Close of Data4, Length);
      If HighLow = 2 Then
         LongString = LongString + PatternString
      Else If HighLow = 1 Then
         ShortString = ShortString + PatternString;
   End;

   If Close of Data5 > 0 Then Begin
      PatternString = "L";
      HighLow = AcmeHighLowIndex(Close of Data5, Length);
      If HighLow = 1 Then
         LongString = LongString + PatternString
      Else If HighLow = 2 Then
         ShortString = ShortString + PatternString;
   End;

   If Close of Data6 > 0 Then Begin
      PatternString = "T";
      HighLow = AcmeHighLowIndex(Average(Close of Data6, Smooth),
      Length);
```

```
        If HighLow = 1 Then
            LongString = LongString + PatternString
        Else If HighLow = 2 Then
            ShortString = ShortString + PatternString;
    End;

    If Close of Data7 > 0 Then Begin
        PatternString = "B";
        HighLow = AcmeHighLowIndex(Close of Data7, Length);
        If HighLow = 2 Then
            LongString = LongString + PatternString
        Else If HighLow = 1 Then
            ShortString = ShortString + PatternString;
    End;

    If Close of Data8 > 0 Then Begin
        PatternString = "S";
        HighLow = AcmeHighLowIndex(Close of Data8, Length);
        If HighLow = 1 Then
            LongString = LongString + PatternString
        Else If HighLow = 2 Then
            ShortString = ShortString + PatternString;
    End;

    {Calculate shares based on risk model}
    N = AcmeGetShares(Equity, RiskModel, RiskPercent, RiskATR);

    {Multiple Pattern Buy Signal}

    If StrLen(LongString) >= MinimumPatterns Then Begin
        {Draw Entry Targets on the Chart}
        If DrawTargets Then
            Condition1 = AcmeEntryTargets("M", BuyStop, 0, 0, 0);
        Buy("Acme LE Market") N Shares Next Bar on BuyStop Stop;
    End;

    {Multiple Pattern Sell Signal}

    If StrLen(ShortString) >= MinimumPatterns Then Begin
        {Draw Entry Targets on the Chart}
        If DrawTargets Then
            Condition1 = AcmeEntryTargets("M", 0, 0, ShortStop, 0);
        Sell("Acme SE Market") N Shares Next Bar on ShortStop Stop;
    End;
End;
```

## Acme N Strategy

*Strategy*

**Table 11.14.** Acme N Strategy

| Signal Name | Long Entry | Long Exit | Short Entry | Short Exit |
|---|---|---|---|---|
| Acme N System | ✔ | | ✔ | |
| Acme Trade Manager | | ✔ | | ✔ |

## Acme N System

*Signal*

```
{*******************************************************************
Acme N System: Use the Range Ratio to find Narrow Range Patterns
*******************************************************************}

Inputs:
    {N Parameters}
    RatioLength1(1),
    RatioLength2(7),
    RangePercent(0.7),
    MaxRangeRatio(0.7),
    RetraceBars(2),
    {Filter Parameters}
    FiltersOn(True),
    FilterLength(14),
    MinimumPrice(20),
    MinimumADX(18),
    MinimumHV(0.5),
    {Position Parameters}
    Equity(100000),
    RiskModel(3),
    RiskPercent(2.0),
    RiskATR(1.0),
    EntryFactor(0.10),
    DrawTargets(True);

Variables:
    N(0),
    ATR(0.0),
    ATRLength(20),
    MA(0.0),
    MALength(50),
    TradeFilter(True),
    BuyStop(0.0),
```

```
   ShortStop(0.0),
   {N Variables}
   NLength1(5),
   NLength2(10),
   NLength3(4),
   LowVolatility(False);

ATR = Volatility(ATRLength);
MA = Average(Close, MALength);

{Set Entry and Exit Stops}

BuyStop = High + (EntryFactor * ATR);
ShortStop = Low - (EntryFactor * ATR);

{Acme N Setup}

Condition1 = AcmeNarrowRange(NLength1, 1) and
AcmeNarrowRange(NLength1, 0)[1];
Condition2 = Low > Low[1] and High < High[1] and Low[1] > Low[2] and
High[1] < High[2];
Condition3 = AcmeNarrowRange(NLength2, 0);
Condition4 = AcmeInsideDayNR(NLength3, 0);
Condition5 = AcmeRangeRatio(RatioLength1, RatioLength2) <= MaxRangeRatio;
LowVolatility = Condition1 or Condition2 or Condition3 or Condition4 or
Condition5;

{Run trade filters}

If FiltersOn Then
   TradeFilter = Close > MinimumPrice and
   ADX(FilterLength) >= MinimumADX and
   AcmeVolatility(FilterLength) >= MinimumHV;

If LowVolatility and
Range <= RangePercent * ATR and
TradeFilter Then Begin

   {Calculate shares based on risk model}
   N = AcmeGetShares(Equity, RiskModel, RiskPercent, RiskATR);

   {Narrow Range}

   TradeFilter = True;
   If FiltersOn Then
      TradeFilter = MedianPrice > MA;

   If TradeFilter and
   AcmeRetraceDown(RetraceBars) and
   TradeFilter Then Begin
      {Draw Entry Targets on the Chart}
      If DrawTargets Then
         Condition1 = AcmeEntryTargets("N", BuyStop, 0, 0, 0);
```

```
        Buy("Acme LE N") N Shares Next Bar at BuyStop Stop;
    End;

    TradeFilter = True;
    If FiltersOn Then
        TradeFilter = MedianPrice < MA;

    If TradeFilter and
    AcmeRetraceUp(RetraceBars) and
    TradeFilter Then Begin
        {Draw Entry Targets on the Chart}
        If DrawTargets Then
            Condition1 = AcmeEntryTargets("N", 0, 0, ShortStop, 0);
        Sell("Acme SE N") N Shares Next Bar at ShortStop Stop;
    End;
End;
```

## Acme NR

*PaintBar*

```
{*****************************************************
Acme NR: Display the narrowest range bar in n bars
*****************************************************}

Inputs:
    RangeLength(10);

If AcmeNarrowRange(RangeLength, 0) Then Begin
    PlotPaintBar(High, Low, "Acme NR");
    Alert("Acme NR Alert");
End
Else Begin
    NoPlot(1);
    NoPlot(2);
End;
```

## Acme NR%

*PaintBar*

```
{*******************************************************
Acme NR%: Display a narrow range bar by % of ATR
*******************************************************}

Inputs:
    RangeLength(10),
    RangeFactor(0.65);

Variables:
    ATR(0.0);

ATR = Volatility(RangeLength);
If Range <= RangeFactor * ATR Then Begin
    PlotPaintBar(High, Low, "Acme NR%");
    Alert("Acme NR% Alert");
End
Else Begin
    NoPlot(1);
    NoPlot(2);
End;
```

## Acme NR2

*PaintBar*

```
{*******************************************************
Acme NR2: Display 2 narrow range bars in a row
*******************************************************}

Inputs:
    RangeLength(5);

If AcmeNarrowRange(RangeLength, 1) and
AcmeNarrowRange(RangeLength, 0)[1] Then Begin
    PlotPaintBar(High, Low, "Acme NR2");
    Alert("Acme NR2 Alert");
End
Else Begin
    NoPlot(1);
    NoPlot(2);
End;
```

## Acme P Strategy

*Strategy*

The Acme P System is a self-contained system with its own exit strategy; thus, it does not use the Acme Trade Manager.

**Table 11.15.** Acme P Strategy

| Signal Name | Long Entry | Long Exit | Short Entry | Short Exit |
|---|---|---|---|---|
| Acme P System | ✔ | ✔ | ✔ | ✔ |

## Acme P System

*Signal*

```
{******************************************************************
Acme P System: Pairs Trading

Requirements
------------

Data1: Stock 1 Intraday
Data2: Stock 2 Intraday
Data3: Stock 1 Daily (hidden)
Data4: Stock 2 Daily (hidden)
******************************************************************}

Inputs:
    Price1(Close of Data3),
    Price2(Close of Data4),
    StandardDeviations(1.5),
    Length(30),
    {Position Sizing Parameters}
    Equity(100000),
    RiskModel(3),
    RiskPercent(2.0),
    RiskATR(1.0),
    {Trade Logging}
    LogTrades(False),
    LogFile("Orders.txt");

Variables:
    N(0),
    HV1(0.0),
    HV2(0.0),
    CV(0.0),
    VolatilityBand(0.0),
```

```
    VolatilityConstant(0.0523),
    UpperBand(0.0),
    LowerBand(0.0),
    Spread(0.0);

If Date <> Date[1] Then Begin
    N = AcmeGetShares(Equity, RiskModel, RiskPercent, RiskATR)
    of Data3;
    HV1 = AcmeVolatility(Length) of Data3;
    HV2 = AcmeVolatility(Length) of Data4;
    CV = Correlation(Price1, Price2, Length);
    VolatilityBand = VolatilityConstant * (HV1 + HV2) * (1 - CV);
    UpperBand = StandardDeviations * VolatilityBand;
    LowerBand = StandardDeviations * (-VolatilityBand);
End;

Spread = (Close of Data1 / Price1) - (Close of Data2 / Price2);

If Spread crosses above LowerBand Then
    Buy("Acme P LE") N Shares This Bar on Close;

If Spread crosses above 0 Then
    ExitLong("Acme P LX +") This Bar on Close
Else If Spread <= StandardDeviations * LowerBand Then
    ExitLong("Acme P LX -") This Bar on Close;

If Spread crosses below UpperBand Then
    Sell("Acme P SE") N Shares This Bar on Close;

If Spread crosses below 0 Then
    ExitShort("Acme P SX +") This Bar on Close
Else If Spread >= StandardDeviations * UpperBand Then
    ExitShort("Acme P SX -") This Bar on Close;

{Log Trades for Spreadsheet Export}
Condition1 = AcmeLogTrades(LogTrades, LogFile, "P");
```

## Acme R Strategy

*Strategy*

**Table 11.16.** Acme R Strategy

| Signal Name | Long Entry | Long Exit | Short Entry | Short Exit |
|---|---|---|---|---|
| Acme R System | ✔ | | ✔ | |
| Acme Trade Manager | | ✔ | | ✔ |

## Acme R System

*Signal*

```
{******************************************************************
Acme R System: Look for Rectangle Breakouts
******************************************************************}

Inputs:
    {R Parameters}
    RectangleLength(4),
    RectangleRange(12),
    RectangleFactor(1.0),
    RectangleRatio(0.3),
    {Filter Parameters}
    FiltersOn(True),
    FilterLength(14),
    MinimumATR(1.0),
    {Position Parameters}
    Equity(100000),
    RiskModel(3),
    RiskPercent(2.0),
    RiskATR(1.0),
    EntryFactor(0.25),
    DrawTargets(True);

Variables:
    N(0),
    ATR(0.0),
    ATRLength(20),
    TradeFilter(True),
    BuyStop(0.0),
    ShortStop(0.0),
    {R Variables}
    InRectangle(False),
    RectangleHigh(0.0),
    RectangleLow(0.0);

ATR = Volatility(ATRLength);

RectangleHigh = Highest(High, RectangleLength);
RectangleLow = Lowest(Low, RectangleLength);

BuyStop = RectangleHigh + (EntryFactor * ATR);
ShortStop = RectangleLow - (EntryFactor * ATR);

If FiltersOn Then
    TradeFilter = ATR >= MinimumATR;

If TradeFilter Then Begin

    {Calculate shares based on risk model}
    N = AcmeGetShares(Equity, RiskModel, RiskPercent, RiskATR);
```

```
{Determine whether or not we are in a rectangle}
InRectangle = AcmeRectangular(RectangleLength, RectangleRange,
RectangleFactor, RectangleRatio);

If InRectangle Then Begin
    {Draw Entry Targets on the Chart}
    If DrawTargets Then
        Condition1 = AcmeEntryTargets("R", BuyStop, 0, 0, 0);
    Buy("Acme LE R") N Shares Next Bar on BuyStop Stop;
    {Draw Entry Targets on the Chart}
    If DrawTargets Then
        Condition1 = AcmeEntryTargets("R", 0, 0, ShortStop, 0);
    Sell("Acme SE R") N Shares Next Bar on ShortStop Stop;
    End;
End;
```

## Acme Range Ratio

*Indicator*

```
{****************************************************************
Acme Range Ratio: Display the ratio of two bar ranges
****************************************************************}

Inputs:
    Length1(2),
    Length2(7),
    LowerLimit(.7),
    UpperLimit(1.3);

Plot2(LowerLimit, "Lower Limit");
Plot3(UpperLimit, "Upper Limit");
If Date <> CurrentDate Then
    Plot1(AcmeRangeRatio(Length1, Length2), "Acme RR");
```

## Acme Rectangle

*Indicator*

```
{******************************************************************
Acme Rectangle: Draw a rectangle
******************************************************************}

Inputs:
    RectangleLength(4),
    RangeLength(12),
    RangeFactor(1.0),
    RangeRatioLimit(0.3);

Variables:
    RectangleHigh(0.0),
    RectangleLow(0.0),
    UpperLine(-1),
    LowerLine(-1);

RectangleHigh = Highest(High, RectangleLength);
RectangleLow = Lowest(Low, RectangleLength);
If AcmeRectangular(RectangleLength, RangeLength, RangeFactor,
RangeRatioLimit) Then Begin
    UpperLine = TL_New(Date[RectangleLength-1],
    Time[RectangleLength-1], RectangleHigh,
    Date[0], Time[0], RectangleHigh);
    If UpperLine >= 0 Then Begin
        If GetBackGroundColor = Black Then
            TL_SetColor(UpperLine, Yellow)
        Else
            TL_SetColor(UpperLine, Black);
        TL_SetSize(UpperLine, 1);
    End;
    LowerLine = TL_New(Date[RectangleLength-1],
    Time[RectangleLength-1], RectangleLow,
    Date[0], Time[0], RectangleLow);
    If LowerLine >= 0 Then Begin
        If GetBackGroundColor = Black Then
            TL_SetColor(LowerLine, Yellow)
        Else
            TL_SetColor(LowerLine, Black);
        TL_SetSize(LowerLine, 1);
    End;
End;
```

## Acme Spread

*Indicator*

```
{*********************************************************************
Acme Spread: Plot the Spread between 2 Securities

Requirements
------------

Data1: Stock 1 Intraday
Data2: Stock 2 Intraday
Data3: Stock 1 Daily (hidden)
Data4: Stock 2 Daily (hidden)
*********************************************************************}

Inputs:
    Price1(Close of Data3),
    Price2(Close of Data4),
    StandardDeviations(1.5),
    Length(30);

Variables:
    HV1(0.0),
    HV2(0.0),
    CV(0.0),
    VolatilityBand(0.0),
    VolatilityConstant(0.0523),
    UpperBand(0.0),
    LowerBand(0.0),
    Spread(0.0);

If Date <> Date[1] Then Begin
    HV1 = AcmeVolatility(Length) of Data3;
    HV2 = AcmeVolatility(Length) of Data4;
    CV = Correlation(Price1, Price2, Length);
    VolatilityBand = VolatilityConstant * (HV1 + HV2) * (1 - CV);
    UpperBand = StandardDeviations * VolatilityBand;
    LowerBand = StandardDeviations * (-VolatilityBand);
End;

Spread = (Close of Data1 / Price1) - (Close of Data2 / Price2);
Plot1(Spread, "Spread");
Plot2(UpperBand, "UB");
Plot3(0, "Zero");
Plot4(LowerBand, "LB");
```

## Acme Trade Manager

*Signal*

```
{*********************************************************************
Acme Trade Manager: Set stops and profit targets
*********************************************************************}

Inputs:
    SystemID(""),
    {Position Management Parameters}
    ExitFactor(0.25),
    StopBars(1),
    ProfitTarget(True),
    ProfitFactor(0.9),
    HoldBars(5),
    DrawTargets(True),
    {Trade Logging}
    LogTrades(False),
    LogFile("Orders.txt");

Variables:
    ATR(0.0),
    ATRLength(20),
    ATRFactor(0.0),
    ProfitBars(0),
    SellStop(0.0),
    SellTarget1(0.0),
    SellTarget2(0.0),
    CoverStop(0.0),
    CoverTarget1(0.0),
    CoverTarget2(0.0);

ATR = Volatility(ATRLength);
ATRFactor = ProfitFactor * ATR;
ProfitBars = IntPortion(HoldBars/2) + 1;

SellStop = Lowest(Low, StopBars) - (ExitFactor * ATR);
ExitLong("Acme LX-") Next Bar at SellStop Stop;
If ProfitTarget Then Begin
    SellTarget1 = High + ATRFactor;
    ExitLong("Acme LX+") CurrentContracts/2 Shares Next Bar at
    SellTarget1 Limit;
    SellTarget2 = High[ProfitBars] + (2 * ATRFactor);
    ExitLong("Acme LX++") CurrentContracts/2 Shares Next Bar at
    SellTarget2 Limit;
End;
If BarsSinceEntry >= HoldBars - 1 Then
    ExitLong("Acme LX") Next Bar on Open;

CoverStop = Highest(High, StopBars) + (ExitFactor * ATR);
```

```
ExitShort("Acme SX-") Next Bar at CoverStop Stop;
If ProfitTarget Then Begin
   CoverTarget1 = Low - ATRFactor;
   ExitShort("Acme SX+") CurrentContracts/2 Shares Next Bar at
   CoverTarget1 Limit;
   CoverTarget2 = Low[ProfitBars] - (2 * ATRFactor);
   ExitShort("Acme SX++") CurrentContracts/2 Shares Next Bar at
   CoverTarget2 Limit;
End;
If BarsSinceEntry >= HoldBars - 1 Then
   ExitShort("Acme SX") Next Bar on Open;

{Draw Exit Targets on the Chart}
If DrawTargets Then
   If MarketPosition = 1 Then
      Condition1 = AcmeExitTargets(SystemID, SellStop,
      SellTarget1, SellTarget2)
   Else If MarketPosition = -1 Then
      Condition1 = AcmeExitTargets(SystemID, CoverStop,
      CoverTarget1, CoverTarget2);

{Log Trades for Spreadsheet Export}
Condition1 = AcmeLogTrades(LogTrades, LogFile, SystemID);
```

## Acme Triangle

*Indicator*

```
{*********************************************************************
Acme Triangle: Plot Triangle Formations
*********************************************************************}

Inputs:
   Length(20),
   Strength(3),
   MaximumSlope(0.5),
   MaximumPivots(3);

Variables:
   FoundHighPivot(False),
   FoundLowPivot(False),
   N(0),
   SH1(-1),
   SL1(-1),
   SH2(-1),
   SL2(-1),
   TH(-1),
   TL(-1),
   HighSlope(0.0),
   LowSlope(0.0),
   ProjectHigh(0.0),
   ProjectLow(0.0);
```

```
N = 1;
SH1 = SwingHighBar(N, High, Strength, Length);
If SH1 <> -1 Then Begin
    N = 2;
    FoundHighPivot = False;
    While FoundHighPivot = False and N <= MaximumPivots Begin
        SH2 = SwingHighBar(N, High, Strength, Length);
        If SH2 <> -1 and High[SH1] < High[SH2] Then
            FoundHighPivot = True;
        N = N + 1;
    End;
End;


N = 1;
SL1 = SwingLowBar(N, Low, Strength, Length);
If SL1 <> -1 Then Begin
    N = 2;
    FoundLowPivot = False;
    While FoundLowPivot = False and N <= MaximumPivots Begin
        SL2 = SwingLowBar(N, Low, Strength, Length);
        If SL2 <> -1 and Low[SL1] > Low[SL2] Then
            FoundLowPivot = True;
        N = N + 1;
    End;
End;


If FoundHighPivot and FoundLowPivot Then Begin
    HighSlope = TLSlopeEasy(High, SH2, SH1);
    LowSlope = TLSlopeEasy(Low, SL2, SL1);
    ProjectHigh = TLValueEasy(High, SH1, SH2, 0);
    ProjectLow = TLValueEasy(Low, SL1, SL2, 0);
    If AbsValue(HighSlope) <= MaximumSlope and
    High <= ProjectHigh and
    AbsValue(LowSlope) <= MaximumSlope and
    Low >= ProjectLow Then Begin
        TH = TL_New(Date[SH1], Time[SH1], High[SH1],
        Date, Time, High);
        TL = TL_New(Date[SL1], Time[SL1], Low[SL1],
        Date, Time, Low);
    End;
End;
```

## Acme Triple Bottom

*Indicator*

```
{*****************************************************************
Acme Triple Bottom: Draw a Triple Bottom line
*****************************************************************}

Inputs:
    LookbackBars(40),
    Strength(3),
    RangeFactor(0.3),
    MALength(50);

Variables:
    ATR(0.0),
    TBBar(-1),
    TBLine(-1),
    AlertString("");

ATR = Volatility(LookbackBars);
TBBar = AcmeTripleBottom(LookbackBars, Strength, RangeFactor);
If TBBar <> -1 Then Begin
    TBLine = TL_New(Date[0], Time[0], Low,
    Date[TBBar], Time[TBBar], Low);
    AlertString = "Acme Triple Bottom";
    If DMIPlus(LookbackBars) > DMIMinus(LookbackBars) Then
        Condition1 = AbsValue(Low - Average(Close, MALength)) <=
        RangeFactor * ATR
    Else If DMIPlus(LookbackBars) < DMIMinus(LookbackBars) Then
        Condition1 = AbsValue(High - Average(Close, MALength)) <=
        RangeFactor * ATR;
    If Condition1 Then
        AlertString = AlertString + " Near " +
        NumToStr(MALength, 0) + " Bar Moving Average";
    If AlertEnabled or Condition1 Then
        Alert(AlertString);
End;
```

## Acme Triple Top

*Indicator*

```
{*****************************************************************
Acme Triple Top: Draw a Triple Top line
*****************************************************************}

Inputs:
    LookbackBars(40),
    Strength(3),
```

```
    RangeFactor(0.3),
    MALength(50);

Variables:
    ATR(0.0),
    TTBar(-1),
    TTLine(-1),
    AlertString("");

ATR = Volatility(LookbackBars);
TTBar = AcmeTripleTop(LookbackBars, Strength, RangeFactor);
If TTBar <> -1 Then Begin
    TTLine = TL_New(Date[0], Time[0], High,
    Date[TTBar], Time[TTBar], High);
    AlertString = "Acme Triple Top";
    If DMIPlus(LookbackBars) > DMIMinus(LookbackBars) Then
        Condition1 = AbsValue(Low - Average(Close, MALength)) <=
        RangeFactor * ATR
    Else If DMIPlus(LookbackBars) < DMIMinus(LookbackBars) Then
        Condition1 = AbsValue(High - Average(Close, MALength)) <=
        RangeFactor * ATR;
    If Condition1 Then
        AlertString = AlertString + " Near " +
        NumToStr(MALength, 0) + " Bar Moving Average";
    If AlertEnabled or Condition1 Then
        Alert(AlertString);
End;
```

## Acme V High Zone

*PaintBar*

```
{*********************************************************************
Acme V High Zone: Indicate when the V High Zone is hit
*********************************************************************}

Inputs:
    VolatilityFactor(0.9),
    Length(10);

Variables:
    VHighZone(0.0);

VHighZone = AcmeVHigh(VolatilityFactor, Length);
If VHighZone > 0.0 and High >= VHighZone Then
    PlotPaintBar(High, Low, "V High Zone");
```

## Acme V Low Zone

*PaintBar*

```
{*****************************************************************
Acme V Low Zone: Indicate when the V Low Zone is hit
*****************************************************************}

Inputs:
    VolatilityFactor(0.9),
    Length(10);

Variables:
    VLowZone(0.0);

VLowZone = AcmeVLow(VolatilityFactor, Length);
If VLowZone > 0.0 and Low <= VLowZone Then
    PlotPaintBar(High, Low, "V Low Zone");
```

## Acme V Strategy

*Strategy*

**Table 11.17.** Acme V Strategy

| Signal Name | Long Entry | Long Exit | Short Entry | Short Exit |
|---|---|---|---|---|
| Acme V System | ✔ | | | |
| Acme Trade Manager | | ✔ | | ✔ |

## Acme V System

*Signal*

```
{*****************************************************************
Acme V System: Anticipate a "V" Bottom based on Linear Regression
*****************************************************************}

Inputs:
    {V Parameters}
    VolatilityFactor(2.0),
    RegressionBars(5),
    RangeFactor(1.0),
    {Position Parameters}
    Equity(100000),
    RiskModel(3),
    RiskPercent(2.0),
    RiskATR(1.0),
```

```
    EntryFactor(0.25),
    DrawTargets(True);

Variables:
    N(0),
    ATR(0.0),
    ATRLength(20),
    MA(0.0),
    MALength(50),
    LRValue(0.0);

ATR = Volatility(ATRLength);
MA = Average(Close, MALength);
LRValue = LinearRegValue(Low, RegressionBars, -1);

{Entry Signal}

If (DayOfWeek(Date) = 1 or DayOfWeek(Date) = 2) Then Begin

    {Calculate shares based on risk model}
    N = AcmeGetShares(Equity, RiskModel, RiskPercent, RiskATR);

    If High < Lowest(High, RegressionBars - 1)[1] and
    Range <= RangeFactor * ATR and
    Low > LRValue and
    Low > MA and
    High > Low[1] Then Begin
        {Draw Entry Targets on the Chart}
        If DrawTargets Then
            Condition1 = AcmeEntryTargets("V", Close + EntryFactor,
            0, 0, 0);
        Buy("Acme LE V") N Shares Next Bar on Close + EntryFactor Stop;
    End;
End;
```

## AcmeCobra

*Function*

```
{*****************************************************************
AcmeCobra: Search for the Cobra Pattern
*****************************************************************}

Inputs:
    Percent(Numeric),
    RangeFactor(Numeric);

Variables:
    ATR(0.0),
    Length(20);

AcmeCobra = 0;
```

```
ATR = Volatility(Length);

If AcmeRangePercent(Open, 0) <= Percent and
AcmeRangePercent(Close, 0) >= (1 - Percent) and
Range <= RangeFactor * ATR Then
    AcmeCobra = 1;

If AcmeRangePercent(Open, 0) >= (1 - Percent) and
AcmeRangePercent(Close, 0) <= Percent and
Range <= RangeFactor * ATR Then
    AcmeCobra = 2;
```

## AcmeDoubleBottom

*Function*

```
{********************************************************************
AcmeDoubleBottom: Find a double bottom formation
********************************************************************}

Inputs:
    LookbackBars(Numeric),
    Strength(Numeric),
    RangeFactor(Numeric);

Variables:
    RangeDelta(0.0),
    HighPivot(0.0),
    LowPivot(0.0),
    LowMinimum(7);

AcmeDoubleBottom = -1;
RangeDelta = RangeFactor * Volatility(LookbackBars);
HighPivot = PivotHighVSBar(1, High, Strength, Strength, LookbackBars);
LowPivot = PivotLowVSBar(1, Low, Strength, Strength, LookbackBars);

If HighPivot <> -1 and
LowPivot <> -1 and
LowPivot >= LowMinimum and
AbsValue(Low - Low[LowPivot]) <= RangeDelta and
AbsValue(Low - Lowest(Low, LowPivot)) <= RangeDelta and
HighPivot < LowPivot and
Low <= Low[1] Then
    AcmeDoubleBottom = LowPivot;
```

## AcmeDoubleTop

*Function*

```
{********************************************************************
AcmeDoubleTop: Find a double top formation
```

```
*****************************************************************}

Inputs:
    LookbackBars(Numeric),
    Strength(Numeric),
    RangeFactor(Numeric);

Variables:
    RangeDelta(0.0),
    HighPivot(0.0),
    LowPivot(0.0),
    HighMinimum(7);

AcmeDoubleTop = -1;
RangeDelta = RangeFactor * Volatility(LookbackBars);
HighPivot = PivotHighVSBar(1, High, Strength, Strength, LookbackBars);
LowPivot = PivotLowVSBar(1, Low, Strength, Strength, LookbackBars);

If HighPivot <> -1 and
LowPivot <> -1 and
HighPivot >= HighMinimum and
AbsValue(High - High[HighPivot]) <= RangeDelta and
AbsValue(High - Highest(High, HighPivot)) <= RangeDelta and
HighPivot > LowPivot Then
    AcmeDoubleTop = HighPivot;
```

## AcmeEntryTargets

*Function*

```
{*****************************************************************
AcmeEntryTargets: Plot the entry points for stop and limit orders
*****************************************************************}

Inputs:
    SystemID(String),
    BuyStop(Numeric),
    BuyLimit(Numeric),
    ShortStop(Numeric),
    ShortLimit(Numeric);

Variables:
    PlotColor(Black),
    BSLine(-1),
    BLLine(-1),
    SSLine(-1),
    SLLine(-1),
    BSString(""),
    BLString(""),
    SSString(""),
    SLString(""),
    BSText(-1),
```

```
    BLText(-1),
    SSText(-1),
    SLText(-1);

AcmeEntryTargets = False;
If LastBarOnChart Then Begin
    If GetBackGroundColor = 1 Then
        PlotColor = White;
    If BuyStop > 0 Then Begin
        BSString = " LE " + SystemID + " Stop ";
        BSLine = TL_New(Date[0], Time[0], BuyStop,
        Date[1], Time[1], BuyStop);
        If BSLine >= 0 Then Begin
            TL_SetColor(BSLine, PlotColor);
            TL_SetSize(BSLine, 1);
            TL_SetExtRight(BSLine, True);
            BSText = Text_New(Date, Time, BuyStop, BSString);
            Text_SetColor(BSText, PlotColor);
        End;
    End;
    If BuyLimit > 0 Then Begin
        BLString = " LE " + SystemID + " Limit ";
        BLLine = TL_New(Date[0], Time[0], BuyLimit,
        Date[1], Time[1], BuyLimit);
        If BLLine >= 0 Then Begin
            TL_SetColor(BLLine, PlotColor);
            TL_SetSize(BLLine, 1);
            TL_SetExtRight(BLLine, True);
            BLText = Text_New(Date, Time, BuyLimit, BLString);
            Text_SetColor(BLText, PlotColor);
        End;
    End;
    If ShortStop > 0 Then Begin
        SSString = " SE " + SystemID + " Stop ";
        SSLine = TL_New(Date[0], Time[0], ShortStop,
        Date[1], Time[1], ShortStop);
        If SSLine >= 0 Then Begin
            TL_SetColor(SSLine, PlotColor);
            TL_SetSize(SSLine, 1);
            TL_SetExtRight(SSLine, True);
            SSText = Text_New(Date, Time, ShortStop, SSString);
            Text_SetColor(SSText, PlotColor);
        End;
    End;
    If ShortLimit > 0 Then Begin
        SLString = " SE " + SystemID + " Limit ";
        SLLine = TL_New(Date[0], Time[0], ShortLimit,
        Date[1], Time[1], ShortLimit);
        If SLLine >= 0 Then Begin
            TL_SetColor(SLLine, PlotColor);
            TL_SetSize(SLLine, 1);
            TL_SetExtRight(SLLine, True);
            SLText = Text_New(Date, Time, ShortLimit, SLString);
```

```
            Text_SetColor(SLText, PlotColor);
        End;
    End;
End;

AcmeEntryTargets = True;
```

## AcmeExitTargets

*Function*

```
{********************************************************************
AcmeExitTargets: Plot the stop loss points and profit targets
********************************************************************}

Inputs:
    SystemID(String),
    StopLoss(Numeric),
    ProfitTarget1(Numeric),
    ProfitTarget2(Numeric);

Variables:
    PlotColor(Black),
    SLLine(-1),
    PT1Line(-1),
    PT2Line(-1),
    SLString(""),
    SLText(-1),
    PT1String(""),
    PT1Text(-1),
    PT2String(""),
    PT2Text(-1);

AcmeExitTargets = False;

If LastBarOnChart Then Begin
    If MarketPosition = 1 Then Begin
        SLString = " LX " + SystemID + "-";
        PT1String = " LX " + SystemID + "+";
        PT2String = " LX " + SystemID + "++";
    End;
    If MarketPosition = -1 Then Begin
        SLString = " SX " + SystemID + "-";
        PT1String = " SX " + SystemID + "+";
        PT2String = " SX " + SystemID + "++";
    End;
    If GetBackGroundColor = 1 Then
        PlotColor = White;
    SLLine = TL_New(Date[0], Time[0], StopLoss,
    Date[1], Time[1], StopLoss);
    If SLLine >= 0 Then Begin
        TL_SetColor(SLLine, PlotColor);
```

```
            TL_SetSize(SLLine, 1);
            TL_SetExtRight(SLLine, True);
            SLText = Text_New(Date, Time, StopLoss, SLString);
            Text_SetColor(SLText, PlotColor);
        End;
        PT1Line = TL_New(Date[0], Time[0], ProfitTarget1,
        Date[1], Time[1], ProfitTarget1);
        If PT1Line >= 0 Then Begin
            TL_SetColor(PT1Line, PlotColor);
            TL_SetSize(PT1Line, 1);
            TL_SetExtRight(PT1Line, True);
            PT1Text = Text_New(Date, Time, ProfitTarget1, PT1String);
            Text_SetColor(PT1Text, PlotColor);
        End;
        PT2Line = TL_New(Date[0], Time[0], ProfitTarget2,
        Date[1], Time[1], ProfitTarget2);
        If PT2Line >= 0 Then Begin
            TL_SetColor(PT2Line, PlotColor);
            TL_SetSize(PT2Line, 1);
            TL_SetExtRight(PT2Line, True);
            PT2Text = Text_New(Date, Time, ProfitTarget2, PT2String);
            Text_SetColor(PT2Text, PlotColor);
        End;
End;

AcmeExitTargets = True;
```

## AcmeFloatChannelHigh

*Function*

```
{*******************************************************************
AcmeFloatChannelHigh: Return the value of the upper float channel
*******************************************************************}

Inputs:
    TheFloat(Numeric);

Variables:
    FloatBars(0);

AcmeFloatChannelHigh = 0;
FloatBars = 0;
If TheFloat > 0 Then Begin
    FloatBars = AcmeGetFloatBars(TheFloat);
    If FloatBars > 0 Then
        AcmeFloatChannelHigh = Highest(High, FloatBars);
End;
```

## AcmeFloatChannelLow

*Function*

```
{****************************************************************
AcmeFloatChannelLow: Return the value of the lower float channel
****************************************************************}

Inputs:
   TheFloat(Numeric);

Variables:
   FloatBars(0);

AcmeFloatChannelLow = 0;
FloatBars = 0;
If TheFloat > 0 Then Begin
   FloatBars = AcmeGetFloatBars(TheFloat);
   If FloatBars > 0 Then
      AcmeFloatChannelLow = Lowest(Low, FloatBars);
End;
```

## AcmeGetFloat

*Function*

This listing contains only a partial list of float values. Refer to Chapter 4 for obtaining and adding a float value to the *AcmeGetFloat* function.

```
{****************************************************************
AcmeGetFloat: Get the float of a given stock
****************************************************************}

Inputs:
   Symbol(String);

Variables:
   ix(0),
   il(0),
   iu(0),
   im(0),
   SymbolFound(False);

Array:
   Symbols[2048](""),
   Floats[2048](0.0);

ix = 1;
Symbols[ix] = "A"; Floats[ix] = 368.5; ix = ix + 1;
Symbols[ix] = "AA"; Floats[ix] = 746.2; ix = ix + 1;
Symbols[ix] = "AAPL"; Floats[ix] = 312.2; ix = ix + 1;
```

```
Symbols[ix] = "ABC"; Floats[ix] = 101.7; ix = ix + 1;
Symbols[ix] = "ABF"; Floats[ix] = 37.0; ix = ix + 1;
Symbols[ix] = "ABFS"; Floats[ix] = 15.1; ix = ix + 1;
Symbols[ix] = "ABGX"; Floats[ix] = 64.7; ix = ix + 1;
Symbols[ix] = "ABI"; Floats[ix] = 141.5; ix = ix + 1;
Symbols[ix] = "ABK"; Floats[ix] = 75.2; ix = ix + 1;
Symbols[ix] = "ABM"; Floats[ix] = 15.8; ix = ix + 1;
Symbols[ix] = "ZBRA"; Floats[ix] = 24.7; ix = ix + 1;
Symbols[ix] = "ZICA"; Floats[ix] = 28.1; ix = ix + 1;
Symbols[ix] = "ZIGO"; Floats[ix] = 7.6; ix = ix + 1;
Symbols[ix] = "ZIXI"; Floats[ix] = 11.4; ix = ix + 1;
Symbols[ix] = "ZOLL"; Floats[ix] = 6.9; ix = ix + 1;
Symbols[ix] = "ZOMX"; Floats[ix] = 28.8; ix = ix + 1;
Symbols[ix] = "ZQK"; Floats[ix] = 12.9; ix = ix + 1;
Symbols[ix] = "ZRAN"; Floats[ix] = 9.5;

SymbolFound = False;
il = 0;
iu = ix + 1;
While SymbolFound = False and (iu - il) > 1 Begin
    im = IntPortion((il + iu) / 2);
    If Symbol = Symbols[im] Then
        SymbolFound = True
    Else If Symbol < Symbols[im] Then
        iu = im
    Else
        il = im;
End;

AcmeGetFloat = 0;
If SymbolFound Then
    AcmeGetFloat = Floats[im] * 1000000.00;
```

## AcmeGetFloatBars

*Function*

```
{*********************************************************************
AcmeGetFloatBars: Calculate the bar number for a float turnover
*********************************************************************}

Inputs:
    FloatValue(Numeric);

Variables:
    TotalVolume(0.0),
    BarIndex(0);

TotalVolume = 0.0;
BarIndex = 0;

If CurrentBar > 0 Then Begin
```

```
    If FloatValue > 0.0 Then Begin
        While TotalVolume < FloatValue and BarIndex < MaxBarsBack Begin
            TotalVolume = TotalVolume + Volume[BarIndex];
            BarIndex = BarIndex + 1;
        End;
    End;
End;

AcmeGetFloatBars = BarIndex;
```

## AcmeGetShares

*Function*

```
{*****************************************************************
AcmeGetShares: Calculate the number of shares based on risk model

RiskModel = 1, Equal Value Units Model
RiskModel = 2, Percent Risk Model
RiskModel = 3, Percent Volatility Model
*****************************************************************}

Inputs:
    Equity(Numeric),
    RiskModel(Numeric),
    RiskPercent(Numeric),
    RiskUnits(Numeric);

Variables:
    MinimumShares(200),
    RiskShares(0),
    ERP(0.0),
    Length(20);

ERP = Equity * RiskPercent / 100;

If RiskModel = 1 and Close > 0 Then
    RiskShares = MaxList(MinimumShares,
    100 * IntPortion(Equity / (100 * Close)));

If RiskModel = 2 and RiskUnits > 0 Then
    RiskShares = MaxList(MinimumShares,
    100 * IntPortion(ERP / (100 * RiskUnits)));

If RiskModel = 3 and Volatility(Length) > 0 Then
    RiskShares = MaxList(MinimumShares,
    100 * IntPortion(ERP / (100 * Volatility(Length))));

AcmeGetShares = RiskShares;
```

## AcmeHarami

*Function*

```
{********************************************************************
AcmeHarami: Search for the extended Harami Pattern
********************************************************************}

Variables:
    RPLimit(0.45),
    RRLimit(0.60),
    Harami1(False),
    Harami2(False),
    Harami3(False);

AcmeHarami = 0;

If Range[1] > 0 and Range[2] > 0 and Range[3] > 0 Then Begin
    Condition1 = Low >= Low[1] and High <= High[1];
    Condition2 = Close > Open;
    Condition3 = AcmeRangePercent(Close, 1)[1] <= RPLimit and
    AcmeRangePercent(Open, 1)[1] >= (1 - RPLimit);
    Condition4 = (Range / Range[1]) <= RRLimit;
    Harami1 = Condition1 and Condition2 and Condition3 and
    Condition4;

    Condition1 = Low >= Low[2] and High <= High[2];
    Condition2 = Low[1] >= Low[2] and High[1] <= High[2];
    Condition3 = Close > Open;
    Condition4 = AcmeRangePercent(Close, 1)[2] <= RPLimit and
    AcmeRangePercent(Open, 1)[2] >= (1 - RPLimit);
    Condition5 = (Range / Range[2]) <= RRLimit;
    Harami2 = Condition1 and Condition2 and Condition3 and
    Condition4 and Condition5;

    Condition1 = Low >= Low[3] and High <= High[3];
    Condition2 = Low[1] >= Low[3] and High[1] <= High[3];
    Condition3 = Low[2] >= Low[3] and High[2] <= High[3];
    Condition4 = Close > Open;
    Condition5 = AcmeRangePercent(Close, 1)[3] <= RPLimit and
    AcmeRangePercent(Open, 1)[3] >= (1 - RPLimit);
    Condition6 = (Range / Range[3]) <= RRLimit;
    Harami3 = Condition1 and Condition2 and Condition3 and
    Condition4 and Condition5 and Condition6;

    If Harami1 or Harami2 or Harami3 Then
        AcmeHarami = 1;

    Condition1 = Low >= Low[1] and High <= High[1];
    Condition2 = Close < Open;
    Condition3 = AcmeRangePercent(Open, 1)[1] <= RPLimit and
    AcmeRangePercent(Close, 1)[1] >= (1 - RPLimit);
    Condition4 = (Range / Range[1]) <= RRLimit;
```

```
    Harami1 = Condition1 and Condition2 and Condition3 and
    Condition4;

    Condition1 = Low >= Low[2] and High <= High[2];
    Condition2 = Low[1] >= Low[2] and High[1] <= High[2];
    Condition3 = Close < Open;
    Condition4 = AcmeRangePercent(Open, 1)[2] <= RPLimit and
    AcmeRangePercent(Close, 1)[2] >= (1 - RPLimit);
    Condition5 = (Range / Range[2]) <= RRLimit;
    Harami2 = Condition1 and Condition2 and Condition3 and
    Condition4 and Condition5;

    Condition1 = Low >= Low[3] and High <= High[3];
    Condition2 = Low[1] >= Low[3] and High[1] <= High[3];
    Condition3 = Low[2] >= Low[3] and High[2] <= High[3];
    Condition4 = Close < Open;
    Condition5 = AcmeRangePercent(Open, 1)[3] <= RPLimit and
    AcmeRangePercent(Close, 1)[3] >= (1 - RPLimit);
    Condition6 = (Range / Range[3]) <= RRLimit;
    Harami3 = Condition1 and Condition2 and Condition3 and
    Condition4 and Condition5 and Condition6;

    If Harami1 or Harami2 or Harami3 Then
        AcmeHarami = 2;
End;
```

## AcmeHighLowIndex

*Function*

```
{******************************************************************
AcmeHighLowIndex: Calculate the High Low Index
******************************************************************}

Inputs:
    Price(Numeric),
    Length(Numeric);

AcmeHighLowIndex = 0;

If Price[1] >= Highest(Price, Length - 1)[2] and
Price < Price[1] Then
    AcmeHighLowIndex = 1
Else If Price[1] <= Lowest(Price, Length - 1)[2] and
Price > Price[1] Then
    AcmeHighLowIndex = 2;
```

## AcmeHook

*Function*

```
{*****************************************************************
AcmeHook: Search for a Hook Pattern
*****************************************************************}

Inputs:
    Length(Numeric),
    Percent(Numeric);

AcmeHook = 0;

If AcmeRetraceUp(Length)[1] and
Low < Low[1] and
AcmeRangePercent(Close, 1) >= (1 - Percent) Then
    AcmeHook = 1;

If AcmeRetraceDown(Length)[1] and
High > High[1] and
AcmeRangePercent(Close, 1) <= Percent Then
    AcmeHook = 2;
```

## AcmeInsideDay2

*Function*

```
{*****************************************************************
AcmeInsideDay2: Search for two Inside Days in a row
*****************************************************************}

AcmeInsideDay2 = False;

If Low > Low[1] and High < High[1] and
Low[1] > Low[2] and High[1] < High[2] Then
    AcmeInsideDay2 = True;
```

## AcmeInsideDayNR

*Function*

```
{*****************************************************************
AcmeInsideDayNR: Find an inside day / narrow range bar
*****************************************************************}

Inputs:
    RangeLength(Numeric),
    Index(Numeric);

AcmeInsideDayNR = False;
```

```
If Range < Lowest(Range, RangeLength - 1)[Index + 1] and
Low > Low[1] and High < High[1] Then
   AcmeInsideDayNR = True;
```

## AcmeLogTrades

*Function*

```
{***********************************************************************
AcmeLogTrades: Log trades to a file for import into a spreadsheet
***********************************************************************}

Inputs:
   LoggingOn(TrueFalse),
   LogFileName(String),
   SystemID(String);

Variables:
   ADXLength(14),
   Length(30),
   TradeString("");

AcmeLogTrades = False;

If LoggingOn and Category = 2 Then Begin
   {Log Closed Positions}
   If BarsSinceExit(1) = 1 Then Begin
      TradeString = GetSymbolName + "," +
         NumToStr(EntryDate(1), 0) + "," +
         NumToStr(EntryPrice(1), 3) + "," +
         NumToStr(ExitDate(1), 0) + "," +
         NumToStr(ExitPrice(1), 3) + "," +
         NumToStr(PositionProfit(1), 3) + "," +
         NumToStr(ADX(ADXLength)[BarsSinceEntry(1)], 0) + "," +
         NumToStr(Volatility(Length)[BarsSinceEntry(1)], 2) + "," +
         NumToStr(AcmeVolatility(Length)[BarsSinceEntry(1)], 3) +
         "," + SystemID + NewLine;
      FileAppend(LogFileName, TradeString);
   End;
   {Log Open Positions}
   If LastBarOnChart and CurrentEntries > 0 Then Begin
      TradeString = GetSymbolName + "," +
         NumToStr(EntryDate(0), 0) + "," +
         NumToStr(EntryPrice(0), 3) + "," +
         NumToStr(Date, 0) + "," +
         NumToStr(Close, 3) + "," +
         NumToStr(OpenPositionProfit, 3) + "," +
         NumToStr(ADX(ADXLength)[BarsSinceEntry(0)], 0) + "," +
         NumToStr(Volatility(Length)[BarsSinceEntry(0)], 2) + "," +
         NumToStr(AcmeVolatility(Length)[BarsSinceEntry(0)], 3) +
         "," + SystemID + NewLine;
      FileAppend(LogFileName, TradeString);
```

```
    End;
    AcmeLogTrades = True;
End;
```

## AcmeNarrowRange

*Function*

```
{****************************************************************
AcmeNarrowRange: Is the specified bar a narrow range bar?
****************************************************************}

Inputs:
    RangeLength(Numeric),
    Index(Numeric);

AcmeNarrowRange = False;
If Range < Lowest(Range, RangeLength - 1)[Index + 1] Then
    AcmeNarrowRange = True;
```

## AcmeOnAverage

*Function*

```
{****************************************************************
AcmeOnAverage: Is the current bar sitting on the moving average?
****************************************************************}

Inputs:
    Length(Numeric);

Variables:
    MA(0.0);

AcmeOnAverage = False;
MA = Average(Close, Length);
If MA >= Low and MA <= High Then
    AcmeOnAverage = True;
```

## AcmePullback

*Function*

```
{****************************************************************
AcmePullback: Search for a Gann Pullback Pattern
****************************************************************}

Inputs:
    ADXLimit(Numeric),
    Length(Numeric);
```

```
Variables:
    PullbackBars(3),
    Percent(0.35),
    RangeLength(5),
    RangeFactor(0.7);

AcmePullback = 0;

Condition1 = AcmeRetraceDown(PullbackBars) = True;
Condition2 = AcmeTail(Percent, RangeLength) = 1;
Condition3 = AcmeCobra(Percent, RangeFactor) = 1;

If ADX(Length) >= ADXLimit and
DMIPlus(Length) > DMIMinus(Length) and
AcmeRangePercent(Close, RangeLength) <= Percent and
(Condition1 or Condition2 or Condition3) Then
    AcmePullback = 1;

Condition1 = AcmeRetraceUp(PullbackBars) = True;
Condition2 = AcmeTail(Percent, RangeLength) = 2;
Condition3 = AcmeCobra(Percent, RangeFactor) = 2;

If ADX(Length) >= ADXLimit and
DMIMinus(Length) > DMIPlus(Length) and
AcmeRangePercent(Close, RangeLength) >= (1 - Percent) and
(Condition1 or Condition2 or Condition3) Then
    AcmePullback = 2;
```

## AcmeRangePercent

*Function*

```
{*********************************************************************
AcmeRangePercent: Calculate the range percentage over n bars
*********************************************************************}

Inputs:
    Price(Numeric),
    Length(Numeric);

Variables:
    RangeHigh(0.0),
    RangeLow(0.0);

AcmeRangePercent = 0.0;
RangeHigh = Highest(High, Length);
RangeLow = Lowest(Low, Length);
If (RangeHigh - RangeLow) > 0 Then
    AcmeRangePercent = (Price - RangeLow) / (RangeHigh - RangeLow);
```

## AcmeRangeRatio

*Function*

```
{*******************************************************************
AcmeRangeRatio: Calculate the Range Ratio
*******************************************************************}

Inputs:
    Length1(Numeric),
    Length2(Numeric);

Variables:
    Range1(0.0),
    Range2(0.0);

AcmeRangeRatio = 0;
Range1 = Average(Range, Length1);
Range2 = Average(Range, Length2);
If Range1 <> 0 and Range2 <> 0 Then
    AcmeRangeRatio = Range1 / Range2;
```

## AcmeRectangular

*Function*

```
{*******************************************************************
AcmeRectangular: Determine whether the region is a rectangle
*******************************************************************}

Inputs:
    RectangleLength(Numeric),
    RangeLength(Numeric),
    RangeFactor(Numeric),
    RangeRatio(Numeric);

Variables:
    ATR(0.0),
    VLength(30),
    RectangleHigh(0.0),
    RectangleLow(0.0),
    RectangleHeight(0.0),
    RangeHigh(0.0),
    RangeLow(0.0),
    RangeHeight(0.0);

AcmeRectangular = False;
ATR = Average(Range, VLength);

RectangleHigh = Highest(High, RectangleLength);
RectangleLow = Lowest(Low, RectangleLength);
RectangleHeight = RectangleHigh - RectangleLow;
```

```
RangeHigh = Highest(High, RangeLength)[RectangleLength];
RangeLow = Lowest(Low, RangeLength)[RectangleLength];
RangeHeight = RangeHigh - RangeLow;

If RectangleHeight > 0 and RangeHeight > 0 Then
    If (RectangleHeight / RangeHeight) <= RangeRatio and
    RectangleHeight <= RangeFactor * ATR Then
        AcmeRectangular = True;
```

## AcmeRetraceDown

*Function*

```
{*****************************************************************
AcmeRetraceDown: Search for an n-bar pullback
*****************************************************************}

Inputs:
    Length(Numeric);

Variables:
    InsideDays(0),
    LowerBars(0);

AcmeRetraceDown = False;
InsideDays = CountIF(Low > Low[1] and High < High[1], Length);
LowerBars = CountIF(Low < Low[1] and High < High[1], Length);
If (LowerBars = Length or
(InsideDays = 1 and LowerBars = Length - 1)) Then
    AcmeRetraceDown = True;
```

## AcmeRetraceUp

*Function*

```
{*****************************************************************
AcmeRetraceUp: Search for an n-bar retracement upwards
*****************************************************************}

Inputs:
    Length(Numeric);

Variables:
    InsideDays(0),
    HigherBars(0);

AcmeRetraceUp = False;
InsideDays = CountIF(Low > Low[1] and High < High[1], Length);
HigherBars = CountIF(Low > Low[1] and High > High[1], Length);
If (HigherBars = Length or
```

```
(InsideDays = 1 and HigherBars = Length - 1)) Then
    AcmeRetraceUp = True;
```

## AcmeTail

*Function*

```
{*******************************************************************
AcmeTail: Search for a Tail Pattern
*******************************************************************}

Inputs:
    Percent(Numeric),
    RangeLength(Numeric);

Variables:
    RP(0.0),
    RP25(0.25),
    RP50(0.50);

AcmeTail = 0;
RP = (AcmeRangePercent(Open, 1) + AcmeRangePercent(Close, 1)) / 2;

Condition1 = RP >= (1 - Percent);
Condition2 = AcmeRangePercent(Close, 1) >= (1 - RP25);
If (Condition1 or Condition2) and
AcmeRangePercent(Low, RangeLength) <= Percent and
AcmeRangePercent(Open, 1) > RP50 and
AcmeRangePercent(Close, 1) > RP50 Then
    AcmeTail = 1;

Condition1 = RP <= Percent;
Condition2 = AcmeRangePercent(Close, 1) <= RP25;
If (Condition1 or Condition2) and
AcmeRangePercent(High, RangeLength) >= (1 - Percent) and
AcmeRangePercent(Open, 1) < RP50 and
AcmeRangePercent(Close, 1) < RP50 Then
    AcmeTail = 2;
```

## AcmeTest

*Function*

```
{*******************************************************************
AcmeTest: Search for a Test Pattern
*******************************************************************}

Variables:
    Length(20),
    SeparationBars(2),
    Half(0.5);
```

```
AcmeTest = 0;

If Low < Lowest(Low, Length - 1)[1] and
NthLowestBar(2, Low, Length) >= SeparationBars and
AcmeRangePercent(Close, 1) > Half Then
    AcmeTest = 1;

If High > Highest(High, Length - 1)[1] and
NthHighestBar(2, High, Length) >= SeparationBars and
AcmeRangePercent(Close, 1) < Half Then
    AcmeTest = 2;
```

## AcmeTripleBottom

*Function*

```
{*****************************************************************
AcmeTripleBottom: Find a triple bottom formation
*****************************************************************}

Inputs:
    LookbackBars(Numeric),
    Strength(Numeric),
    RangeFactor(Numeric);

Variables:
    Delta(0.0),
    HighPivot1(0.0),
    LowPivot1(0.0),
    HighPivot2(0.0),
    LowPivot2(0.0);

AcmeTripleBottom = -1;
Delta = RangeFactor * Volatility(LookbackBars);
HighPivot1 = PivotHighVSBar(1, High, Strength, Strength, LookbackBars);
LowPivot1 = PivotLowVSBar(1, Low, Strength, Strength, LookbackBars);
HighPivot2 = PivotHighVSBar(2, High, Strength, Strength, LookbackBars);
LowPivot2 = PivotLowVSBar(2, Low, Strength, Strength, LookbackBars);

If HighPivot1 <> -1 and
LowPivot1 <> -1 and
HighPivot2 <> -1 and
LowPivot2 <> -1 and
AbsValue(Low - Low[LowPivot1]) <= Delta and
AbsValue(Low - Low[LowPivot2]) <= Delta and
AbsValue(Low - Lowest(Low, LowPivot2)) <= Delta and
HighPivot1 < LowPivot1 and
HighPivot2 < LowPivot2 and
Low <= Low[1] Then
    AcmeTripleBottom = LowPivot2;
```

## AcmeTripleTop

*Function*

```
{******************************************************************
AcmeTripleTop: Find a triple top formation
******************************************************************}

Inputs:
    LookbackBars(Numeric),
    Strength(Numeric),
    RangeFactor(Numeric);

Variables:
    Delta(0.0),
    HighPivot1(0.0),
    LowPivot1(0.0),
    HighPivot2(0.0),
    LowPivot2(0.0);

AcmeTripleTop = -1;
Delta = RangeFactor * Volatility(LookbackBars);
HighPivot1 = PivotHighVSBar(1, High, Strength, Strength, LookbackBars);
LowPivot1 = PivotLowVSBar(1, Low, Strength, Strength, LookbackBars);
HighPivot2 = PivotHighVSBar(2, High, Strength, Strength, LookbackBars);
LowPivot2 = PivotLowVSBar(2, Low, Strength, Strength, LookbackBars);

If HighPivot1 <> -1 and
LowPivot1 <> -1 and
HighPivot2 <> -1 and
LowPivot2 <> -1 and
AbsValue(High - High[HighPivot1]) <= Delta and
AbsValue(High - High[HighPivot2]) <= Delta and
AbsValue(High - Highest(High, HighPivot2)) <= Delta and
HighPivot1 > LowPivot1 and
HighPivot2 > LowPivot2 and
High >= High[1] Then
    AcmeTripleTop = HighPivot2;
```

## AcmeVHigh

*Function*

```
{*****************************************************************
AcmeVHigh: Find the V High Price
****************************************************************}

Inputs:
    VolatilityFactor(Numeric),
    Length(Numeric);

AcmeVHigh = 0.0;
If HighW(1) > 0 and
Volatility(Length) > 0 Then
    AcmeVHigh = HighW(1) + (VolatilityFactor * Volatility(Length));
```

## AcmeVLow

*Function*

```
{*****************************************************************
AcmeVLow: Find the V Low Price
****************************************************************}

Inputs:
    VolatilityFactor(Numeric),
    Length(Numeric);

AcmeVLow = 0.0;
If LowW(1) > 0 and
Volatility(Length) > 0 Then
    AcmeVLow = LowW(1) - (VolatilityFactor * Volatility(Length));
```

## AcmeVolatility

*Function*

```
{*****************************************************************
AcmeVolatility: Calculate the annualized historic volatility
*****************************************************************}

Inputs:
    Length(Numeric);

Variables:
    DaysInYear(365),
    DaysInMonth(30),
    DaysInWeek(7),
    TimeFactor(0.0);

AcmeVolatility = 0;

If Close > 0 and Close[1] > 0 Then Begin
    If DataCompression >= 2 and DataCompression < 5 Then Begin
        If DataCompression = 2 Then {Daily}
            TimeFactor = DaysInYear
        Else If DataCompression = 3 Then {Weekly}
            TimeFactor = DaysInYear / DaysInWeek
        Else If DataCompression = 4 Then {Monthly}
            TimeFactor = DaysInYear / DaysInMonth;

        AcmeVolatility = StdDev(Log(Close / Close[1]), Length) *
        SquareRoot(TimeFactor);
    End;
End;
```

# References

[1] Bollinger, John (2002) *Bollinger on Bollinger Bands*. McGraw-Hill, New York, New York

[2] Bulkowski, Thomas N (2000) *Encyclopedia of Chart Patterns*. John Wiley & Sons, New York, New York

[3] Connors, Laurence A and Linda Bradford Raschke (1995) *Street Smarts, High Probability Short Term Trading Strategies*. M. Gordon Publishing Group, Malibu, California

[4] Cooper, Jeff (1996) *Hit and Run Trading, The Short-Term Stock Traders' Bible*. M. Gordon Publishing Group, Malibu, California

[5] Cox, John C and Mark Rubinstein (1985) *Options Markets*. Prentice Hall, Englewood Cliffs, New Jersey

[6] Crabel, Toby (1990) *Day Trading with Short Term Price Patterns and Opening Range Breakout*. Rahfeldt & Associates, Jupiter, Florida

[7] Darvas, Nicolas (1960) *How I Made $2,000,000 in the Stock Market*. Carol Publishing Group, New York, New York

[8] Davidowitz, Steven (1977) *Betting Thoroughbreds*. Penguin Books, New York, New York

[9] Dunnigan, William (1956) *New Blueprints for Gains in Stocks & Grains*. Financial Times Pitman Publishing, London, England

[10] ———— (1957) *One-Way Formula for Trading in Stocks & Commodities*, Financial Times Pitman Publishing, London, England

[11] Edwards, Robert D and John Magee (1948) *Technical Analysis of Stock Trends*. John Magee, Springfield, Massachusetts

[12] Epstein, Richard A (1967) *The Theory of Gambling and Statistical Logic*. Academic Press, San Diego, California

[13] Farley, Alan S (2001) *The Master Swing Trader*. McGraw-Hill, New York, New York

[14] Fosback, Norman (1976) *Stock Market Logic*. The Institute for Econometric Research, Fort Lauderdale, Florida

[15] Gartley, Harold M (1935) *Profits in the Stock Market*. Lambert-Gann Publishing Co., Pomeroy, Washington

[16] Hirsch, Yale and Jeffrey A Hirsch (2001) *Stock Trader's Almanac*. The Hirsch Organization, Old Tappan, New Jersey

[17] LaBier, M. Rogan (2001) *The Nasdaq Trader's Toolkit*. John Wiley & Sons, New York, New York

[18] McLaren, William (1986) *Gann Made Easy*. Gann Theory Publishing, Tallai, Queensland, Australia

[19] McMillan, Lawrence (1993) *Options as a Strategic Investment*. Simon & Schuster, New York, New York

[20] Neter, John and William Wasserman (1974) *Applied Linear Statistical Models*. Richard D. Irwin, Inc. Homewood, Illinois

[21] Niederhoffer, Victor (1997) *The Education of a Speculator*. John Wiley & Sons, New York, New York

[22] Nison, Steve (1991) *Japanese Candlestick Charting Techniques*. New York Institute of Finance, New York, New York

[23] ———— (1994) *Beyond Candlesticks*. John Wiley & Sons, New York, New York

[24] Reverre, Stephane (2001) *The Complete Arbitrage Handbook*. McGraw-Hill, New York, New York

[25] Schabacker, Richard (1932) *Technical Analysis and Stock Market Profits*. Financial Times Pitman Publishing, London, England

[26] ———— (1934) *Stock Market Profits*. Financial Times Prentice Hall, London, England

[27] Schwager, Jack D (1989) *Market Wizards, Interviews with Top Traders*. New York Institute of Finance, New York, New York

[28] ———— (1992) *The New Market Wizards*. John Wiley & Sons, New York, New York

[29] Selby, Samuel M (1974) *CRC Standard Mathematical Tables*. CRC Press, Cleveland, Ohio

[30] Stridsman, Thomas (2001) *Trading Systems that Work*. McGraw-Hill, New York, New York

[31] Sun-Tzu and Roger Ames, Translator (1993) *Sun-tzu: The Art of Warfare*. Ballantine Books, New York, New York

[32] Sweeney, John (1996) *Campaign Trading*. John Wiley & Sons, New York, New York

[33] Taylor, George Douglass (1950) *The Taylor Trading Technique*. Lilly Publishing Company, Los Angeles, California

[34] Tharp, Van K (1999) *Trade Your Way to Financial Freedom*. McGraw-Hill, New York, New York

[35] Vince, Ralph (1990) *Portfolio Management Formulas*. John Wiley & Sons, New York, New York

[36] ———— (1992) *The Mathematics of Money Management*. John Wiley & Sons, New York, New York

[37] Williams, Ted and John Underwood (1971) *The Science of Hitting*. Simon & Schuster, New York, New York

[38] Woods, Steve (2000) *The Precision Profit Float Indicator*. MarketPlace Books, Columbia, Maryland

[39] Zweig, Martin (1986) *Winning on Wall Street*. Warner Books, New York, New York

# Index

# Colophon

| | |
|---|---|
| *Text Font* | Adobe Caslon Pro (a favorite of Ben Franklin) |
| *Code Font* | LucasFont TheSansMono Condensed |
| *Charts* | TradeStation 2000*i* |
| | TradeStation 6 |
| *Data Sources* | HistoryBank.com® |
| | Nasdaq Historical Data Services |
| | NYSE Market Data Services |
| | Pinnacle Data Corporation |
| *Internet* | www.acmetrader.com |
| | www.barrons.com |
| | www.bloomberg.com |
| | www.bollingerbands.com |
| | www.briefing.com |
| | www.cboe.com |
| | www.cme.com |
| | www.equis.com/free/taaz/ |
| | www.floatanalysis.com |
| | www.holdrs.com |
| | www.impactopia.com |
| | www.investors.com |
| | www.ivolatility.com |
| | www.marketvane.net |
| | www.metastock.com |
| | www.nasdaqtrader.com |
| | www.neovest.com |
| | www.nysedata.com |
| | www.onechicago.com |
| | www.tickquest.com |
| | www.traderbot.com |
| | www.traders.com |
| | www.tradestation.com |
| | www.wdgann.com |

# TITLES FROM ACME TRADER

MARK R. CONWAY AND AARON N. BEHLE

## PROFESSIONAL STOCK TRADING
*System Design and Automation*

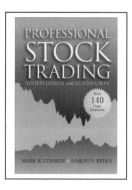

Learn the science and art of equities trading from professional hedge fund managers. The book contains over one hundred examples of actual trades, with supporting commentary and annotated charts. Starting with a trading model, the book develops a series of advanced long/short trading systems, culminating with two unique market models. Track the traders through a typical trading day as they analyze charts and watch as the trades unfold. Finally, learn several new approaches to day trading using traditional technical analysis techniques applied to shorter time frames.

2003/336 PAGES/HARDCOVER
ISBN 0-9718536-4-9

MARK R. CONWAY AND AARON N. BEHLE

## PROFESSIONAL STOCK TRADING
*Technical Analysis Software*

This software is a complete trading platform for the professional trader. All of the source code is fully disclosed, including systems and indicators for strategies such as pair trading, float analysis, and linear regression. The entire process is automated – money management, stock selection, position sizing, and trade management. Charts are annotated with price patterns, trade targets, and technical analysis indicators. The software can be applied to all time frames and is designed for both the day trader and position trader. Requires Windows and TradeStation.

2003/SOFTWARE/CD-ROM
ISBN 0-9718536-5-7

## ORDERING INFORMATION

ONLINE      HTTP://WWW.ACMETRADER.COM

EMAIL       SALES@ACMETRADER.COM

WRITE       ACME TRADER LLC
            237 MOODY STREET
            SUITE 565
            WALTHAM, MA 02453